D0982339

M. M. Daffinger

FRANZ GRILLPARZER

M. M. Daffinger

MARIE VON SMOLENITZ

"Allmacht ist deine Macht, O Schönheit, mächtige Herrin;
Was dein Szepter berührt, ändert das Wesen, die Art.
Als ich am Fenster sie sah, in papiernen Wickeln die Locken,
Glaubt ich die Charis zu sehn, weißliche Rosen im Haar."

Franz Grillparzer

A CRITICAL BIOGRAPHY

DOUGLAS YATES

SOMETIME READER IN GERMAN IN THE
UNIVERSITY OF ABERDEEN

'You call me poet—I deserve it ill:
It is not I who write the life I live—
Who would in poetry my title give
Should call me poem, poet not, I feel.'
F. G., *Self-Confession*

VOLUME I

BASIL BLACKWELL
OXFORD
1964

First printed 1946
Reprinted 1964

PRINTED IN GREAT BRITAIN FOR
BASIL BLACKWELL & MOTT LTD. BY
THE COMPTON PRINTING WORKS (LONDON) LTD. LONDON, N.1.
AND BOUND BY
THE KEMP HALL BINDERY, OXFORD

To my Wife

PREFACE

THE chapters comprising this volume cover only about the first half of Grillparzer's life and works. Though the need for a handy biography of this dramatist in English has long been felt, it is unfortunately still impracticable to supply it in full. The essential critical apparatus for the later works is still incomplete; indeed, even one portion relating to those treated here (*Wke* I. 18–19, Vienna, 1939) has proved to be unavailable in British libraries.

The point of view maintained in this study (as in *Der Kontrast zwischen Kunst und Leben bei Grillparzer*, Berlin, 1929) is no longer unfamiliar to Grillparzer enthusiasts. At the same time there is new and even startling evidence of its correctness in these pages; they therefore contain quotations from poems and documents in the original language and somewhat detailed treatment; it would only invite controversy if far-reaching statements were made and not substantiated as far as possible. This applies more particularly to the period after 1822, though the treatment of 'Sappho' (this chapter was first printed in *German Studies* presented to H. G. Fiedler, Oxford, 1938) has also of necessity been elaborate. The kind of Grillparzer biography really required, an authentic guide in briefer form, will no doubt emerge from these and subsequent efforts. It may perhaps be claimed meanwhile that the present volume contains not altogether insignificant results as regards both the interpretation of Grillparzer's works and the more general issue of poetic self-revelation in literary masterpieces. That portion of the poet's life and works remaining to be treated gives promise of hardly less reward. Appendices to the second volume will include translations of documents, poems quoted in full, and such other material as may seem desirable.

In acknowledgement of various kinds of assistance I wish first to thank my wife, and thank her deeply, for all the indispensable help she has given me in trying conditions of health during the past years of my adherence to this project: the work is dedicated to her in all earnestness and devotion. My gratitude is also due to Professor F.E. Sandbach, my friend and former teacher, from whom I derive my esteem for this dramatist, for constant encouragement, advice, and aid, including the reading of typescript and proofs. His sudden death, while these pages are still in the press, has grieved me more than I can say. Among my friends and colleagues I should like to thank Professor A. Cameron for help with the poem 'Todeswund', Mr. A. A. Parker for help with the Spanish 'kiss and tell' poem, and Dr. W. Witte for numerous ungrudging services. To the Carnegie Trust for the Universities of Scotland I offer my thanks for facilitating the publication of this volume, as also to the editors and publishers for their advice and encouragement; the delay in printing is due to influences beyond their control.

D. Y.

ABERDEEN, *Jan.* 1944

My father died without having been able to bring his critical biography of Grillparzer to a close. The first volume is being reprinted without addition or alteration, except for the correction of misprints; but the decision not to make any revisions has only been taken after careful review of more recent literature on Grillparzer. In the years since this volume first appeared a number of full-length studies have been published; they include Josef Nadler's *Franz Grillparzer* (Vaduz, 1948), Gerhart Baumann's *Franz Grillparzer und das österreichische Wesen* (Vienna, 1954) and Walter Naumann's *Grillparzer. Das dichterische Werk* (Stuttgart, n.d.). In each case, however, the general approach to Grillparzer's life and works is different in angle from my father's; and because of this dissimilarity of method these (and other) studies have not contained new evidence of such a nature as might have warranted revision of the present volume. More relevant is Rudolf Stiefel's work *Grillparzers 'Goldenes Vließ'. Ein dichterisches Bekenntnis* (Basler Studien zur deutschen Sprache und Literatur XXI, Berne, 1959), the first section of which, *Der Mensch*, is of interest as an extended interpretation of the trilogy based upon a point of view similar to that which my father maintained.

In the introduction to his book, Stiefel formulates, with welcome clarity, a reminder of the proven fruitfulness of the biographical method of criticism as it has been applied to Grillparzer; and the hope remains that reminders such as this may inspire the research necessary for the eventual completion of my father's study with a second volume worthy of the first.

W. E. Y.

DURHAM, *Sept.* 1963

CONTENTS

FRANZ GRILLPARZER

INTRODUCTION

WHEN we hear it said that Grillparzer is the greatest of those who sought to follow in the footsteps of Goethe and Schiller, and hear him quoted as saying that he would have been content to remain standing where they stood, do we realize how he resembled and represented them inwardly, not merely as regards the 'classical' quality of his dramatic works, but as a poet who fulfilled, or sought to fulfil, their conjoint conception of the poet's mission? If Schiller in his poet's pursuit achieved sublime self-abnegation, and Goethe, on the other hand, supreme self-expression, Grillparzer in his activity seems to combine them both. Of Goethe it is often lightly held that his works were basically a self-aid to, and subordinate to, living; and of Schiller that his were artistic conquests, won counter to his life's adversity. In Grillparzer life and art are wed: each fulfils itself through its counterpart, and thus both achieve their proper consummation. But there was not constant harmony between the partners in this union of life and art; rather was it in their ever-recurring contrasts—the underlying theme of all Grillparzer's dramas—that the conditions for this poet's life-activity were alone provided. The 'Kontrast zwischen Kunst und Leben' is an expression of real meaning as employed by him.

This contrast is a reality—or at any rate not a mere abstraction—and its sense is the opposite to that which commends itself at first blush to us. For Grillparzer, as for any poet worth his salt, the formula does not connote a vague incompatibility between poetry and reality, but rather—since the former is the object of his striving—the contrast between creative art and contented living, between effort and repose, or ambition and contentment, or duty and desire, or necessity and freedom. It is in fact a universal contrast, equated with that which governs all our lives. There is hardly a limit to the number of terms one might propose as respectively analogous to those of art and life. That is why this contrast in its various aspects was able to inspire Grillparzer's handling of so many human conflicts, all of them dramatic actions reducible ultimately to terms of the schism between the subject and the world—as experienced by the poet.

The case for examining the correlation between Grillparzer's experience and his work rests on this fact, the more especially in that this inter-dependence results with him from quasi-deliberate intention, as he repeatedly betrays. He treated in his dramas his own emotional crises—connected with his pursuit; his personal conflicts and higher moral issues reappear in transposed re-presentation and dramatical disguise.

Fifteen years ago the statement that Grillparzer's dramas were fundamentally personal in origin, lyrical in inspiration, and in final analysis *Künstlerdramen* one and all, seemed to cause surprise; nowadays it does so no longer, and Erich Hock writes: Aus lyrischem Drang greift Grillparzer zum Drama, um zu offenbaren—und zugleich zu verhüllen. Was als allgemein gültig über Persönliches hinaus erkannt war, wurde im Drama gestaltet'.[1] At the same time there is no doubt that this impulse, thus described as lyrical, is in reality *par excellence* the true dramatic impulse, denoting the fulfilment of this leading form of art. A poet who once responds to it, as Shakespeare clearly did, is done with mere 'observation' and invention. What would we not give to possess as much of Shakespeare's life-story as we do of Goethe's? If we could descry the origins in his life's experiences of so much that is vital, authentic, original and true in his works, these would not lose, but would gain in intensity and value for us, because we should better understand them and perceive their truth aright. In certain cases, doubtless, like that of 'Troilus and Cressida', we might ultimately judge them biased or subjective, the product of a mood.

And so it is with Grillparzer, but that we do possess his data. In the Vienna edition of his works, now completed as far as the works treated in this volume are concerned, we have a critical apparatus which rivals that available for Goethe; nothing that is documented relating to Grillparzer, whether apparently inconsequential or otherwise, has been wittingly suppressed. The following chapters include certain crucial judgements which could never have been formed without such an edition. The critical literature of the past about Grillparzer bears witness to the need of it, being strewn with crudest evidence of the lack of adequate biographical data. At the same time such premature surmisings point to the prevalence of a deep-rooted conviction among admirers of this great man, that his life and personality—those of a true artistic genius—indeed conceal the clue to his

[1] Cf. 'Das Schmerzerlebnis und sein Ausdruck in Grillparzers Lyrik', 1937, p. 27.

literary interpretation. Grillparzer's significant experience of life, his own admission implies, willy-nilly permeates all his works:

> 'Du nennst mich Dichter? Ich verdien' es nicht.
> Ein andrer sitzt, ich fühl's, und schreibt mein Leben,
> Und soll die Poesie den Namen geben,
> Statt Dichter fühl' ich höchstens mich Gedicht'.

Thomas Mann, in words belonging to a different context, seems to offer an interpretation of this epigram: 'So weitgehend eins sind Werk und Leben des Dichters, daß man, genau genommen, nur eines zu nennen brauchte und von dem Werke als seinem Leben, von dem Leben aber als seinem Werk sprechen könnte'.[1] The present experiment in biographical criticism or critical biography was conceived in this sense.

Grillparzer is indeed like Shakespeare (whose life Keats described as a poem, too, or an allegory, and his plays as the commentary to it); Grillparzer is the German Shakespeare, a greater dramatist than others of his tongue, because he not only had the real dramatic instinct and impulse, but was the first great German dramatist of a leading theatrical centre with an established stage-tradition—Old Vienna, then still the true cultural capital, if no longer the political centre of the German-speaking world. Grillparzer's drama is pre-eminently stageworthy, standing or falling with the acting art—it is not book-drama merely, like that of his more serious German rivals, not drama worthy of the state-aided theatre only and incapable of spontaneous popular support. It is true that like Schiller and in different degree Goethe, Grillparzer was a master playwright who betrays consciousness of his poetic mission. In this he may seem to differ from Shakespeare; but he is of Shakespeare's breed, though his great masterpieces still await universal recognition. Like every artist he is prized for his greatest achievement, the tragedy with which this volume ends; yet other works of his are hardly inferior; and even his less successful dramas are manifestly of that quality which produces perfection in favourable conditions.

There is always, however, this overriding consideration: even more significant than a poet's individual works are his works, biographically interpreted and inter-related, in their totality—in virtue of the picture they afford of the poet's personality and for the sake, in favourable circumstances, of the 'story of his life' which 'taking the ear strangely' they profoundly and subtly reflect. This truth was perhaps first recognized by the contemporary reviewer (in *Globe*, 1826) of

[1] Cf. 'Lotte in Weimar', Stockholm, 1939, p. 250.

Goethe's *Oeuvres Dramatiques*, when these first appeared in Stapfer's French translation. It was a judgement in which Goethe himself acquiesced, just as Grillparzer would no doubt have done regarding his own products.

The position is admirably summed up, from a slightly different angle, by a modern critic in the following statement: 'The work of any particular creative writer may, or may not, contain incidents taken from his personal life, but that which gives tone, direction, individuality and depth to his creations is an intimate reflection of himself—of his own mind and temperament. There are no exceptions. Therefore whoever sets out to draw a picture of such a writer looks for his likeness first of all in his works'.[1]

[1] Desmond MacCarthy, *Sunday Times*, Aug. 26, 1945.

CHAPTER I

YOUTHFUL WORKS

I. 'BIEDERMEIER' OR TRAGIC POET?

FRANZ Grillparzer was born on January 15, 1791, in Vienna, where he spent his whole life except for a few brief journeys to other countries, from which he always returned with the firm conviction that he could not exist anywhere outside his beloved native city and the beautiful resorts within range of it; and he died in Vienna on January 21, 1872. Yet he often complained, and not without cause, that the conditions which prevailed in Austria were far less favourable to his artistic activity and personal development than those of certain other countries might have been; and his biographers commonly speak of him as a victim of those conditions, physical, psychological, racial, and political, and as being in consequence a somewhat pathetic figure and truly representative of the Austria of his day.

It is true that the outward appearance he presents of a prematurely aged, embittered, and disappointed city official, together with our knowledge of many circumstances in his public life, seem to support this view. But when we look more closely and discover the intimate nature of his personal tragedy and private fate, and realize that his works are primarily an expression of this, the national and historical aspect of Grillparzer's existence acquires a relatively more limited significance and validity, and we are disposed to examine the life and works of this great dramatic poet in a more personal as well as in a more general human light.

2. CHILDHOOD

With regard to Grillparzer's actual ancestry it is perhaps hardly surprising that nothing is known which explains in any degree satisfactorily the presence in him of those qualities which constitute his genius, since this seems to be the rule with individuals of really outstanding endowment; and when we learn that the most diligent scrutiny of official records discovers nothing more illuminating than that his grandfather was a cooper by trade and came of Upper Austrian peasant stock, and that the mother's side of the family, formerly millers by trade, cannot be traced further back than the end of the seventeenth century either, we are disposed to accept with equanimity

the fact that these results afford but slender ground for eugeni
speculation. Yet consideration of the character and circumstances o
Grillparzer's parents clearly has a claim to our attention, even if i
were only for the sake of discovering what factors in his upbringin
and early environment may have influenced the development of hi
unquestionable gifts.

Among such known characteristics of his parents there are indee
few which are not actually recorded by Grillparzer himself in filia
piety (in which he was by no means deficient) and in sharpene
recollection of the formative experiences of his childhood and youth
In his autobiography he narrates that his father was a lawyer, a strictl
conscientious and punctilious man, but very reserved in character
Of his father's true inner nature the poet is able to give little account
since his occupation and natural reserve prevented him from devotin
himself to his children; and he died before the poet reached the ag
of eighteen, after years of illness and distress on account of the wars
which had brought about a decline in the family prosperity and onl
aggravated his habitual moroseness. His outward bearing was somewhat stern and aloof, he avoided society, but was a lover of nature
Almost his sole joy was in the cultivation of his flower garden, o
allotment. Only on long walks, accompanied by his whole family
or by his eldest son alone, did he seem to become happy and com-
municative. From the fact that on such occasions his father took
pleasure in naming the islets of the Danube according to his own fancy
after the manner of explorers, Grillparzer concludes that he must hav
allowed his imagination some play in earlier years, and adds that eve
later nothing pleased his serious-minded parent more than the ghos
and adventure stories he supplied him with, over which he woul
often sit till late into the night.

His mother, the poet tells us, was a good soul, worried by he
children, always tidying up after them, but herself none too tidy i
her ways, a woman who lived only for music, of which she was
passionate devotee. Unlike the father, she was intensely religious, o
almost morbid temperament, and subject to hallucinations. He
children may well have been obsessed with dread of having inherite
these unstable qualities of mind and character. The youngest boy
Adolph, drowned himself at the age of seventeen, leaving a not
behind (hardly reassuring for his brother Franz, who was himsel
given to gloomy forebodings of the same nature): 'Wenn einstenz de
Franz sich verheurathen sollte und Kinder bekommt, so soll er ihne

warnen, daß sie nicht mir gleich werden'.[1] On the other hand, it is not improbable that the boy was here alluding merely to an alleged propensity for 'thieving', with which he had apparently been too severely reproached by members of the family, including especially Franz.[2] Grillparzer's remaining brothers, Karl and Camillo, were both afflicted in different ways; the former caused him gravest anxiety in later life, falsely accusing himself, in a fit of temporary insanity in 1836, of embezzlement; and Camillo, who was very effeminate, suffered like the poet himself from fits of melancholy and brooding introspection. The mother herself, when she was in her fifty-second year, after a long and distressing illness at that critical stage, put an end to her own life.

Anna Franziska, or as she described herself on her marriage certificate, with her mother's Christian names, Anna Maria,[3] was the daughter of Christoph Sonnleithner, a Dean of the Viennese Law Faculty, whose home was a favourite rendezvous for lovers of art and music, among them Haydn and Mozart. It was in the house of his son Ignaz, a centre of Viennese musical culture, that Schubert first produced so many of his immortal songs.

Anna Franziska Sonnleithner married Dr. Wenzel Grillparzer on January 12, 1789, at the age of twenty-one. The bridegroom inscribed himself as aged twenty-six and failed to give his full name. It is assumed from this circumstance that he was ignorant of the date and locality of his birth, which is now known to have been on May 17, 1760, making him seven years older than his wife, and not four, as was formerly supposed.[4]

Of the four children, all sons, who sprang from this marriage Franz Seraphikus was the eldest. He was supposed to be his father's favourite child, though he himself declares that his father gave no evidence of this; and, seeming to have little in common with any of his brothers, Franz was allowed to grow up in isolation, a lonely inhabitant of those forbidding apartments in the Bauernmarkt (leased by the father, according to Grillparzer's account, when they were artificially illuminated) which were the gloomy haunt of his childhood's days.

His mother attempted to instruct him in music in her nervous unmethodical way, inflicting on him the 'torture of his boyhood' as he describes these lessons. From a professional instructor, who as an

[1] B. 95 [i.e. 'Wke.' (hist.-krit. Gsmtausg.) Abtlg. III, Briefe und Dokumente, Nr. 95].

[2] Cf. B. 95: 'Da ich immer mehr und mehr in das stellen hineingekommen wäre, so habe ich denn Entschluß gefaßt mir selbst das Leben zu nehmen./Vill belogen und betrogen haben ich die Mama und den Franz, doch bitte ich um Verzeihung, und mir nicht fluchen'.

[3] Cf. B. 306. [4] Cf. 'Grillparzers Ahnen', Vlg. d. Lit.Ver., Vienna, 1915, p. 5.

instructor was equally incompetent through indolence and neglect, Grillparzer subsequently learned little more.

At the age of about six he was sent to a private school consisting of two classes. As he had already learnt to read he was put into the upper class and thus failed to receive instruction in other rudiments. But his reading progressed and seems to have been his one delight.

Soon afterwards play-acting began, but was soon interrupted. Grillparzer's first experiences of the theatre, which he was able to visit but seldom as a child, filled him with admiration for stage effects, magical transportations, transformations, and the like; and it is worth noting that his taste for such effects is not entirely overcome even by the time he came to write his maturest work for the stage.

3. EDUCATION

In his ninth year, instead of being sent immediately to the Gymnasium, the boy began to receive instruction from private tutors; but this proved so unsatisfactory that his father had to bribe the entrance-examiner for the second year's class at the Gymnasium in order to secure admission to this class for his backward son.

This took place in 1800. He was a pupil there for four years, and though he laboured there under the same disadvantages as at the private school, not having mastered the elements of his school subjects and failing to impress his instructors in any way favourably, at the end of this period he received a certificate entitling him to continue his studies in a kind of finishing course at the University of Vienna. By this time he had access to his father's library and read with delight such works as Cook's 'Voyages', Buffon's 'Natural History', certain dramatic works, including 'Hamlet', 'Lear', and 'Nathan der Weise' (his father possessed no works by Goethe or Schiller) and above all Guthrie and Gray's 'World History' in a translation occupying over 90 volumes, which he declares he devoured, and which is in fact the source of inspiration for most of his youthful works.

This reading had been preceded by that of a volume of the 'Arabian Nights', which he had borrowed from the bookshelf of a maiden aunt and prized above everything, along with Goethe's 'Götz' and 'Clavigo', Schiller's 'Wallensteins Lager', and particularly Gozzi's 'Rabe' (Il corvo), which he much preferred to the works of Shakespeare, Goethe, and Schiller that he already knew.

In connection with this reference to his aunt, who dwelt along with two sisters in the house of his maternal grandmother, where

Grillparzer took part in amateur dramatics again, he tells of his consciousness of a certain impediment in their speech, which he too had inherited from his mother, and how, like Demosthenes, he finally mastered it by speaking with pebbles in his mouth and was thus rid of an embarrassment which had considerably aggravated his natural disposition to shyness.[1] His self-consciousness about his name,[2] which he thought ugly, remained with him for many years; he refused at first to allow it to appear on his playbills.

At the university Grillparzer discovered he was possessed of some literary ability, though it found expression in very modest beginnings, including a comedy which caricatures his professors and which was written to rival his older friend Mailler's efforts in tragedy. Even in this earliest attempt at dramatic work it is worth noticing, however, that Grillparzer fashions from living models and not from literary ones.

His autobiographical description of how he and Mailler, who came to regard him as a 'wayward genius', had originally grown acquainted is of interest because of its account of the genesis of that literary achievement, a schoolboy's essay on the 'Passage of Time'. This had attracted the older boy's attention, and Grillparzer narrates how a sudden flash of insight inspired the effusion. It is the first example of his exaggerated faith in this process and effect of the *furor poeticus*. His inability to recapture this deceptive mood after his youth, even when his best work was being done, was wont to fill him with misgivings as to the decline of his poetic gifts.

When his intermediate course at the university was over, the results being on the whole no more satisfactory than those of his earlier education, Grillparzer, in order to please his father, became enrolled in the faculty of Law and Political Science in 1807. The results of his examination at the end of his first semester were so unsatisfactory, however, that Grillparzer grew disgusted with this youthful torpor of his and resolved to mend his methods; by the end of his first year he was able by dint of sincere effort to achieve distinction in his results. This was before his law studies proper had commenced. He completed these too with success, and it was assumed by his teachers that he would take up the profession of law. But the young man had actually made no plans of any kind for a career.

[1] In a note 'Zu Fixlmüllners Charakteristik', written in 1828 for his satire 'Das Prius oder Die Bekehrung, ein rührendes Drama für Beamte' begun in 1821, but never completed, Gr. speaks of the same matter. Cf. T. 1673 [i.e. 'Wke.', Abtlg. II, Bd. 7 ff., Tagebücher und Literarische Skizzenhefte, Nr. 1673].

[2] Recorded in the same place T. 1673, cf. also T. 1652–63.

With his friend Mailler, who had meanwhile died, Grillparzer had continued his literary efforts. They had read Schiller's early dramas together and seen 'Fiesko' on the stage. Under the influence of these works, especially of 'Don Carlos', he had slowly developed his own first tragedy, 'Blanka von Kastilien' (1808–09), which he later held to bear resemblance to its model in two salient particulars at any rate: its change of plan in the middle, and its inordinate length.

Together with friends, particularly Wohlgemuth and Altmütter, Grillparzer pursued during the years of his juridical studies, but independently of these for the most part, his real intellectual inclinations. Altmütter seems to have played an important part in Grillparzer's awakening to something like a belief in his own genius; the author is undoubtedly still mindful of this in his account of this time, written at the age of sixty-two. In his autobiography he explains, with his dramatic skill revealed in the narrative, how it was through an old nurse that he had made the acquaintance of Wohlgemuth and his circle of friends, who were a year ahead of him in their studies, and how they had exchanged ideas in a somewhat purposeless way until Altmütter appeared in their midst, his eyes alight with humour and intelligence. Georg Altmütter, whose most intimate and devoted friend he was to become, won his heart at this first meeting. Then follows an account with Grillparzer's repeated asseverations of Altmütter's brilliance, of how they spent every morning and every evening together at the home of their mutual friend during the successive years of their studies; an account of the activities of the Academy of Sciences' and the 'Journal of Folly' which the circle ran under Altmütter's inspiration; and not least, of the episode when he and his friend mounted the pedestal of the monument on the Kahlenberg, twin-geniuses surveying an immeasurable panorama, with their native city beneath: all this speaks eloquently of Grillparzer's consciousness of his debt to this friend, who replaced Mailler 'more than tenfold' and obviously inspired him with ambition and confidence, probably for the first time in his life.

It was in this circle that his 'Blanka von Kastilien' took shape. Moreover, Wohlgemuth's father, a great friend and constant supporter of the Leopoldstädter Theater, encouraged amateur dramatic productions in which Grillparzer participated. Yet in spite of these beneficial influences he was by no means certain that he possessed the necessary talent for drama; and so all his other dramatic plans remained fragments, except the one-act play 'Die Schreibfeder' (1807–09), and later the one-act comedy 'Wer ist schuldig?' (1811), neither of which was published, however, or even put forward by the young poet for publication, as was the more ambitious 'Blanka.'

4. EARLIER YOUTHFUL WORKS

'Die Schreibfeder' and 'Blanka' belong to the first, 'Wer ist schuldig?' to the second, of two principal phases in Grillparzer's early development as reflected in his dramatic exercises and experiments. The year 1810 marks a long pause in his productivity. The main differences, rather of degree than kind, in the two periods are manifested in the varying use of his literary models, in his technique, and in his fashioning from personal experience.

This last tendency is the most significant, and it becomes the most salient one. In the numerous instances of this drawing upon personal experience for the treatment of stock situations and attitudes there is nothing remarkable, even when we encounter it early. But we soon discover that the tendency has an important bearing on a central problem of Grillparzer's which is best conveyed perhaps by Hilda Schulhof in the introduction to the *Jugendwerke*, in words which aptly characterize these youthful 'confessions':

> 'Versuche sind Fragen. Wie die Worte des frühen Tagebuchs "Bin ich ein guter Mensch oder nicht?" in das Ringen nach Selbsterkenntnis, aber auch in den Kampf des sich bildenden Charakters hineinleuchten, so deuten die verschieden gestimmten Erwägungen über die eigene künstlerische Begabung auf die Kämpfe des werdenden Talentes hin. "Ich habe mich oft sehr unzweideutig . . . über mein Talent zur dramatischen Dichtkunst erklärt, und dennoch ist es gewiß, daß ich nicht vollkommen, wenigstens nicht zu allen Zeiten über dieses mein Talent im Reinen bin' (Tagebuch I, 19_{27}) und 'Werde ich je mehr als mittelmäßiger Dichter werden, oder nicht? Dieß ist die Frage an deren richtiger Beantwortung ich beinahe verzweifle" (I, 17_{25}). Die Jugendwerke sind die Fortsetzung, Ausgestaltung und Verkörperung dieser bangen Erwägungen und zweifelnden Fragen, deren Antwort nach errungenem Siege das stolze "anch' io" ward.'[1]

The first period of his dramatic attempts is naturally less rich in evidence of this truth than the later, and in the earlier phase the experimental nature of his exercises, his dependence on external sources for suggestion, is correspondingly greater.

Among his very earliest diary notes are those familiar pronouncements which reveal his consciousness of this dependence: Meine Nachahmungssucht übersteigt allen Glauben. Alle meine Ideen

[1] 'Wke.', Abtlg. II, Bd. 3, p. vii.

formen sich nach jüngst gelesenen (T.59). Wenn Göthe, Schiller und Shakespeare über mich einen Konkurs eröfneten ich müste affenkahl dastehen (T.168).

Grillparzer's propensity for drastic, sensational self-criticism, as here exemplified, is indulged not merely in imitation of Rousseau, but reveals an unusual capacity in him, characteristic of his singular personality, that of the born dramatic poet, a capacity which was to bear remarkable fruit in his subsequent work.

The general character of Grillparzer's earlier youthful works from 1806 to 1809 is determined by his reading (in which history figures prominently, his Gray and Guthrie, in particular, providing him with characters, motives, and conflicts) and by his interest in the theatre and amateur dramatics. Through his historical reading his attention was directed to the subject matter of classical drama, to the study of which Schreyvogel's 'Sonntagsblatt' had conducted him. His interest in the popular stage productions of his native city, on the other hand, enabled their influence too to make itself felt in hardly less degree.

The early fragments 'Lukretia Creinwill' (1807) and 'Rosamunde Klifford' (1808) are clearly influenced by the later Schiller. Verse-form, structure, motivation, and manner are his, though the prominence given to lengthy monologues in the iambic verse of 'Rosamunde Klifford', and in other early fragments, points to the influence of Schiller's early (prose) works too, such as 'Die Räuber' and 'Fiesko'. The iambic style, combined with end-rhymes, and running sometimes to strophic form, exercises such a hold on him, however, that it is liable to crop out in the midst of prose utterance itself. Schilleresque words, images, and comparisons permeate the youthful works, though the selection is determined by the unformed theatrical taste of one still impressed by popular drama.

The influence of Shakespeare and Goethe in these fragments is displayed in certain features too, highly coloured ones from 'Richard III', 'Macbeth', 'Lear', and 'Götz'. But Shakespeare in the original (or even in faithful translation) was unknown to Grillparzer at this time and only influenced him through Schiller; that is to say, only such images of Shakespeare's as resembled those in Schiller are in evidence. And with regard to Goethe's influence at this time, Grillparzer wrote in his autobiography:

> Zwar gefiel mir Goetz von Berlichingen, er entzükte mich sogar, aber die naive Ungezwungenheit, die in diesem Drama herrscht, machte mich, einen jungen Menschen von 14 bis 15 Jahren glauben, es gehöre eben kein so großes Genie dazu, um so etwas zu schreiben, besonders da

ich in meiner Fantasie genug Materiale zu haben glaubte, um wohl auch etwas Ähnliches zu verfertigen. . . .'

At the time of his attempt at another historical drama, his fragment entitled 'Robert Herzog von der Normandie', dating from three years later than the time to which this passage refers, his relation to Goethe was practically unchanged. It was still circumscribed by his attitude to 'Götz', with its clashing of weapons and accoutrements, as conceived by the child who with his brothers and playmates improvised for their homely stage along the lines of the popular 'Ritterstück' of Vienna.

This childish pastime, in fact, together with the attraction of the popular theatre which inspired it, was what first induced Grillparzer to attempt to write for the theatre. Thus he did not actually begin as an imitator of the classical dramatists. His first piece was the straightforward farcical comedy 'Die unglücklichen Liebhaber', to which we have already referred, and not the stiff classicistic effort of 'Lukretia Creinwill'. And this is of importance for his whole development. The Lokalposse, the Viennese musical comedy and melodrama, were his models; his 'Zauberwald' belongs to the succession of operatic adaptations of Shakespeare for the popular Viennese stage. His 'Robert Herzog von der Normandie', too, in so far as it includes motives from Goethe and Shakespeare, does so only at second-hand through the influence of the Viennese Ritterstück. A similar observation applies to his farcical comedies, like 'Die unglücklichen Liebhaber' and 'das Narrennest'; in so far as they reflect the influence of Molière, it is only through the agency of popular pieces in the tradition of Molière's comedy.

In 'das Narrennest' (Autumn, 1808), which is the last effort in Grillparzer's first period (except 'Blanka', which continued to occupy him till the beginning of 1810, and the poetic tableau 'Irenens Wiederkehr'), we discover an additional feature which justifies its bracketing with 'Die unglücklichen Liebhaber' (Spring, 1806). In the earlier comedy he had introduced figures from among those he had actually come to know in real life, the professors who taught at the university. In 'das Narrennest' he causes his friends to appear, and in the person of 'Franz Seraphin Klodius Storch, ein Dichter' we discern an early exercise in self-caricature. The Christian names are his own, and Storch is a reference to his figure and gait. He is further described as—

'elegant gekleidet, hat Brillen auf der Nase, mit einer fantastischen Figur, seine Gestalt ist dürr und mager, besonders zeichnen sich die Beine hierin aus, er spricht schnell und lispelt ziemlich stark, auch verzerrt und verschiebt er von Zeit zu Zeit die Achseln und Arme'.

This satirical description corresponds to a milder reality. Grillparzer attached great importance to his attire. At all times he suffered from feelings of inferiority, even when he commanded the admiration of his friends and achieved success in his university studies; he was in consequence not always erect and at ease in his bearing, but 'twisted and distorted his arms and shoulders from time to time'. Further instances of this unsparing self-criticism are contained in the later portrayals of Fixlmüllner, including reference to his volubility (to which Grillparzer's natural taciturnity at times gave place); his *poète sifflé*, too, has shifty eyes, a pale complexion, and shows a tendency to stoop.

In all these self-portrayals it is Grillparzer's conception of his unsuitability to be what he strove to become, a poet, that acts as a painful stimulus, and nearly all the other examples in the *Jugendwerke* of figures which are intended to compare or contrast with his opinion of himself are conceived in reference to the same excessive feeling of frustration and mortification.

An apparent exception only from this generalization about Grillparzer's self-portrayals (as considered apart from his utilization of isolated personal experiences in these early dramatic experiments as occasion arose) is found in his 'drama', 'Die Schreibfeder', where the figure of Wilhelm Brand is represented in the same relation to Franz Moser as was Grillparzer's to his own father. The representation in this piece of his father's obstinacy in executing at all costs any undertaking he had set his mind upon, his unconditional fulfilment of his given word, and his sudden outbursts of uncontrolled anger which so terrified his family, these are features recorded by Grillparzer elsewhere. So also is the statement that such outbursts were frequently succeeded by equally unexpected changes to geniality and gentle outpourings of romantic feeling, which in their turn endeared him to all their hearts. The father complained bitterly of his son's poetic inclinations and prophesied that he would come to a bad end; his own education having been neglected (as Grillparzer explains), he failed to sympathize with his son's educational and cultural progress. And so in 'Die Schreibfeder' Wilhelm is misjudged and misunderstood, though he never ceases to strive to win Franz Moser's affection; and the whole work, a simple comedy in its lay-out, becomes almost a tragedy with this conflict as between father and son, partaking of Grillparzer's own experience, for its theme. The 'Schreibfeder' conflict ends happily, however, whereas Grillparzer and his father were never reconciled, and even on his death-bed the father turned his back on his weeping son, replying to his protestations of affection that it was now 'too late'.

This extravagant and inconsiderate indulgence by the father of his own emotions and self-regard caused his son unnecessary unhappiness, remorse, and self-reproach. Such treatment, and the father's general rigour of attitude towards his family dependants, which was perhaps bred of the timid self-repression of his cramped personality, left an indelible mark on Grillparzer's nature. It is not too much to say that he was irreparably damaged in self-confidence thereby and in the broad power to take himself and life as he found them—though this in turn was favourable, we shall observe, to his artistic outlook.

Not that Grillparzer entirely mistrusted himself or unconditionally accepted his father's teachings. His 'Schreibfeder' comedy was written before his father's death in 1809, being completed by the beginning of that year, and it contains incidentally a first crude attempt to deal in comedy form with the ethics of truth-telling and promise-keeping. Unjustly accused of telling a lie over a most trivial matter, the mislaying of a pen, Wilhelm incurs disfavour, banishment, and disinheritance by his foster-parent, whose fitful tendencies to relent and forgive are frustrated by his recollection of an oath extracted from him by his own father, never to sanction the slightest divergence from truthfulness; so that the unedifying conflict between him and Wilhelm is unresolved until the missing article is accidentally recovered, the youth's honour vindicated, and his wounded pride healed. Grillparzer's delineation of this conflict makes it appear probable that early in life he felt not only unsettled in his mind as to the unconditional validity of certain principal tenets in his father's unimaginative moral code, such as the one which is summed up in the now familiar formula of 'Weh dem, der lügt', but that he also suffered acutely under the humiliations to which by his father's treatment he was so constantly exposed.

Such evidence as this of Grillparzer's early tendency to grapple earnestly with life's problems suggests that he acquired it in great part through this relationship to his father. His inability to ignore these problems, to take life as normal beings do—even his loss of confidence in himself—lie (paradoxical though it may seem) at the root of the impulses to which we owe his works.

An interesting example of how his dramatic creations reflect his self-criticism is contained in his portrayal of Maria de Padilla in 'Blanka v. Kastilien'. She is a character about whom he is unable to make up his mind. The extent to which he appears to identify himself with this 'villainess' is characteristic of his regular procedure in dramatic creation, and an examination of it here will render more intelligible some of the poet's later identifications with, or assimilations to, himself of characters from entirely different walks of life and in entirely different circumstances from his own. 'Es ist ausgemacht: ihr hervorstechendster Zug ist Herrschbegierde, nicht Neigung zum Großen....' But it appears that she was originally qualified for greatness, the poet reminds himself. He would not need to emphasize this if he were not actually trying to comprehend her conduct in terms of his own nature, by attributing motives to her that are paralleled again and again in the self-criticism of his diaries:

> 'Ich stelle sie mir nämlich so vor: Sie war ein Mädchen ohne feste Grundsätze, durch ihren äußerst niederträchtigen Bruder verzogen, und schon früh erstickt jeder Keim zum Guten, der wirklich in ihrer Seele lag'.

It is the defective upbringing imputed to her which is here of account, not of course the circumstance that she received it at the hands of her brother in particular:

> 'Doch konnte seine Erziehung nie einen gewissen Trieb nach Großem aus ihrem Herzen reißen, der aber durch alle Umstände und Verhältnisse in Herrschsucht und Sucht zu glänzen, Wohlgefallen an phantastisch großen Handlungen ausartete. Es ist nicht sowohl Geldgeiz, Hang zum Laster, was sie gleich anfangs an den König fesselte, als vielmehr eine ungezähmte Begierde viel zu sein, zu heißen, zu gelten, mit einem Worte bekannt (berühmt oder berüchtigt, einerlei) gefürchtet zu werden, zu herrschen'.

It is as if the author were anxious to clear Maria's character from suspicion of inherently vicious tendencies: having put her in his own place, so to speak, not merely imagining himself in hers, he seems concerned to defend and justify her there. But he wrote these words for his own guidance, and in them he is trying to convince himself (without much success) that in Maria's circumstances he himself would have been capable of her crime, or rather that she needed, in order to be capable of it, no worse a nature than his own.

> 'Nun muß sich Maria entschließen, Blankan zu ermorden. Verträgt sich dieser Entschluß mit ihrem Charakter? Maria ist nicht grausam, nicht lasterhaft, sie ist nur herrschsüchtig, und eben hieraus, glaube ich, fließt natürlich ihr Beistimmen in den gräßlichen Plan ihres Bruders'.

The whole passage (T. 38) indicates Grillparzer's instinctive procedure in dramatic creation, which was to draw upon his own experience and observation of himself, in order to render his characters true to life and seek to ensure that his motivation should be valid. We are reminded in this of Scherer's account of Goethe's own procedure, where he states (in reference to 'Werther'): 'Der enge Anschluß an die Wirklichkeit bot die Gewähr einer hohen poetischen Wahrheit und Wahrscheinlichkeit!'

In the same connection it is of importance to anticipate the interesting entry in Grillparzer's diary at the time of his composing 'Sappho' during the summer of 1817. It seems to establish by Grillparzer's own confession what is here observed as his practice in character delineation; it is quoted only in part here, but will be given in full in its proper place:

> 'Ich glaube, daß das Genie nichts geben kann, als was es in sich selbst gefunden. . . . Also sollte Shakespeare ein Mörder, Dieb, Lügner, Verräther, Undankbarer, Wahnsinniger gewesen seyn, weil er sie so meisterlich schildert? Ja! Das heißt, er mußte zu dem allen Anlage in sich haben, obschon die vorherrschende Vernunft, das moralische Gefühl nichts davon zum Ausbruch kommen ließ' (T. 221).

Grillparzer's claim does not go far enough. Not only is it true that the genius must himself harbour the qualities and propensities he so convincingly interprets; his audience must harbour them too, or his representation could not reach their hearts and understanding, nor as dramatic art endure. As Goethe wrote in pregnant words:

> 'Nur sämtliche Menschen leben das Menschliche'.

Grillparzer was proceeding aright. In the works that belong to the second phase of his apprenticeship his practice of identifying his central characters with himself is more marked. In his mature works it is the rule.

5. LATER YOUTHFUL WORKS

The poet always remembered the time extending from his eighteenth to his twenty-fifth year as a period of dispirited inaction. He lacked the power and endurance to complete a single one of his more ambitious works; yet he himself states that his mind was actively engaged.

Outward circumstances weighed heavily upon him. After his father's death, in the last year but one of his university course, he had to find means to provide for himself. His professors secured part-time occupation for him as tutor to two young gentlemen, who paid so well that his own needs were supplied and something left over for his family. At the same time his forgotten tragedy suggested itself to him as a possible source of income. With the help of Wohlgemuth and

Altmütter a copy was made, and Grillparzer handed it to his uncle, then Secretary to Graf Palffy, lessee of the Hofburgtheater, which continued under private management until 1817. After a long delay, during which his uncle reported: 'Es ist sehr lang; ich sehe kein Ende', Grillparzer's manuscript was returned to him with the verdict that Graf Palffy considered it unsuitable.

The effect on Grillparzer of this refusal was to confirm for him his father's prophecy and strengthen him in his revolve to bid farewell to poetry, dramatic poetry in particular, for good and all.

In the meantime the end of his studies was approaching, and one of his professors proposed to him the acceptance of a permanent post as tutor in law studies to the nephew of Graf v. Seilern. He accepted, though the salary was small, in order no longer to be a burden and anxiety to his mother, and because of his distaste for the thought of entering the civil service. This was in the Spring of 1812.

In one of the most delightful and entertaining passages of his autobiography Grillparzer describes his new employer, Graf v. Seilern, as being more of a caricature than a reality. For his gluttony he is remembered in 'Weh dem, der lügt'. But the year spent in this family was not without profit for Grillparzer. He had access to the library, after he had eased the rusty lock, where he found many English works, the property of the Count's grandfather, who had been Ambassador in London, and Grillparzer was thus encouraged to improve his knowledge of our language. He became acquainted with Shakespeare's works in the original at this time, and by the end of the year there is evidence in his writings that he was familiar with Schlegel's translations, which afforded him a far more adequate understanding and appreciation of the works studied than the crude prose versions of Eschenburg's which he had consulted hitherto.

The summer he spent with the family at one of their country seats; after their return he completed the year in service as general tutor to the nephew (no longer merely as his tutor in law-subjects). In February, 1813, he secured employment as unpaid learner-assistant in the Viennese Court Library.

But in the summer of 1813 he made arrangements to accompany the family into the country again, this time to a lonely residence in Moravia, near the Hungarian boundary. He was giving service which was hardly appreciated, for when he fell seriously ill in the autumn and the doctor represented his illness as contagious he was removed to the cottage of a local quack doctor and subsequently abandoned there—the family having departed—to perish or recover for all they cared. This is the place he describes as Ottokar's hiding-place, when for a time he lay hidden beyond human ken:

> 'Ein ärmlich Badhaus steht dort in der Tiefe,
> Von Menschen abgesondert und Verkehr,
> Da hielt er vierzehn Tage sich verborgen;
> Ein Ort, zum Sterben mehr, als um zu leben!'

When he eventually did recover, he made his way back to Vienna, where he was received as one returned from the dead. Under the care of his mother, for whom he had cried out so unceasingly in his delirium, and of the doctor who had attended his father, he was safely nursed through a serious relapse. The doctor, pressing Grillparzer's hand on the occasion of his last visit, would accept no payment; for he declared that his case was one of the few in his practice for which he as a doctor could take a little credit. He had not expected his patient to survive.

After his recovery Grillparzer resumed his teaching activity, for it was his only source of income, and continued his occupation as unpaid apprentice at the Hofbibliothek. These two occupations ended with the year 1813. At the end of this year he entered upon his career as a civil servant, having received his university certificate in November and being urged to take this step, with a view to making some practical provision for his own future and the care of his family dependants. With varying success and in various capacities he continued in this service for twenty years before attaining to the modest dignity and security of his appointment as 'Archivdirektor der allg. Hofkammer' in 1832.

Grillparzer's heart was never in this work, though this is hardly to be conceived as a personal reproach. Austrian government officials were not accustomed to take their official duties too seriously, and Grillparzer subsequently came to regard his own as of very secondary importance compared to the services he was rendering as a distinguished Austrian poet. He looked for privileges and preferment in the state civil service, as a recognition of his literary merits and as an alternative form of state-poet patronage not otherwise budgeted for in the national economy. It is hardly necessary to point out that this was a view not shared by some of his influential superiors in sinecure posts, who eventually had the dubious satisfaction of seeing the poet obliged to conform to appearances and toe their (imaginary) line.

The first years of Grillparzer's civil service career fall within the period he spoke of as one of outward inaction. Evidence of the activity and preparation going on within him is contained in his account of this time, including the year of leisure to pursue his own interests which his apprenticeship under the indolent officials of the Court Library afforded. He applied his time principally to the study of languages, especially that of the Greek Classics (with all the resources of the library to hand) and Spanish, the literature which was to have such a profound influence on his future development.

Influenced in part by Schlegel's example, Grillparzer had early determined to acquaint himself with treasures of foreign literature by learning to understand them in the original. To this end he had added to his command of the classical languages and of French that of Italian and English. He had also already concerned himself to some extent with Spanish, an interest aroused by Bertuch's translation of Don Quixote and comments on the Spanish poets, and further stimulated by Schlegel's translations of Calderon, which our poet (unconsciously in search of suitable material for the exercise of his young powers) believed he could surpass. His method of pursuing his Spanish studies further at the library consisted therefore in a laborious undertaking to render 'La vida es sueño' into German in the rhyming metre of the original, which involved in the first place looking up the meaning of nearly every word. He eventually completed one hundred and eighty lines, reaching the middle of the first act. More than two years later, at the end of the time we have referred to as Grillparzer's later youthful period, this experiment was to bring the young poet to the notice of Schreyvogel at the Hofburgtheater and thus lead to his first success.

The period from 1811–16 was itself still one of doubts and misgivings, and it is even richer than the earlier one in dramatic exercises and experiments reflecting these doubts. Before the end of the first period, in such a way as to influence quite clearly the fragment 'Irenens Wiederkehr', Grillparzer's attitude to Goethe had changed. Again it was Schreyvogel's 'Sonntagsblatt' which guided him. In February, 1808, it had praised 'Pandoras Wiederkunft', the model which Grillparzer's work reflects, as his title suggests. Grillparzer admits in his diary on June 20, 1810, that he came to gaze 'with indescribable delight into the depths of Goethe's inexpressibly delicate feeling'. He learned to think highly of 'Faust' and to despise Schiller (at that time) by contrast: 'Margaretens rein himmlische Engelsgestalt gleitete an meinem trunkenen Auge vorüber' (T. 92). And then he adds the familiar words (quoted below) referring to the impression which 'Tasso' made on him, leading him to recognize himself in every feeling and expression of Goethe's poet. He read 'Iphigenie', 'Clavigo', 'Egmont', and despairing of ever achieving anything of value in poetry, he discarded all his previous efforts as failing to satisfy his new standards; but before long he was engaged anew in ambitious dramatic experiments, which reveal from now on the influence in particular of Goethe and Shakespeare and mark on every page his progress in technique, historical study, and psychological insight. His language and his interest in the faithful observation of character, particularly his portrayals of woman's nature, indicate his debt to both. To this period for example seems to belong Grillparzer's observation of 'das Dämonische' in Juliet's, as also in Egmont's, nature; in Juliet it is entirely associated, in Shakespeare's representation, with her experience of love. She is, like certain characters now delineated by Grillparzer (for example, Gianetta in Act I, Sc. 3 of 'Seelengröße') and like the later Hero, forgetful of all previous ties, 'deaf to warning', 'blind to danger', and reveals in her bearing 'was die Weiber befällt, wenn eine wahre Liebe eine Beziehung auf die Sinne bekommen hat'.

Associated with this observation of Juliet—and here we again anticipate—is Grillparzer's representation of his Bertha in 'Die Ahnfrau' in the episode following upon the fatal wounding of her father by Jaromir; when Tybalt is killed by Romeo, Juliet's love at once prevails over her grief; and Bertha in her love for Jaromir has no ears nor regard for what is reported to her about her father, but listens only for news of Jaromir:

> Hauptmann Ihr auch hier, mein holdes Fräulein,
> Darauf war ich nicht bereitet.
> Hilfe wollt' ich hier begehren,
> Nicht des Unglücks Bote sein.
> Euer Vater ist—
> Bertha (schnell) Und er?
> Hauptmann Wer mein Fräulein?
> Bertha Und — die Räuber?
> Hauptmann Noch ist es uns nicht gelungen.
> Ach und Euer Vater —
> Bertha Nicht?
> Nun habt Dank für eure Botschaft.

Grillparzer's representation of the conflicting emotions in Bertha's breast after this tragic happening, so well exemplified in Juliet's case, is the most genuinely dramatic passage in the whole work of 'Die Ahnfrau'. The motive as applied in this early piece is still clearly derivative. It might serve in this form as an example of what results when a so-called 'Bildungserlebnis' alone is operative. The contem-

porary critic of the 'Eipeldauer Briefe' expressed his judgement o
this feature in Grillparzer's earliest venture with customary uncon
ventionality as follows:

> der *Offizier* kumd und erzählt der Bertha, daß ihr *Vater* verwundt iss –
> mein *Bertha* zeigt aber so weni *Theilnahm* an'n sterbend'n *Vatern*, daß'
> sogar 'n blöd'n Offizier auffallt — m'r sieht ihr vielmehr a *Freud* an
> wie's *hörd*, daß ihr'n *Rauberamant'n* nix g'scheh'n iß — da häd i g'ra
> vor der *Mannstoll'n Perschon salveni* ausspeib'n mög'n.'[1]

Yet Grillparzer's employment for Bertha of this 'literary experience
denotes a genuine interest in human nature, coupled with a speculativ
and imaginative insight into Shakespeare's art, which only awaite
his own experience as a stimulus to enable him to endow it with th
compelling truth which distinguishes it as applied in the mature
Hero.

In his 'Spartakus' and 'Alfred der Große' fragments Grillparzer'
debt to Goethe and Shakespeare is immediately apparent; though no
more so than the fact that his identification of himself with the characte
and circumstances of the leading figure in each piece constitutes th
initial incentive to these dramatic efforts. It has been observed by
biographers of Grillparzer that the theme of 'Spartakus', that of th
gladiators' revolt against their Roman oppressors, like Alfred's struggl
against England's Danish invaders in the later work, reflects his own
patriotic feeling in that time of his people's oppression by the hate
French. Though this is true, of Alfred more particularly, it is a mistake t
regret the fact that, like 'Alfred der Große', 'Spartakus' too remaine
unfinished for the specific reason that it might have established fo
Grillparzer a reputation like Kleist's, attendant upon such works as hi
'Hermannsschlacht'. In 'Alfred' political tendency is present, thoug
it is hardly the prime motive, as it certainly is not in 'Spartakus'. Th
subjective feeling with which Grillparzer's Spartakus is imbued wa
not calculated to constitute him the type of military hero whos
example might have served to inspire Grillparzer's compatriots t
similar behaviour. His treatment by Grillparzer arises from feeling
on the author's part that have less to do with patriotic fervour an
heroics than with poetic ambition and striving. In 'Spartakus', in
'Alfred', and in his still later 'Heinrich IV', Grillparzer created characters which were the object of his envy and admiration, the embodiment of his own longings and ambitions. His Spartakus i
compounded of elements which serve 'nur als Hülle für das eigen

[1] 'Briefe des neu angekommenen Eipeldauers', Jh. 1817, H. 5, Brf. 2, p. 42 f.

Erleben' and tones 'die der eigenen Stimme zur Verstärkung dienen'.[1] In 1811, when Grillparzer so eagerly began this work, the following passage interprets his subjective conception of Spartakus:

> 'Nicht zu gemeinem Thun ist der gebohren,
> Zum Welterretter hat ihn Zeus erkohren'.

It was part of the poet's plan, however, to represent his hero as involved in tragedy because he was unable to resist the besetting temptations of love and avoid the unhappy consequences for himself of feminine perfidy—an early appearance of this personal motive. Little more than a year later Grillparzer in despondent mood rejects the implications of all this (T. 146): 'Wenn ich mir jetzt die Idee, die mich bei der Ausarbeitung des Spartakus begeisterte, bedenke, so schaudre ich, und es ist mir kaum begreiflich, sie je gehabt zu haben'. It would be 'scarcely conceivable' that he should reject the idea in such terms unless he had in fact related it to himself.

Directly opposed, in spirit, to such works as 'Spartakus', 'Alfred der Grosse', and 'Heinrich IV' (a work in which Grillparzer seeks what Volkelt describes as 'humoristische Selbstbefreiung von seiner Zwiespältigkeit') are those which give expression to what the same author describes as 'das Ideal des stillen Sinnes', such as 'Irenens Wiederkehr' and the earlier 'Robert, Herzog von der Normandie'. It becomes immediately clear that this ideal takes its origin from Grillparzer's feelings of insufficiency and inability to achieve his ambition which are so frequently recorded in his diaries and reflected in his works. These feelings cause the author unhappiness, and he is induced (when in this defeatist mood) to condemn ambitious strivings and declare 'worin eigentlich das Glück besteht: in Selbstbegrenzung und Seelenfrieden'. These un-Faustian words occur in an account written in 1822 of a rejected plan dating back to 1813, a plan to continue and complete Goethe's 'Faust' by causing the hero to embrace this quietistic ideal through his sense of responsibility for Gretchen's unhappy fate.[2]

Certainly the most striking feature of Grillparzer's early works and fragments, as indeed of his whole dramatic works, is the evidence they contain of his tendency to draw upon his feelings and experience as a would-be poet, and upon the results of his psychological introspection. Of the remaining fragments the most interesting in this respect are 'Die Pazzi' and 'Friedrich der Streitbare'. In the characters of Francesko Pazzi and Jerindo Frangipani the author accuses himself of weaknesses and deplores his own shortcomings and unhappy fate. His notes on

[1] Cf. 'Wke.', II. 3, p. xx.

[2] Cf. 'Wke.', II, 4, p. 242 (Faust plan).

these characters [1] can leave no one in doubt that they were intended to give expression to his feelings of despair at the disadvantages and misfortunes which hindered him from realizing his poetic ambition. Both of them feel themselves to be unjustly treated, to be outcasts from society, and are aggrieved that they should have failed to achieve recognition.

> 'In dieser Wendung liegt ... die Sehnsucht des heranwachsenden Künstlers nach der Anerkennung, die ihm noch versagt wird', as Hilda Schulhof says. 'Die Charaktere des Pazzi und Frangipani tragen Keime des Künstlerdramas in die beiden Stücke'.[2]

Pazzi is a rebel in 'consciousness of his unattractive nature, his humble birth, his educational deficiencies and consequent fear of being despised', the young poet writes. In this feeling of humiliation he avoids society and is dissatisfied with himself and the world, because of his very inclination to strive for the opposite goals. 'Because he could not shine in society, he had shunned it'. This fragment still occupied Grillparzer's attention after he had long since invalidated it in its actual quality as a self-portrait by poetic achievements and a personal popularity that were of wide renown. In Frangipani Grillparzer actually gives voice to his longing for the encouragement and support which he later received from Schreyvogel. In all respects Lorenzo and the Herzog are the counterparts of Pazzi and Frangipani, and they are equipped with the gifts and virtues which the latter lack. They are on an equal footing with the characters of Alfred and Heinrich IV referred to above.

> 'Es lockte den jungen Grillparzer, wie so manchen mühsam Strebenden und mit sich Ringenden, das leicht erreichte Glück, Selbstsicherheit und Erfolg in einer Gegenfigur darzustellen'.[3]

With these and numerous other dramatic experiments and plans Grillparzer worked intermittently until the beginning of the year 1816. The author's practice, observed particularly in this second period, of identifying himself with his subjects is outwardly revealed in the youthfulness of his principal characters; Spartakus and Heinrich IV (married men in Grillparzer's sources) are treated as Goethe treated the historical Egmont—a married man with seven children and a wooden leg, as Schiller insists—and for the same sufficient reason; all are represented as young unmarried men.

[1] ibid., pp. 215 ff., 329 ff. [2] Cf. 'Wke.', II. 3, p. xxi. [3] ibid., p. xxii.

6. 'DIE AHNFRAU'

Yet when we come to examine 'Die Ahnfrau' we seem to discover little material that is obviously characteristic of the author in this sense. For though Jaromir (if he, and not the ghost herself, be regarded as the principal figure) is youthful enough, neither he nor any of the other figures (they are hardly characters) in the play bear clear evidence of being conceived along the lines we have discussed.

This circumstance is doubtless attributable to the fact that the work came to be written as the result of external pressure brought to bear on Grillparzer; and the fantastic elements in the subject-matter of this 'in every sense premature' product tempt us to underestimate the fundamental subjectivity in his conception of Jaromir's character and destiny. Yet the formula applied by him to this work: 'Der Arme, dem sich ab ein Gott gewendet', would itself suffice to illuminate the essential kinship between this 'robber chieftain' and the poet himself. In this important respect 'Die Ahnfrau' appears as a work which, like those which were to follow it, continues naturally the development which Grillparzer had more or less consistently followed in his dramatic works up to the beginning of 1816.

Even after the success of 'Die Ahnfrau', as a result of the adverse criticisms which this work encountered, Grillparzer's doubts as to the genuineness of his dramatic gifts (so often reflected in his youthful works) were not overcome. In a letter to Adolf Müllner he makes the following confession:

> 'Von Natur schüchtern und unbeholfen, durch frühes Unglück zur Schwermuth und Selbstpeinigung gestimmt, hatte ich früh dem Glauben an meine Dichtergabe und mit ihm der Lust des Lebens entsagt. Schwer ward mirs aus dem dumpfig-warmen Medium das meine Phantasie brütend um sich geschaffen hatte hervorzutreten in den erkältenden aber zugleich erstärkenden Tag. Herrn Schreyvogels väterlicher Sorge gelangs mein Widerstreben zu besiegen. Aber als nun seine Vaterhand jenes beschrieene, in jeder Hinsicht zu früh geborne Wesen aus mir hervor gezogen hatte, und von allen Seiten die Hunde des kritischen Donners heulend darüber herstürzten, da kehrten alle Qualbilder früherer Tage zurück' (B. 98).

The manner in which Schreyvogel came to play this part, one which nevertheless earned him Grillparzer's lasting gratitude, is vividly recounted in the 'Selbstbiographie', the principal source of information about the genesis of 'Die Ahnfrau'.

On June 5, 1816, Schreyvogel's translation of Calderon's *La vida es sueño* having been performed in the Hofburgtheater, Grillparzer's translated fragment of the same drama was published, without Grillparzer's consent, side by side with Schreyvogel's version in the 'Wiener Modenzeitung'. It was used thus by Hebenstreit, an opponent of Schreyvogel's, to the decided disadvantage of the latter, as the basis of a bitter attack on Schreyvogel's dramatic ability. When Grillparzer shortly afterwards received a message from Schreyvogel saying how deeply hurt he was that the son of a former friend of his should lend himself to such an unworthy intrigue against him, Grillparzer explained in reply that he had unwittingly been made a party to this attack. Schreyvogel gladly accepted his explanation and asked Grillparzer to visit him. On June 22nd a meeting took place, the beginning of an intimate friendship which lasted until Schreyvogel's death in 1832.

The 'fatherly interest' which Schreyvogel took in Grillparzer's dramatic aspirations evoked from him the confession that he had conceived a plan which he had not taken the trouble to execute for two reasons; first, he had resolved to renounce dramatic poetry for ever; and secondly, he hesitated to treat a subject that seemed at best suited for the popular suburban stage. He had no wish to put himself on a level with a class of writers he had always despised—even though he considered that he had enough poetry in him to render the sensational subject-matter worthy of his treatment.

He narrated his plan in detail to Schreyvogel, who exclaimed enthusiastically 'Das Stück ist fertig. Sie brauchen es nur niederzuschreiben'; and overriding Grillparzer's scruples, he extracted from him a promise to consider it further. They probably talked of Müllner's fate-tragedy 'Die Schuld', and even at this first meeting Schreyvogel seems to have drawn attention to the relation it bore to Grillparzer's projected drama.

The author names two literary sources for 'die Ahnfrau' in his account. During the first four months of the year he had suffered a serious illness and he may have read these sources during the early part of that time.

One of them seems to have been a German adaptation in a Viennese pirated edition of the story of the eighteenth-century French brigand 'Louis Mandrin'. It was the manner of the brigand's capture that struck Grillparzer. He had sought refuge from his pursuers in a castle, where he was loved—according to Grillparzer's recollection—by a servant girl. She had no knowledge of his true identity. He was captured in her room. Grillparzer states that the tragic implications in this relationship, or rather in this exposure (he emends), made a deep impression upon him. We shall probably not go astray in supposing that the motive for this lay in the young poet's own habitual reflections upon himself as little better than an impostor. It is, however, to be remarked that in the source referred to, as in Grillparzer's finished work, the girl is *not* a servant girl or of lowly origin, but is of noble birth, and her lover is a young man of passionate nature, clever, witty, of boundless ambition and other adventurous characteristics.

The second source mentioned by Grillparzer seems to have been an adaptation of a section of the 1797 German translation 'Die blutende Gestalt mit Dolch und Lampe' from M. G. Lewis's 'Ambrosio or The Monk', a novel which, appearing first in 1795 in London, was described by Scott as 'a romance in the German taste' and by Schlegel as 'one of the most popular so-called original publications imitated from inferior German sources'. One of these sources was Benedikt Naubert's version of the popular ghost story 'Die weiße Frau', which Grillparzer may also have used.

In Grillparzer's source it is the identity of appearance between the last descendant of an ancient family and the ghost of her original ancestress which suggested itself to the young author as a feature offering possibilities for gruesome stage effects. On one occasion the girl's lover mistakes her for the ghost, and on another, that of a projected elopement, he mistakes the ghost for the girl.

One morning near the beginning of June, 1816, when he was lying in bed, so Grillparzer declares, the two ideas joined together in his mind and mutually supplemented each other, the bandit issuing forth as a lineal descendant himself of the guilty ancestress, whose spirit, subject to a curse, could find no peace.

Grillparzer seems to have dismissed the idea of executing his plan, and for a time he saw no more of Schreyvogel. On August 12, however, they met again by chance. As he approached, Schreyvogel called out: 'Wie steht's mit der Ahnfrau?' and Grillparzer replied despondently: 'Es geht nicht'. To which Schreyvogel responded that he had once given the same answer to Goethe and had been assured: 'Man muß nur in die Hand blasen, dann geht's schon'.

These characteristic words of the great master, even at second-hand, fired Grillparzer's imagination. His innermost spirit was stirred, he declares. Before his walk was over he had started to compose the opening lines of his piece: 'Nun wohlan, was muß, geschehe!'—in the trochaic verse characteristic of the Spanish drama and rendered attractive to him through his study of Calderon; the latter's 'Devocion de la Cruz' presents the robber motive in combination with those of incestuous passion and attempted parricide, and also embraces the theme of expiation, as in Grillparzer's piece. He admits, however, that he would probably not have risked the Spanish verse-form for the German stage but for the example of Müllner.

These features were combined with other literary influences, the language especially of Grillparzer's piece being obviously affected by his studies of Schiller, Goethe, and Shakespeare. In addition there was the influence of the Viennese popular theatre with its numerous dramatized robber and ghost stories, 'Volksmärchen' like Grillparzer's own. This influence is the earliest, the most far-reaching, and the most recognizable of all.

The action of the piece is briefly as follows: The ancestress of a noble house has been slain by her husband for infidelity, and a curse has been pronounced upon her spirit, which was doomed to wander until her tainted progeny has perished from the earth. Hence she haunts the castle which is the abode of the only surviving branch of her family. Her maternal instincts prompt her to warn Count Borotin's only child Bertha of impending danger. Bertha has fallen in love with a stranger who has rescued her from bandits in the woods. The stranger turns out to be Jaromir, a robber chief and also Bertha's own brother, who was thought to have been drowned, but was actually kidnapped in his infancy. The count assists some soldiery in their efforts to exterminate the brigands and is accidentally killed in the dark by Jaromir, his unrecognized son, who, incidentally, is armed with the dagger with which the Ahnfrau herself was originally slain. Bertha dies of grief (or may be supposed to poison herself after the curtain of the penultimate act), and Jaromir is killed in the ancestral vault by the embrace of the Ahnfrau whom he mistakes for her. Thus the ancient guilt of the Ahnfrau is expiated, and her spirit can rest in peace.

Commenced on August 13, 1816, this play was completed in its first version in very little over a month, by September 15th. Each act as it was finished, the first act after only four days, was carried to Schreyvogel, who corrected and criticized very considerably and subsequently revised the complete work. He demanded an extension and motivation of the fate-idea in the piece, so that the living generation should be represented as doomed 'because they were of sinful descent' and not, as it were, gratuitously. He also insisted upon sharper characterization and the elimination of many repetitions and extravagant expressions. These matters received Grillparzer's reluctant attention, and the second version thus came to be prepared, the one on which the shorter stage version and the first printed edition are based, with five acts instead of four, the original third act being divided to form the third and fourth acts of the piece as we know it now. Grillparzer revised the work for its sixth edition in 1844, making, however, only a few minor alterations.

'Die Ahnfrau' profited considerably in content and form by Schreyvogel's aid and criticism. It is true that it thus became a fate-tragedy proper, instead of remaining a ghost-play with all the makings of a fate-tragedy in it. Even in Grillparzer's first version the decisive incidents are not determined by the will of the characters, who are indeed dominated by a fore-ordained fate against which they vainly struggle. There is also, hanging on the wall, that familiar theatrical property of this *genre*, the 'fateful' dagger. Jaromir subsequently wields it to slay his father, who dying declares:

> 'Das hat nicht mein Sohn gethan,
> Tiefverhüllte, höhre Mächte
> Führten seine schwanke Rechte,

just as Jaromir in Act IV of this first version exclaims of the same deed:

> Ja, der Wille ist der meine
> Doch die That ist dem Geschick'.

And is it anything but that familiar motive of fate-tragedy, not merely incest, but insane incestuous passion, that impels Jaromir to lust after Bertha, even when he knows her to be his sister? There is no trace of plausible motivation for this action. Its purpose is to exploit the popular audience's superstitious horror of such unnatural passion and at the same time to drive Jaromir into the Ahnfrau's embrace.

In the versions prepared for the very successful production of the play on the stage in January and February, and for the first printed edition in May, 1817, considerable cuts were made and lengthy instructions introduced relating to gruesome stage effects. This effectively completed the process of exposing Grillparzer's 'Ahnfrau' to the censure of contemporary literary critics. Hebenstreit was unsparingly vindictive:

> 'Ich halte diese Arbeit für recht schlecht: denn es ist durchaus nicht zu läugnen, daß hier Verbrechen durch Verbrechen gesühnt werden und die Charakteristik im wahren Sinne erbärmlich ist'.

Müllner formed his own unfavourable opinion, which Grillparzer at first tried to refute; 'die Anhfrau in ihrer gegenwärtigen Gestalt ist nicht *meine* Ahnfrau'.

There is some truth in this. For even if we hold the view that th
play is essentially a fate-tragedy from the start, it is nevertheless per
missible to say with Emil Reich in reference to the subjective characte
of Grillparzer's creation: 'Fremde Einwirkung verzerrte die unsern
Poeten nur halbbewußt vorschwebende, aus den bittersten Kümmer
nissen der eigenen Existenz entsprungene Idee'.[1] This original feelin
of gloomy foreboding was undoubtedly Grillparzer's own. Jaromi
is an unhappy character in being an outcast from society through n
fault of his own, in possessing, like Pazzi and Frangipani, a passionat
and violent nature, and in being a foredoomed victim of an unhapp
fate. There can be no doubt regarding the subjective nature o
Grillparzer's portrayal of his 'Armer, dem sich ab ein Gott gewendet',
nor of the gloomy and pessimistic atmosphere of the whole piece
Referring to his original version he describes it as a 'Gespenstermär-
chen mit einer bedeutenden menschlichen Grundlage'. The misfortunes and decline of Grillparzer's own family, those disqualification
of birth and upbringing reflected elsewhere in his youthful works
and his despondency at being unable to achieve his ambition an
destiny are all reflected in 'Die Ahnfrau'. In this sense it constitute
no departure from his regular dramatic practice.

[1] Reich, E.: 'Franz Grillparzers Dramen', Dresden, 1909[3], p. 46. In the latest edition of thes lectures Reich even speaks of Schreyvogel's 'Verunstaltung' of Grillparzer's original con-ception and text; cf. 'Grillparzers Dramatisches Werk', Vienna, 1938[4], p. 43.

[2] Cf. Jugenderinnerungen im Grünen, G. 84, 15 [i.e. 'Wke.', I. 10–12, Gedichte, Nr. 84, 15] l. 121.

CHAPTER II

'SAPPHO'

'SAPPHO' is a work which, in spite of all that has been written about it, and for all its apparent simplicity of action and outline, still presents certain unsolved difficulties which stand in the way of its satisfactory interpretation and appreciation. It reflects, in a completer sense than has hitherto been shown, its author's mind and feeling, and his actual observations and experiences at the time of its creation. Like 'Die Ahnfrau' itself this work too, though ostensibly less subjective, was based on a profound inner conviction of the author.

Grillparzer always resented criticism which described his 'Ahnfrau' as being merely sensational. At the time of the first bitter attacks upon it he determined, in vindication of his injured pride, that his next work should afford no excuse for criticism on similar grounds. He would choose a subject permitting entirely objective and dramatic as opposed to subjective and theatrical treatment, one which did not depend on robbers, ghosts, and bangs for effect, 'die Räuber-, Gespenster- und Knall-Effekte' of his 'Ahnfrau'. It was his wish to prove to himself and the world that he was capable of relying solely on the poetic quality of his products.[1]

The wisdom of Grillparzer's determination to avoid in future the crude theatrical effects of his 'Ahnfrau' is self-evident. His distrust of his own feelings and his wish to keep them out of his next work may perhaps appear to be less well founded. A passage in recent musical criticism, however, fits Grillparzer's case exactly, when Mr. W. J. Turner writes of Stravinsky: 'His desire to achieve the impersonal is undoubtedly genuine, but I believe it is because he is a good and serious enough artist to have real ambitions and to be conscious of his special weakness—which is to be too personal and primarily emotional.'[2] Yet we must remember that Grillparzer's works, like those of the artist to whom these words refer, nevertheless derive their real interest and value from this weakness duly controlled;

[1] He may well be held to have taken to heart the kindly encouragement of the 'ald'r g'scheid'r Herr' of the so popular Eipeldauer Briefe (Jh. 1817, H. 5, Br. 2, p. 52): 'wann der *jungi Mann* aso fortfahrd, und amahl ein'n *lieblichern Geg'nstand anfasst,* so waxt uns in ihm a *dramatischer Dichter* empor, den (i sags ganz ohni Scheu) *Deutschland* no nie *aufz'weis'n* g'habt had'.

[2] *New Statesman and Nation,* Feb. 22, 1936, p. 262.

only then shall we be suitably prepared for considering the goo intentions with which he took up his work on 'Sappho'.

I. OBJECTIVE INTENTIONS

On June 29, 1817, Grillparzer met an acquaintance, Dr. Joël who proposed to him that he should write an opera libretto for th composer Weigl on the subject of 'Sappho'. Grillparzer's reply wa that the subject was suitable for a tragedy. The story attracted him he afterwards declared, because it seemed particularly well adapte to the simple kind of treatment he had in mind: the more so, n doubt, as, according to the aesthetic convention of Grillparzer's day classical antiquity was the domain of nobility, simplicity, and objec-tivity in art.

> 'Ich ... suchte ... nach einem Stoff, der es mir möglich machte, i der Behandlung eine Ruhe walten zu lassen, die mich vor der Gefah des Selbstmitspiels bewahrte, die mir des Strebens um so würdige schien, je fremder sie meiner Individualität ist, und je mehr ich ver-zweifelte sie je zu erreichen. Schon in früher Zeit hatte mich Sappho' Ende begeistert ...'.

At the time when these lines were written to Müllner,[1] who con-sidered the early acts of 'Sappho' unsatisfactory, because writte without enthusiasm, Grillparzer was still in a mind to defend hi new work on the strength of the first two acts. In doing so he wa quite sincere, and not merely concerned to refute Müllner's criticism He deplored the fact that he had not been able to sustain the effor of remaining entirely objective in his treatment, that is to say, objec-tive and dramatical as opposed to subjective and lyrical, or theatrical perhaps. He then gives his account of the change which took plac as the result of an averred interruption through illness when engage on the middle of the piece, and adds:

> 'Ich sah sehr wohl den Kontrast ein, in dem die beiden Hälften de Stücks gegen einander standen, aber ich war immer bereit die Parthi der geliebten ersten Hälfte gegen die letzte zu nehmen'.[2]

This document informs us of Grillparzer's point of view at a tim before 'Sappho' had actually been produced. The evidence so give

[1] 'Wke.', III. 1, B. 104 (Erster Entwurf), p. 97, ll. 15–24. Müllner had written from Weißen-fels about a fortnight earlier, on Feb. 14, 1818: 'Sie fingen an ohne Begeisterung; aber sie kan Ihnen im Fortgang. Ist es nicht so? Darum ist der Anfang schlecht, Mittel und Ende göttlich' ibid., p. 91, ll. 8–10.

[2] Loc. cit. (Zweiter Entwurf), p. 103, ll. 21–24.

of his original intention, more especially his recognition that he had failed to fulfil this intention, is important, quite apart from the fact that he may have been wrong in preferring the first part of his play to the more spontaneous and unpremeditated second part, or that he may have subsequently somewhat modified his opinion as the result of 'Sappho's' unforeseen success.

There is, in principle, no doubt that Grillparzer was mistaken in this preference. If he had actually been successful in carrying out his original intention his work could hardly have commanded the interest that it does.

> 'Der Vorsatz auch des größten Meisters kann immer nur der Anstoß, nie der Inhalt und Umfang eines echten Dichterwerks sein',

as Gundolf says in reference to 'Sappho', adding the significant words:

> 'Wer die Idee eines Werks mit seinem Bewußtsein durchdringen könnte, wäre ein flacher Poet, und wessen Werk nicht mehr ist als sein Dichter davon weiß, lebt nicht über die kurze Dauer seiner Theorien hinaus'.[1]

It is instructive to observe that originally Grillparzer seems to have thought differently as regards the composition of his 'Sappho' and that in the letter to Müllner he offers excuses for what really least needed excuse in a genuine poet's work.

Perhaps it is an understanding of this truth, and not merely reserve, that fortunately prevents the greatest poets, as a rule, from volunteering information about their original intentions, as well as about the personal experiences, the real origins, the private thoughts, associated with what is expressed in their works. For when they observe the inevitable modification and transfiguration which these elements have undergone, and the wider significance which through poetic treatment they have acquired, these poets must feel that whatever they might attempt to confess of the process by which this took place could only limit the potential implications of what they have expressed. An attractive, characteristic, though isolated, example of this attitude is found in Goethe's reply when, pressed for an interpretation, he opened wide his eyes and echoed mysteriously Faust's words: 'Die Mütter! Mütter! 's klingt so wunderlich!', or in his declaration that his 'Faust' was 'incommensurable'. On how many matters, profound as well as intimate, did he not prefer to remain silent when he could have helped if he would, even regarding the main purport of his 'Faust', wisely leaving his readers to imagine and

[1] 'Jb. d. Freien Deutschen Hochstifts', Fr. a. M., 1931, Fr. Gundolf, 'Fr. Grillparzer', pp. 9–93, cf. p. 34 f.

his critics to explain, if they could, what he really might have meant to express!

Grillparzer's admissions about a cardinal aspect of his original poetic intentions in 'Sappho' are of importance, therefore, because they invite discussion of the history of its composition and afford guidance towards a just analysis and interpretation of the work. He knew that in some manner beyond his actual control the development of his idea had insensibly changed. What he failed to realize at the time of writing his letter to Müllner was that this was not in itself undesirable. He naïvely supposed that the distraction of an aching tooth had been responsible for the change, not that his original conception had been itself in some way inadequate. He was certainly not aware of the truth that if his work was to transcend mediocrity it must have freedom to shape itself unhampered by strict adherence to his initial purpose.

2. SUBJECTIVE THEME—AN 'ARTIST-TRAGEDY'

It is commonly held that the short time which elapsed between Grillparzer's conception of 'Sappho' and his setting to work upon the play itself virtually excludes the possibility of his having intended from the outset to bring out what we now regard as the distinctive psychological content of this tragedy. On the very evening of the day of his conversation with Dr. Joël he set down his scenario, and on the following day he was at work upon his play. With regard to the scenario Sauer writes in his Introduction to 'Sappho':

> 'Aus dem Szenarium folgt aber weiter, daß Grillparzer zunächst nur die rein menschlichen Züge des Stoffes anzogen, daß sich ihm das Liebes- und Eifersuchtsdrama zuerst gestaltete, ohne daß ihm die tieferen Grundideen des Werkes bereits ganz deutlich gewesen wären. . . . Das Werk vertiefte sich mehr und mehr erst während der Ausarbeitung. Sappho zog ihn zuerst als Weib und später als Künstlerin, als Dichterin an. Zum Künstlerdrama wurde das Werk erst allmählich ausgestaltet. Das Künstlerische ist das Sekundäre'.[1]

The question whether Sappho's being a poetess may be regarded as secondary or incidental to Grillparzer's original plan is, however, debatable. The scenario, a mere sketch of the projected action of the play, does not suffice to establish Sauer's contention. Grillparzer's words in the letter to Müllner convey the impression that even in his

[1] 'Wke.', I. 1, p. lxxxiv.

original conception he regarded the fact as one of prior and not secondary importance:

> 'Ich verfiel auf Sappho. . . Ein Charakter, der Sammelplatz glühender Leidenschaften, über die aber eine *erworbene* Ruhe, die schöne Frucht höherer Geistesbildung, den Szepter führt, bis die angeschmiedeten Sklaven die Ketten brechen und dastehen und Wuth schnauben . . .'.[1]

A number of Grillparzer's sayings afford a kind of commentary to this conception of his heroine's character. It is essentially his own conception. As far back as 1808 Grillparzer had expressed in his diary the conviction that a poet must possess violent passions (T. 32):

> 'ich *habe* heftige Leidenschaften . . . und gewiß das muß ein Mensch besizen, der nur einigermaßen Anspruch auf den Namen eines Dichters machen will'.

A little earlier he had written the following words, which are invariably associated with his portrayal of Sappho:

> 'Ich bin *rachgierig*, und zwar so, daß ich außer mir selbst komme, wenn ich diese Leidenschaft nicht in vollem Maaße befriedigen kann. . . . Diese Leidenschaft äußert sich besonders wenn die *Eifersucht* ins Spiel kömmt. . . . Eifersucht schließt bei mir ganz den Gebrauch der Vernunft aus. . . . Ich bin überzeugt, daß ich eine Untreue der Geliebten blutig . . . rächen würde'. (T. 17).

These passages perhaps throw light on the phrase, 'Ein Charakter, der Sammelplatz glühender Leidenschaften'; the words 'über die aber eine *erworbene* Ruhe, die schöne Frucht höherer Geistesbildung, den Szepter führt' recall the concluding words of the diary note written while he was composing 'Sappho' during the summer of 1817. The passage, we saw, affords strong evidence of Grillparzer's practice of identifying himself with his central characters. And since he invokes Shakespeare in justification of his own implied procedure (in respect here to the passion of jealousy), it is of interest to observe that modern criticism tends to endorse Grillparzer's remarkable insight into Shakespeare's living art. Running through almost everything that Shakespeare wrote after 1600 Mr. J. Dover Wilson detects a strain that he associates with 'the commonplace derangement known as jealousy, jealousy of the same kind as, if not identical with, that described so savagely in the Sonnets', an excessive human passion which the poet exorcizes, 'confesses' (in Goethe's meaning), interprets, or reveals, in works like 'Troilus and Cressida', 'Othello', 'The

[1] Loc. cit. p. 97, ll. 25-28.

Winter's Tale', 'Cymbeline', and 'Hamlet'.[1] And before re-quoting Grillparzer (with his reference, among other things, to Shakespeare's 'madness') it may also be appropriate to recall a judgement of Mr. T. S. Eliot's, which Mr. Dover Wilson supports: 'The "madness" of Hamlet lay to Shakespeare's hand'.[2] Grillparzer's passage about his own and Shakespeare's procedure seems to establish on his own confession what we observe in Sappho as an example of his practice in character delineation (T. 221):

'Man hat sehr viel über die Gabe großer Dichter gesprochen, die verschiedenartigsten, ihrem eigenen Selbst fremdartigsten Leidenschaften und Charaktere zu schildern, und Manche haben gar viel von Beobachtung und Studium des Menschen gesagt und gemeint, Shakespeare habe in Bierhäusern, unter Karrenschiebern und Matrosen die Züge zu seinen Macbeths und Othellos zusammengesammelt, und dann wenn das Bündel voll gewesen, sich hingesetzt und ein Stück d'raus zusammengesetzt. Ganz gut

' "Das rühmen die Schüler aller Orten
Ist aber noch keiner ein Weber geworden!"

'Ich glaube, daß das Genie nichts geben kann, als was es in sich selbst gefunden, und daß es nie eine Leidenschaft oder Gesinnung schildern wird, als die er selbst, als Mensch, in seinem eigenen Busen trägt; daher kommen die richtigen Blicke, die oft ein junger Mensch in das menschliche Herz thut, indeß ein in der Welt Abgearbeiteter, selbst mit schärferm Beobachtungsgeist Ausgerüsteter nichts als 100mal gesagte Dinge zusammenstoppelt. Also sollte Shakespeare ein Mörder, Dieb, Lügner, Verräther, Undankbarer, Wahnsinniger gewesen seyn, weil er sie so meisterlich schildert? Ja! Das heißt, er mußte zu dem allen Anlage in sich haben, obschon die vorherrschende Vernunft, das moralische Gefühl nichts davon zum Ausbruch kommen ließ. Nur ein Mensch mit ungeheuren Leidenschaften kann meiner Meinung nach dramatischer Dichter seyn, ob sie gleich unter dem Zügel der Vernunft stehen müssen und daher im gemeinen Leben nicht zum Vorschein kommen. — Ich wollte, irgend ein Dichter läse das!'

That these concluding words have a bearing upon Grillparzer's personal conception and presentation of Sappho is clear. She, *the poetess*, was to be revealed in circumstances in which her pent-up passions should actually break forth. She was to be shown as discontented with her lonely lot as a poetess, just as Grillparzer was discontented, and as seeking belatedly to partake of 'life', thus exposing herself (through the inevitable thwarting of her desires) to the risks

[1] Cf. J. Dover Wilson, *The Essential Shakespeare*, Cambridge, 1932, p. 118 f., and *What Happens in Hamlet*, Cambridge, 1935, p. 306 f.
[2] T. S. Eliot, *The Sacred Wood*, London, 1920, p. 93.

nd consequences of such an outburst. For the same inherent passions which, held in restraint, are a qualification for art, prove, because of heir very violence, a danger to the happiness and well-being of the oet in real life, which so readily affords situations that greatly excite hem. Grillparzer considered this to indicate the special need for estraint on the poet's part and to be an example of the hardship attenlant upon poetic endowment. This theme hardly seems to justify he judgement that 'Sappho' was planned to be an *Eifersuchtstragödie* ather than a *Künstlertragödie*. For it was Sappho the poetess who was nvolved in this tragedy, and her fate was to be an original interpretaion by Grillparzer of the *malheur d'être poète* in an aspect revealed to im in the first place by observation of his own nature.

The phrase *malheur d'être poète* occurs in the letter to Müllner, mmediately following upon the words last quoted, and the context upports the present argument:

> '. . . Dazu gesellte sich, sobald das Wort: *Dichterin* einmal ausgesprochen war, natürlich auf der Stelle der Kontrast zwischen Kunst und Leben (wenn die Ahnfrau unwillkürlich gewissermaßen eine Paraphrase des berüchtigten d'Alambertischen *malheur d'être* geworden ist, so dürfte wohl die Sappho ein in eben dem Sinne wahres *malheur d'être poète* in sich fassen). Mit einem Wort, der Gedanke ergriff mich und ich war, als ich zur Ausführung gieng, begeisterter, als je in meinem Leben'.[1]

Influenced, no doubt, by Grillparzer's supposed change of plan, auer seems to assume that Grillparzer in fact added this motive of the ontrast between art and life to his original conception, gradually orgetting his first intention of showing that Sappho incurred guilt nerely through her passionate character and despotic behaviour. But we have seen that in Grillparzer's original conception the cause or this behaviour actually lay within her as a poetess. In spite of auer's judgement, based on the scenario, the original plan must herefore, no less than the finished work, be regarded as that of an rtist-tragedy.

A pencil drawing of the final scene made by Grillparzer presumably on the morning after meeting Joël, before the work was commenced, lepicts Sappho with averted gaze bidding farewell to the kneeling air.[2] It seems permissible to interpret this as showing that the oetess is about to commit suicide, not blaming anyone else for her ate, but recognizing that her own nature, that of a poetess, has etrayed her into behaving *unworthily*.

[1] Loc. cit., p. 97, l. 29; p. 98, l. 6.
[2] 'Wke.', I. 17 (Apparatband), p. 174, and Tafel I, Zeichnung zum V. Akt der 'Sappho'.

3. INFLUENCE OF 'TASSO'

The same aspect of the *malheur d'être poète* is paralleled in Goethe' 'Tasso', undoubtedly the most important literary influence discernibl in Grillparzer's tragedy. 'Tasso' was a work which he prized ver highly. In 1810 he wrote in his diary (T. 92):

> 'Felsenfest ward meine Liebe für Göthen durch Tasso'n gegründe Konnte diese Dichternatur dem Dichter fremd sein? Ich selbst glaub es zu sein der als Tasso sprach, handelte, liebte; nur Worte, so schie es mir, hatte Göthe meinen Gefühlen gegeben; ich fand mich in jeden Gefühle, in jeder Rede, in jedem Worte. . . . ich bethete Göthe a Und doch schreibt sich von dieser Zeit auch der Anfang meines Trüb sinns, meiner Melancholie her'.

This influence was present (as Grillparzer knew)[1] from the start, an it affords the aptest explanation of Grillparzer's expression in th Selbstbiographie when he says of Goethe (in words that hav generally so far escaped precise explanation):

> 'Er erwähnte meiner "Sappho", die er zu billigen schien, wori er freilich gewissermaßen sich selbst lobte, denn ich hatte so ziemlic mit seinem Kalbe gepflügt'.

His theme, he says in effect, was borrowed from Goethe; Grillparze admits that in using it he was in a sense 'poaching on Goethe' preserves'.[2] More than twenty years later he used almost the sam words in a conversation with Zimmermann, and it is justifiable t assume that Grillparzer was aware of having been influenced b 'Tasso' to treat the *malheur d'être poète* theme from the point of viev natural to himself.

Grillparzer was equally aware, however, that his treatment of th 'Tasso' theme fell short of Goethe's and that he was not so fitted fo the task of representing in his heroine a poetess by nature, nor in hi drama an example of the tragic contrast between genius and the world

> 'Ein Meister hätte vielleicht verstanden', he explains to Müllne 'Sappho'n selbst im Sturme der Leidenschaften die Farbe, die die Dicht kunst ihrem *Charakter* gab, sichtbar zu machen; ich, weniger geschickt mußte *vor* dem Sturme eine Kraft anschaulich machen, die mit unter di erregenden Kräfte des Sturms selber gehört'.[3]

[1] Cf. *Brief an Müllner* (I. Entw.), p. 100, ll. 1–3, where Grillparzer refers to 'Tasso' (an 'Correggio'), insisting on his own conviction that there is 'eine natürliche Scheidewand zwische Kunst und Leben'!

[2] This is the modern equivalent to Samson's metaphor, Judges xiv. 18, 'If ye had not *plowe with my heifer*, ye had not found out my riddle', a premeditated taunt and provocative allusio to the manifest intimacy of the Philistine wedding guests with his young bride, their kinswoman

[3] 'Brief an Müllner', p. 99, ll. 11–16.

'his passage explains that though Grillparzer's intention was similar o Goethe's in 'Tasso', he felt that he had to content himself with treatment of the contrast between 'art' and 'life' (not genius and he world); a treatment, moreover, which presents 'art', then 'life', hen 'art' again, alternately.

In view of this we might be disposed to agree with Petsch when, peaking of the opening acts, he says:

> 'die Sappho des ersten Entwurfes ist im Grunde gar keine wahre Künstlernatur; als ein sinnlich veranlagtes, leidenschaftliches Wesen hat sie sich vorschnell einem Beruf gewidmet, der die volle Hingabe des Menschen verlangt'.[1]

3ut it is hardly an opinion that Grillparzer would himself have ndorsed, except perhaps mistakenly (after completing 'Sappho') as egards the complete self-sacrifice which is here alleged to be denanded by the poet's profession. Grillparzer was himself so preoccupied with the thought of this sacrifice that from now on he makes t in different aspects and presentation almost involuntarily the underying theme of all his works. This conviction was founded, with Grillparzer, as it was with Beethoven, on 'the profound instinctive knowledge of genius that solitude (withdrawal from the world, or what Grillparzer calls "Sammlung") was necessary to the highest development of his creative power'.[2] If, however, this requirement is understood to imply as much as it seems to imply in Grillparzer's final treatment of 'Sappho', the almost complete renunciation of contact with life, the virtual divorcement of art and life, it is clearly invalid. The finished work seems to express as its teaching this extreme view, with the difference that for the later 'Sappho' the world is well lost. The original conception, however, even apart from this difference, does not necessarily imply so much. It may be interpreted as conveying no more than the author's conviction that the poet's nature renders him peculiarly apt in contact with life to offend against convention; and that consequently he must restrain his own impulses (not specifically on behalf of his art) more than ordinary people need to do. This again is (superficially appraised) the 'teaching' of 'Tasso', and we must regard it as the lesson which Grillparzer derived from the work; it corresponded to his own conviction before 'Sappho' was commenced.

[1] O. E. Lessing, 'Gr. u.d. neue Drama', reviewed by R. Petsch in 'Euphorion', xiv (1907), p. 163.

[2] Cf. J. W. N. Sullivan, 'Beethoven', London, 1931, p. 183.

4. THE MOTIVE OF AGE-DISPARITY

If it becomes clear in this way that Grillparzer's original plan fc 'Sappho' grew out of a personal conviction thus strengthened, th question arises as to what foundation existed for his belief that th work was objectively conceived, and that it was in part so execute until a change in the train of his thoughts caused the introduction c what he felt to be subjective elements.

The letter to Müllner commences with a statement that Grillparze originally had a twofold object:

> 'Erstens lebte der Stoff wirklich in mir und zwang mich ihn nac außen hinzustellen, zweitens wollte ich mir dabei selbst eine Aufgab machen'.[1]

The first of these reasons must be understood to refer not only to th mere 'material', but also (perhaps primarily) to the conviction w have discussed.[2] Grillparzer had no reason to suspect that it wa peculiar to himself, or in any way subject to qualification. He ha found it expressed in 'Tasso'. In numerous 'artist-plays' and 'educa tion- or vocation-novels', too, deriving their inspiration from 'Tassc and 'Wilhelm Meister' (which' like 'Sappho' itself they 'dilute c travesty'),[3] the romantics had given it wide currency. Grillparze regarded it as a proper (a 'natural') theme for the kind of work h had intended.

In addition to this would-be 'objective' motive regarding Sappho' nature Grillparzer's play contains two others which have indeed a air of being calculated, and which presumably contributed to th poet's persuasion that he had in fact conceived the work objectively.

The Sappho legend, as it presented itself to Grillparzer, told ho the poetess Sappho fell violently in love with Phaon; she was suppose to have persecuted the innocent youth with her attentions and finall to have taken the plunge from the Leucadian rock into the sea i sheer despair.

The two remaining principal motives which may be regarded a supplied by Grillparzer are his introduction of Melitta and his stres on the disparity between the ages of Sappho and Phaon.

It has frequently been claimed for Melitta that she is introduced t create a situation considered to be a favourite one with Grillparze that of a man loved by two women. She has also been said to embod Grillparzer's ideal of young womanhood at the time (and attemp

[1] Loc. cit., p. 97, ll. 6–9. [2] Cf. Sauer's comments in 'Wke'. I. 1, lxxxiii f.
[3] Gundolf, loc. cit. ('Jb. d. Fr. Dt. Hochstifts), p. 36.

have been made to identify her with one or other of his acquaintances). Both these views are beside the mark: the central figure is Sappho, not Phaon; and Melitta has, in German stage parlance, only the *naives Fach*.[1] She owes her presence primarily to dramatic necessity.

The importance which attaches to Melitta in 'Sappho' is best shown by Grillparzer's own words to Frau v. Littrow-Bischoff:

> 'Sappho springt ins Meer, weil Phaon ihr die Gegenliebe weigert; das konnte keinen triftigeren Grund haben, als weil er eine Andre liebte, und damit ist alles gegeben'.[2]

Tempting as it is to suggest, as Sauer does, that Melitta existed in Grillparzer's mind in contrast to Sappho as Lottchen Pichler did to the *femmes savantes* of her mother's literary salon, such as Mme de Staël and Dorothea Schlegel, or that she derives from some particular literary source, these conjectures can have little bearing on the interpretation of the main theme of the work. It is, indeed, not improbable that in his portrayal of this 'liebes Mädchen mit dem stillen Sinn' Grillparzer had some one in mind, possibly a figure of flesh and blood, in accordance with his usual practice and the whole nature of his dramatic art. It is true, too, that some such contrast as Sauer refers to had struck Grillparzer, as the poem 'Das Urbild und die Abbilder' shows. That he was mildly attracted to Charlotte Pichler is known. And lastly it may be conceded that this girl's character as depicted in the poem 'Frühlingsgedanken' and in her mother Caroline Pichler's correspondence with Therese Huber does show certain affinities to Melitta's. On the other hand, the reader of what follows in these pages may be equally prepared to entertain the conjecture that Melitta was modelled, if we can speak of modelling in reference to a figure so slight, on one of Sophie Schröder's daughters, Minna perhaps.

But this brings us no nearer to an understanding of Grillparzer's motive for insisting as he actually does that Sappho's relation to Phaon, which is more central, is that of 'ein Weib, das einen *jüngern*

[1] If she embodied Grillparzer's ideal of womanhood, the same would be true of other comparatively negative characters such as Bertha (in 'Melusina') and Kreusa, who also occupy secondary roles. These characters do reflect, incidentally, Grillparzer's (intermittent) *ideal of quiet happiness*, but they fall properly to be considered in this respect only in relation to figures like Mirza, along with certain characters in the youthful works, which seem to reflect a prevailing 'ethical conviction' of Grillparzer's in favour of this ideal within the works in which they appear. A lucid account of these is contained in Ilse Münch, 'Die Tragik in Drama und Persönlichkeit Fr. Grs.', Berlin, 1931, pp. 8–19 (Jugenddichtungen), though she quite fails to point out the subjective nature of this defeatist mood of Grillparzer's.

[2] A. v. Littrow-Bischoff, 'Aus dem persönlichen Verkehre mit Fr. Gr.', Vienna, 1873, p. 79 f.

Mann liebt'. Late in life Grillparzer complained that Sophie Schröder (the actress who took such an interest in the young poet and made the success of his *Ahnfrau*) was much too old for Sappho's part.[1] Actually she was nothing of the kind, and Grillparzer was only moved to this complaint when he met the youthful Charlotte Wolter and learnt the effect of her performance in the rôle of the poetess. This effect had been to correct outwardly, from the audience's point of view, an inherent defect in Grillparzer's treatment. The Sappho of mature age generally failed to win sympathy. In fairness to Sophie Schröder it must be affirmed, however, that she, 'Germany's greatest tragedienne',[2] triumphantly overcame the poet's deliberately introduced handicap and was by no means outshone by Mme Korn as Melitta when the work was first presented with such astonishing success. Grillparzer assured Atterbom, the Swedish poet who was in Vienna with Rückert at the time, that her performance was a revelation to him and that she interpreted his Sappho to the last inflexion of her voice.[3] She had such sentiments to express to Phaon as that in bidding him follow her and in bestowing her favour on him, an obscure youth, she, who was already famous when he was still but a child, was conferring a distinction upon him which he could not have deserved (l. 112)—though she does not put it so bluntly as that. It is clear that she has taken advantage of his innocence. He modestly represents himself as an instrument on which she plays (l. 158). An indication, moreover, of her age in relation to his and Melitta's is conveyed in her reference to the fact that a number of her former protégées are now counted among Mitylene's *beste Bürgerinnen.*

In the passages near the end of Act I commencing with the words: 'Was kann ich Arme denn dem Teuren bieten?' (l. 370), Sappho feels that she no longer merits nor can claim the bounty of youth and love in Phaon's person; she longs to unlive the past, obliterate even the memory of its joy and woes (including: 'Der Freundschaft und der—

[1] Cf. A. v. Littrow-Bischoff, 'Aus dem persönlichen Verkehre mit Fr. Gr.', pp. 102 ff., 109 ff. This remark dates from 1866. Many critics of 'Sappho' have welcomed the statement. Grillparzer's judgement in the same year, however, expressed to Zimmermann, 'Gespräche, Abtlg. ii (vol. 5, 1863–71), p. 196 f., is as follows: 'Die Wolter ist eine Sappho fürs Auge, sagen Sie. Gut wär's; die Schröder war's auch. . . . Der Abstand soll zu klein sein zwischen der Sappho und der Melitta; den kann ich nicht groß genug haben. . . . Die Melitta ist ein albernes Mädel. Das begreift sich, die Sappho muß ein gut Stück älter aussehen, und doch nicht übel sein'. It is true that by continuing to appear in the role of the poetess long after she had passed her prime Sophie Schröder somewhat exceeded this demand. So, in due course, did Charlotte Wolter.

[2] As Ludwig I of Bavaria described her. Cf. Wurzbach, 'Biogr. Lex. d. k. Österr.', xxxi. 325.

[3] 'Gr. Gespräche', Abtlg. II. 1, p. 89.

Liebe Täuschungen', l. 120)[1] in order to enter a strange untrodden fairyland of love with Phaon. In reality, she declares:

> 'Da steh' ich an dem Rand der weiten Kluft,
> Die zwischen ihm und mir verschlingend gähnt' (ll. 395–6).

For in her youth Sappho had renounced all quiet happiness and domestic joys in her pursuit of ambition, when (like Grillparzer himself) she experienced 'des Beginnens schwankendes Bestreben', 'des Vollbringens wahnsinnglühende Lust' (ll. 49–50); and now she longs to return and partake of what might formerly have been hers, but fears that it is too late, because she is no longer young and fresh and innocent. The withered laurel is a symbol of her state.

Then, turning, she reflects that for the riches which Phaon offers she can recompense him, in different kind, by the achievements of her art, her past and future songs:

> 'Seinem Reichtum
> Kann gleichen Reichtum ich entgegen setzen,
> Der Gegenwart mir dargebotnem Kranz
> Die Blüten der Vergangenheit und Zukunft' (ll. 419–22).

She then invokes, in Grillparzer's rendering of Sappho's famous ode, the aid of Aphrodite (as often in the past) towards the realization of her amorous desires.

However much he may subsequently have regretted it, Grillparzer deliberately established this disparity between Sappho and Phaon, and it was for this reason that he sought to give compensatory stress to Sappho in her quality as a poetess in her first appearance on the stage. 'Sappho ist in der Katastrophe ein verliebtes, eifersüchtiges, in der Leidenschaft sich vergessendes Weib; ein Weib das einen *jüngern* Mann liebt', he says in the letter to Müllner: 'In der gewöhnlichen Welt ist ein solches Weib ein eckelhafter Gegenstand. . . .' He insists, we observe, at this time, on the *alternde Frau* and on the questionableness of her attitude towards Phaon, viewed from the conventional standpoint.

> 'War es nicht durchaus nothwendig, sie noch vor dem Sturm der Leidenschaften so zu zeigen, wie sie in ihrem gewöhnlichen Zustande war, damit der Zuseher die Arme bemitleide, statt sie zu verabscheuen? Wenn es mir gelungen ist, den Zuschauer, so sehr er in der Mitte des

[1] As the 'Eipeldauer' puts it (Jh. 1818, H. 8, Br. 3, p. 42): 'Wir *wiss'n* dass di *Mamsell Sapho* als a *g'fühlvolls Dichterherz* in *Punckt* der *Amourschaftn*, God sey Danck a Wengerl *was midg' macht* had, das had unser dermahliger *Lieblingskoch*, seiner *Pflicht gemäss* keinesweges *verschwieg'n*'.

> Stücks geneigt seyn muß, die Parthie des unschuldigen Paares zu nehmen, dennoch mit seinem Interesse auf Sappho'n fest zu halten, so gebührt ein Theil des Verdienstes vielleicht auch dem ersten Akt.[1]

The assumption that Sappho's fame and achievement as a poetess would compensate for a multitude of personal faults was a natural and characteristic one for the romanticism of Grillparzer's time.

5. GRILLPARZER'S REAL-LIFE SOURCE

But, we ask ourselves, in view of the fact that Grillparzer imposed upon himself an almost insuperable handicap by introducing a motive so damaging to the character of his heroine as that of the obvious disproportion between her own and Phaon's age, what prompted him to do so? It was not a salient feature in the legend, nor does it appear as a motive in any one of the works that have so far been generally accepted as influencing Grillparzer in the conception and execution of his tragedy.[2] This surely is a significant circumstance.—It is perhaps a somewhat startling conjecture, but it nevertheless seems probable enough that the idea of representing Sappho as an almost middle-aged woman resulted from Grillparzer's immediate experience, his knowledge of Sophie Schröder's notorious liaison with the young Daffinger. However surprising the suggestion may seem that Grillparzer had deliberately introduced such a personal and commonplace motive into a purposefully 'classical' work, we may find confirmation for it in the facts that his own and Sophie Schröder's contemporaries were equally astonished at its introduction; and that this same incongruous motive is chiefly responsible for what is unsatisfactory about the piece.

A valuable though neglected contribution to criticism of 'Sappho'

[1] 'Brief an Müllner', loc cit., p. 99.

[2] Grillparzer went to work without consulting any previous treatments of the same subject-matter, unless Backmann is right in supposing that he read Gubitz's monodrama, deriving from it perhaps the suggestion for Sappho's apotheosis (cf. 'Zur Entstehungsgesch. der "Sappho"' in O. Katann, 'Grillparzer-Studien', Vienna, 1924, pp. 122 ff.).

Sauer shows, in 'Werke.' I. 1, that reminiscences of Wieland's 'Agathon' and 'Aristipp', as of Mme de Staël's 'Corinne' may well have associated themselves with Grillparzer's original plan. Backmann supports Sauer's notes regarding the possible influence of Ovid's 'Heroides', particularly on account of the motive of age-disparity (loc. cit., pp. 118 ff.). He considers that Fénelon's 'Télémaque' influences Grillparzer (chiefly in the same direction), ibid., pp. 98 ff. He also seems to favour (cf. 'Wke.' I. 17, p. 141) G. M. Howe's theory regarding the importance of Am. v. Imhoff's 'Schwestern von Lesbos' as 'A Probable Source of Grillparzer's "Sappho",' 'Journal of Eng. & Germ. Phil'. xxii (1923), pp. 503 ff.

The impression which remains when all these suggestions have been considered is that they range too far in search of literary sources and explanations for what may equally well be presumed to have lain immediately to Grillparzer's hand.

is contained in Alex. v. Weilen's 'Geschichte des Burgtheaters'.[1] The following passage from it, not otherwise readily accessible, is quoted in full and will serve to advance the present argument (p. 30):

'Indem Grillparzer in Form und Geist der Dichtung nach klassischem Ausdrucke ringt, wählt er einen Stoff, den er selbst als eine "Fiakeridee" bezeichnet hat, ganz aus dem Leben Wiens und seiner Zeit heraus erfaßt. Das alternde Weib, das mit einer jüngeren Nebenbuhlerin um den Geliebten streitet—man findet es wieder in Bäuerles Memoiren . . . man findet es wieder in Possen, welche die mannstolle alte Schachtel der mitleidlosen Lächerlichkeit preisgeben. Ein Neuling auf dem Wiener Boden, wie Costenoble, hat ganz richtig gesehen, wenn er schreibt: "Die Liebesgeschichte und Eifersucht könnten ebenso gut zwischen einer Wiener Putzmacherin, einer ihrer Mamsellen und einem Ladendiener vorgehen — es würde nicht an Wahrheit verlieren'. Und die Bedenken, welche gegen den tragischen Schluß laut wurden, sie wurzeln in dem erstaunten Gefühle der Zuseher, eine volkstümliche, lustspielmäßig anmutende Begebenheit auf eine Höhe geschoben zu sehen, auf die ihr nicht jedermann zu folgen vermochte.

Kaum ein anderes Werk Grillparzers ist so ganz auf den Boden bestimmter theatralischer Verhältnisse gestellt wie dieses. Die künstlerische Vereinsamung Sophie Schröders, wo findet sie höheren Ausdruck als in der Gestalt Sapphos? In dem mächtigen Pathos der Rede, in dem vernichtenden Liebesbedürfnis lebte das theatralische und persönliche Wesen dieser Frau, die sich mit verzehrender Leidenschaft in die Arme nichtiger junger Burschen stürzte. Gar mancher Phaon hat in ihrem Leben eine bedeutsame Rolle gespielt, und auch von Melittas, die ihr den Freund entrissen, wußte ihr vielgeprüftes Herz zu erzählen.'

It will be observed that there is no mention of Daffinger in this, and there would be no need to mention him, perhaps, if we did not require evidence to confirm v. Weilen's assurances. Moreover, the work of Grillparzer's under discussion reflects the beginning only of his relations to Daffinger: in their development these are of profound importance for an understanding and interpretation of later works. At the same time it is with the actress Sophie Schröder and the way in which her circumstances came to be reflected by Grillparzer (and acted by her) in the person of Sappho that we are at present chiefly concerned.

The attitude of Sophie Schröder's contemporaries, that of the

[1] Alex. v. Weilen, 'Das K.-K. Hofburghtheater seit seiner Begründung' in O. Teuber, 'Die Theater Wiens', Wien, 1906, ii. 2. Halbbd., 2. Teil. E. Reich, 'Grillparzers dramatisches Werk', Vienna, 1938[4], p. 58, virtually dismisses what he underestimates as v. Weilen's claim that Grillparzer was 'halb unbewußt durch Sophie Schröder zur "Sappho" mit angeregt worden'. My own claim goes much further than this. It was formulated independently of v. Weilen's.

Viennese public in particular, to her person and her art was exactly Grillparzer's when he assumes that Sappho's unconventional action was compensated for by her artistic achievements. On the strength of her reputation as an artist of genius Sophie Schröder could behave in her private affairs very much as she pleased without scandalizing her admiring public and intimate acquaintances. They were more solicitous for her welfare than censorious of her conduct when in the year 1816 the famous and gifted actress, at the age of thirty-five formed an illicit union with a young Viennese painter who was nine years her junior.[1]

It is reasonable to assume that this affair with Daffinger engaged Grillparzer's interest and concern. The intimate friendship formed between him and Sophie Schröder since the 'Ahnfrau' days, based upon mutual esteem for each other's art, and gratitude on Grillparzer's part, pre-supposes this. Nor is it perhaps irrelevant to observe that Grillparzer found Daffinger, with whom he now became acquainted through Madame Schröder, in a relationship to her which he knew he might have occupied himself.

Apart from the fact that Daffinger was so much younger than Sophie Schröder, being but one year older than Grillparzer himself this youthful portraitist (who had acquired a considerable reputation through the opportunities afforded him at the time of the Congress of Vienna) was thought to be unsuited to her in other respects. He was of lowly origin, uneducated, and unmannerly, 'ein Kind des Volkes ein Urwiener vom Liechtentalgrund'. It appears to have been over-looked that Phaon is conceived along almost parallel lines and in fact used originally to be so presented on the stage.[2] His 'würdelose Schelt-worte' in Act III (like his 'Schmähungen' in Act V) which Kleinberg mistakenly regards as 'eine Entgleisung des Dichters (wenn man nicht zu gekünstelten Deutungen greifen will)'[3] are evidence of this faithfu

[1] Even M. G. Saphir, who gives an intimate account of Sophie Schröder, his acquaintance among his 'Lineamente zu Schauspieler-Bildnissen', dedicated to her in his 'Berlin Theate Almanach für 1818', pp. 259 ff., declines to take advantage of the tempting opportunity fo scurrilous comment afforded by the actress's sensational and unfortunate third marriage to young actor named Kunst in 1825, one of her many lovers, who was nearly twenty years he junior (a step from which, according to Wurzbach, not even the personal intercession of Kaise Franz could dissuade her). This consideration from M. G. Saphir is the strongest evidence fo the kind of respect which Sophie Schröder inspired.

[2] In C. L. Costenoble's excellent diaries: 'Aus dem Burgtheater 1818–37, Tagebuchblätter' 2 vols., Vienna, 1889, the following interesting comment appears: 'Fichtner (a young acto who wanted to marry [Melitta-] Betty Schröder) war ein noch roherer Phaon als der *Lümme* Grillparzers, vol. II, p. 75, Sept. 10, 1831 (Costenoble's italics). This points to an origina conception of Phaon's role quite different from the prevailing one, which Costenoble woul have described as 'unerträglich flau' (cf. vol. I, p. 148).

[3] A. Kleinberg, 'Fr. Grillparzer', etc., 'Aus Natur u. Geisteswelt', no. 513, p. 37.

eproduction of Daffinger's character. L. Grünstein describes Daffin-er's relationship to Mme Schröder, who had been twice married for the first time at the age of fourteen) and was the mother of a son wenty years old, three daughters in their 'teens (on the elder ones f whom Daffinger soon forced his attentions) and a young boy, in erms remarkably reminiscent of Grillparzer's treatment:

'eine seltene und seltsame Verbindung, . . . die im Zeichen einer eruptiven Sinnlichkeit einsetzt und nach einer mehrjährigen, durch Haß und Eifersucht getrübten Gemeinschaft, zuletzt noch in der ungebundenen Leidenschaftlichkeit des Weibes und dem jähen Überdruß des Mannes, ihren schmerzlichen, in seiner Auswirkung nahezu tragischen Ausklang findet'.[1]

In a letter written on January 19, 1817, to Rahel Varnhagen (for-unate in her fourteen years younger mate) Sophie Schröder describes er vain search for true happiness in love, and she does so in terms vhich remind us of Sappho's regrets: 'Ach . . . wenn ich ein stilles äusliches Glück an der Seite eines mir *ganz gleichgesinnten*, *gleich-ühlenden* Wesens verleben könnte . . .' In this letter, which has been lescribed as a 'Herzensdokument der Frauen der Romantik',[2] she peaks further of her separation from her second husband and her nion with Daffinger. In the misgivings which she entertained with egard to the result of this effort to win happiness we may discern an ndication that she had perused 'Sappho' (as she had actually done by his time) with unusual interest, recognizing in it a prophetic reflection f her own approaching disillusionment:

'Ich will es Ihnen nicht leugnen, daß ich in diesem Augenblick in einem Verhältnisse stehe, wo ich mich bemühe dieses Glück aufzufinden—aber gelingen, ach gelingen, wird es glaube ich kaum. Ein junger guter hübscher für alles Gute und Schöne empfänglicher Mann hat sich mit vieler herzlichen Innigkeit an mich geschlossen—er sucht alles auf, mich davon zu überzeugen, er sieht meinen Augen meine Wünsche ab, und erfüllt sie, soviel in seinen Kräften ist—das alles ist gut, *sehr* gut—aber dennoch, dennoch stoße ich zuweilen auf Härten in diesem wirklich vortrefflichen Gemüt, die mich verwundern, die mich fester überzeugen —es gibt kein *ganz vollkommenes* Glück zwischen Mann und Weib. . . .'

he mentions a further cause for anxiety, one which Grillparzer had oreshadowed, and she does so again in terms which echo Sappho's

[1] Leo Grünstein, 'M. M. Daffinger und sein Kreis', Vienna, Leipzig, 1923, p. 14.
[2] Hn. Stümcke, Introduction to 'Die Briefe von Sophie Schröder, 1813-68' in 'Schriften der esellschaft für Theatergesch.' xvi, xxvi, Berlin, 1910–16.

extravagant railing against *der rauhe* Phaon for his 'Undank',[1] his inconstancy:

> '. . . Doch gesetzt auch, ich irrte, gesetzt auch, es gelänge mir, was bei einem *guten, gefühlvollen* Menschen vielleicht nicht ganz unmöglich ist, diese Härten durch Beharrlichkeit und Sanftmut auszugleichen und mich so dem Ziele meiner Wünsche zu nähern, würde ich auch verhindern können, daß ein *Ungeheuer* welches jetzt die Welt beherrscht—Unbestand—sich zwischen mich und mein Glück stellt? Und wenn es auch nur Furcht davor ist . . .'[2]

One thing is certain, the writer of this letter was singularly well adapted for the rôle of Sappho. And she continued to be so qualified long after this experience. As late as 1831 Immermann learns in Munich, where she was at that time, 'daß die 50jährige Sappho noch immer ihren jugendschönen Phaon verlange'.[3]

At the time when Grillparzer's play was being written and prepared for the stage Sophie Schröder was absent from Vienna on tour. The fact that she was not considered in the first place for the rôle of Sappho is really eloquent, for there was obviously no one better suited, as an actress and by experience, for the part. In his 'Selbstbiographie' Grillparzer, for reasons we can well understand, declares that she, 'in deren Fach die Sappho gehörte', was not reckoned on to take the part because she was at that time not merely on tour, but 'abroad', that is, in Germany, having quarrelled with the theatre authorities in Vienna and threatened not to return; and that for this reason the rôle of Sappho had to be given to Mme Löwe, who was unsuited to it. We have evidence of Sophie Schröder's periodic differences with the Hofburgtheater authorities, but none to show that any existed during her *Kunstreise*, as it is correctly described, in 1817. Schreyvogel and Grillparzer probably assumed that if they delayed the production of the play till she returned she would resent its implications, or at least refuse to expose herself to the risk of being vulgarly identified in her person with Sappho, or of seeming to exploit the undesirable notoriety which she had gained. On September 26, 1817, Schreyvogel wrote to Böttiger in Dresden about the new play: 'Die Rolle ist nicht für Mad. Schröder bestimmt, wovon sie jedoch vorderhand nichts zu wissen braucht.'[4] Why the concealment, we ask, if as stated in the 'Selbstbiographie' she was not expected

[1] l. 1281, ll. 1204 ff., 1290 ff. [2] Loc. cit., vol. I, Brief 98, pp. 144 ff.
[3] Cf. 'Allg. deutsche Biog.' xxxii, p. 527.
[4] 'Gespräche', II. Abtlg. (vol. i, 1791-1831), p. 37.

to return?[1] Surely, if there had been any fear that she would not return, Schreyvogel would normally have wanted Sophie Schröder to hear that the young Grillparzer had written a new play, a 'Sappho' tragedy, in the hope of enticing her back. It seems indeed likely that Grillparzer and Schreyvogel were anxious to cast and, if possible, produce 'Sappho' before Sophie Schröder could return and for the reasons mentioned frustrate or complicate matters for them.

On her return to Vienna at the beginning of December, 1817, however, Sophie Schröder immediately took possession of the rôle.[2] Yet it cannot be supposed that she failed to recognize the obvious parallel between her own and Sappho's experience. Late in life she admitted to Emilie Ringseis that she identified herself with Grillparzer's Sappho, whose fate had once been her own.[3] This admission on her part, coupled with our knowledge of Grillparzer's intimacy with her, and associated with his own and Schreyvogel's misgivings, tends to confirm the impression, which v. Weilen's judgement supports, that it was she who from the start provided in her person and circumstances the real source of the most striking motive in Grillparzer's conception of 'Sappho'. We may even be justified in stating that this was the immediate source of the work itself, or in other words that at the time when the legend of Sappho and Phaon was mentioned to Grillparzer by Joël he had promptly associated it with the parallel problem—for him—of Sophie Schröder's behaviour, so conducive to tragedy, and resolved to treat it dramatically. If so, it is scarcely accurate to speak of the motive of age-disparity, or that of Sophie Schröder's person and circumstances, as being *added* by Grillparzer to the material of 'Sappho', or objectively supplied by him; he did not deliberately introduce the motive or superimpose it: the expression *Grillparzer's Schröder-'Sappho'* might justifiably be coined to characterize his conception and treatment of the piece from the start.

[1] E. Reich, loc. cit., 3rd ed., p. 59, believes that Schreyvogel's letter proves that he thought Sophie Schröder too old for the part. There is no authority for this. It is significant too that this is not the reason for excluding her which Grillparzer himself alleged.

[2] 'Die energische Frau hat ihre Rolle vor sich auf dem Bette liegen und scheint vor Begierde zu brennen, die Sappho und *dabei zugleich ein Bischen auch sich selbst* zu spielen', wrote Grillparzer in a letter to Böttiger on February 20, 1818, 'Wke.' III, p. 94, ll. 2–5 (italics mine).

The first performance of 'Sappho' had to be postponed until after the birth in March of Sophie Schröder's first child by Daffinger, which was baptized at St. Stephan's on May 9, 1818, named Moritz after his father, and entered as the son of Theresia Bürger (Sophie Schröder's maiden name). Near this entry appears the intrusive comment: 'angeblich', which (characteristically enough) the person making it gratuitously supplied.

[3] E. Ringseis, 'Erinnerungsblätter', Freiburg i. Br., 1896, p. 66. Sophie Schröder rejected the suggestion made to her on this occasion that Sappho was really too old to be able to command Phaon's devotion!

6. 'THE POET'S SAD RESPLENDENT FATE'[1]

If we accept this as the true account of how the plan for 'Sappho' came to be conceived we may discern at the same time that in Grillparzer's over-eagerness to proceed with his 'Fiakeridee'[2] lay the source too of the principal artistic defect in the poetic work that grew out of it. If he had given the matter longer consideration he might well have thought it inadvisable to risk alienating sympathy from his heroine by making her appear as old as his model for her really was, in addition to causing her to behave as she did. On the other hand this may have been an integral part of his original design, a part of the 'Aufgabe' which he boldly undertook because of its bearing upon his personal conviction regarding the artistic temperament and the *malheur d'être poète*: namely, to reveal his artist-heroine's behaviour (like Sophie Schröder's) as by no means censurable or *ekelhaft*, in spite of her age. But if a marked disparity of age between Sappho and Phaon was envisaged from the first this involved Grillparzer in difficulties before the end of the work; it caused him to depart from his original conception, not without damage to its logical accomplishment. This is the change of plan he seems to have had in mind in his admission to Müllner. He may not have been conscious of making it deliberately, he may even have forgotten how he originally intended to motivate his catastrophe, but the fact remains that he had to sacrifice adequate motivation of Sappho's end.

Grillparzer's original intention was to show that Sappho was by her poetic nature a woman of violent passions. She was a poetess by virtue of this fact, but only when she exercised restraint over her true nature. He intended to represent her as a victim finally of her own passions, when she made her belated, pitiable, and tragic attempt to find love-happiness. At the time of commencing to write his play he certainly harboured no lofty belief in the divinity of Sappho's nature and calling. On the contrary, she is at first portrayed as being genuinely dissatisfied with her lot as a poetess, and in this she has much in common with Grillparzer himself at the time. When he commenced writing 'Sappho' he was dissatisfied in the same way, and in speaking of the hardship of the poet's lot he is not merely

[1] This corresponds to Grillparzer's formula (in Jugenderinnerungen im Grünen, G. 84, 15, l. 122) for the theme of his 'Sappho': 'Des Dichters blendend, trauriges Geschick'. Note its subjective character and the extent to which the epithets mutually exclude and even contradict one another as symptomatic of the whole work.

[2] 'Gleich und Gleich gesellt sich gern'—e.g., not Sappho=Phaon, but Phaon=Melitta. This 'cabman's idea' (popular, proverbial theme) is the one to which that described as fundamental to the work forms a kind of corollary.

exploiting a literary motive, but is giving expression to his own feelings. In reference to this point we may recall Scherer's words:

> 'Wir kennen die dunkle Gestalt mit dem geheimen tiefen Leiden in der Brust. Sie ist der stille Hausgeist, der die europäische Poesie der zwanziger Jahre durchwandelt. Auch Grillparzer kann sich den Stimmungen des Weltschmerzes nicht entziehen. Die Figur der Sappho ist daraus empfangen'.[1]

At this time, moreover, Grillparzer had an additional reason for discontent. Contemporary criticism of his 'Ahnfrau', 'jenes beschrieene, in jeder Hinsicht, zu früh geborne Wesen',[2] had provided special cause for his dissatisfaction with the poet's lot—'des Dichters trauriges (but not *blendendes*) Geschick'. Sappho is represented, in 'deserting' her art, as being actuated by considerations and motives of which Grillparzer at this time distinctly approved. In introducing Phaon to her people, she explains:

> 'Er war bestimmt, in seiner Gaben Fülle,
> Mich von der Dichtkunst wolkennahen Gipfeln
> In dieses Lebens heitre Blüten-Täler
> Mit sanft bezwingender Gewalt herabzuziehn.
> An seiner Seite werd' ich unter euch
> Ein einfach stilles Hirtenleben führen',

and we are reminded of what Scherer and Volkelt, among others, have said about Grillparzer in respect to this same longing. And when Sappho explains to Phaon later on:

> 'Umsonst nicht hat zum Schmuck der Musen Chor
> Den unfruchtbaren Lorbeer sich erwählt,
> Kalt, frucht- und duftlos drücket er das Haupt
> Dem er Ersatz versprach für manches Opfer',

we realize that Grillparzer is giving expression to feelings which he himself experienced. This means that the existing conclusion to the work, where opposite (and equally subjective) feelings prevail, could not have been premeditated.

There can be no question that at the outset Grillparzer had no intention of representing Sappho's desertion of her art as her real dramatic guilt. But his representation of her character, conduct, and situation, and in particular of her age in relation to Phaon's, drove him later to represent as pre-eminently unpardonable her seeking to partake of the common joys of life.

[1] W. Scherer, 'Vorträge und Aufsätze *etc.*' Berlin, 1874, p. 215 f.
[2] 'Wke.', III., 1 (no. 98, An Adolf Müllner, Jan 21, 1818), pp. 88, ll. 18–19.

It is because the Sappho of the first plan was so much older than Phaon, and because she behaves as she does in a situation of her own creating, showing such traits as selfishness, spite, anger, jealousy meanness, cruelty, violence, and cunning, that Grillparzer saw even then that nothing short of a great compensating emphasis on her merits as a poetess could rescue her for the play. But in the course of the execution of his work he must also have come to see that Sappho was nevertheless alienating herself too much from the sympathy of the audience. The principal reason for this was that she was not youthful enough. To let her commit suicide for reasons that had first suggested themselves to him, not so much because of unrequited love or injured pride, be it said, as because of her very behaviour and in desperation over the *malheur d'être poète*, would not have been sufficient. It had been clear to Grillparzer from the very beginning (*vide* his pencil drawing of the final scene) that after Sappho's 'unclassical' outburst in the middle acts consequent upon the inevitable thwarting of her misdirected desires, she could only become a tragic heroine if she were made to see the error of her ways and atone nobly for the wrong she had done. In the finished work, however, she fails to do so. Grillparzer must have felt that he was unable to contrive this successfully, though without necessarily becoming conscious of the principal cause; instead, his conception of the wrong she had done insensibly became changed. In the course of writing the work his confidence in his own gifts was restored to him, and he came to look upon Sappho's guilt as consisting not in her conduct after renouncing her art, but in the very fact that she had deserted it.

Nothing, of course, can change the fact that Sappho's real dramatic guilt, even in the finished work, results from her character, situation, and behaviour, and not merely from her having 'deserted' her art. As Caroline Pichler wrote in her excellent contemporary review:

> 'Sappho selbst hat wohl nur darin gefehlt, daß sie in einem Alter wo ihr Jugendreitz verblüht war, den Jüngling, der ihr durch nichts als seine Schönheit und grenzenlose Verehrung für sie merkwürdig wurde, sogleich mit allem Feuer der Leidenschaft ergriff, und ihre, aus seinem betäubten, geblendeten Wesen zurück gestrahlte Glut, für die eigne Empfindung seines Herzens hielt. Das hat die Kunst nicht zu verantworten'.[1]

[1] 'Wke.', III. 1, B. 149. The critique is *not* by Th. Huber, as I have shown elsewhere, but by Caroline Pichler herself. Cf. 'Euphorion' xxvi, Heft 2 (1925).

But Grillparzer's point of view, or what he refers to as his 'Gemüths-
age',[1] had altered. As Petsch puts it:

> 'Tatsächlich scheint Grillparzer den Konsequenzen seiner ersten Konzeption nachher aus dem Wege gegangen zu sein; aber ich sehe das Neue eben . . . in der Erhebung Sapphos zu einer Höhe, wo von einer eigentlichen Leidenschaftstragödie kaum mehr die Rede sein kann . . . . Hat sich die Heldin kurz vorher, als sie die entflohene Melitta zurückzuholen befahl . . . in einer relativ ruhigeren Stimmung *bewußt* für den Weg der Leidenschaft *entschieden*, so tritt sie uns nun hoheitvoll, zur Entsagung fähig, entgegen, als sei das Ganze bloß eine Verirrung der großen Künstlerin gewesen, die freilich nicht mehr zu der verlassenen Höhe begierdeloser Reinheit wieder aufsteigen kann'.[2]

Sappho never really comes to see the error of her ways, and her
ıtonement takes the form of almost condescending forgiveness. She
elieves that she had formerly wrongfully deserted her art and her
ods in order to partake of the meaner joys of life.

> 'Ihr habt der Dichterin vergönnt zu nippen
> An dieses Lebens süß umkränzten Kelch,
> Zu nippen nur, zu trinken nicht'.

t was to this insight that Grillparzer had now come as a result of the
elf-confidence and satisfaction with his lot which he had acquired
vhile composing the work. He achieves the feat of making Sappho
nore appealing to most of his audience and of exonerating her from
lame by stressing (partly unconsciously, but of inner conviction)
he divinity of her calling, and raising her to more than human
ıeights.

The Sappho of the closing scenes feels that she has betrayed her
ıigher calling in lowering herself to the level of mere human beings,
vho live to experience and enjoy. This is the only error which she,
n her 'Dichterstolz', is capable of recognizing now. Sappho is some-
hing higher than life and owes it no explanation. She overlooks her
uilt, namely, that she had behaved as 'ein in der Leidenschaft sich
ergessendes Weib', in a manner unworthy of herself as a woman,
ıot merely as a poetess. She, like Grillparzer himself, is now only
onscious of having sinned against her art, of having wrongfully
uccumbed to feelings of dissatisfaction with her lot. She feels
ncapable of regaining her former Olympian heights. She is a broken

[1] An Müllner, loc. cit., p. 103, l. 16.

[2] Petsch, loc. cit. Here, as in the previous passage quoted from this review, it will be observed
ıat Petsch supports the 'Leidenschaftstragödie'-theory. This does not accord with the evidence
onsidered above, and I now no longer associate myself with Petsch in this respect. The
nplications of his expression *begierdelose Reinheit* are also unacceptable. See next note.

woman. Having betrayed her poetic genius, as she believes, sh
appeals to the gods to summon her to themselves:

> 'O gebt nicht zu, daß eure Priesterin
> Ein Ziel des Hohnes werde eurer Feinde,
> Ein Spott des Toren, der sich weise dünkt.
> Ihr bracht die Blüten, brechet auch den Stamm!
> Laßt mich vollenden so wie ich begonnen,
> Erspart mir dieses Ringens blut'ge Qual'.[1]

And so she dies, as the legend demands; death, we must feel, is th
only escape.

We see now that the 'contrast between art and life' has taken on
very different aspect from that with which the play began. Grill
parzer has forgotten his theme of the poet's inherent excessive passion
(like Tasso's) and the pitfall they presage. He is also no longe
suffering from feelings of *Weltschmerz* or *le malheur d'être poète*: h
no longer feels dissatified with his lot as a poet, nor longs to partak
of the (forbidden) joys of *life*; but is convinced, in his new-foun
'Dichterstolz', of the exalted nature of his genius ('des Dichte
blendendes Geschick'!) and feels now no hardship in renouncin
everything in favour of his *art*.

7. THE AUTHOR OF 'SAPPHO'

Nor was this new attitude unwarrantable in him. He had accom
plished a vast stride in his art. The tremendous success of 'Sapph
on the stage, though we admit that it was materially contributed t
by Sophie Schröder's remarkable performance,[2] was by no mear
unmerited on the poet's part. Psychologically and poetically (as i
confirmed by Börne's and Byron's discriminating praise), structurall
and technically, the work is of high quality. With regard to Gril
parzer's interesting representation of Phaon's and Melitta's 'awaken

[1] I. Münch's interpretation of Sappho's suicide: 'Sie fühlt, daß sie sich niemals dauern halten könnte auf der Höhe des reinen Schauens' (loc. cit., p. 33), which is based on these lin (justifiably so?), implies acquiescence in the erroneous conception of 'pure contemplation' the poet's ideal unchanging state. This is consequently just as subjective and arbitrary as th poet's unsatisfactory motivation for suicide analysed above.

[2] The following passages from Costenoble's diaries bear upon this observation (I, p. 9 Sept. 2, 1820): 'Jedes Theater, welches keine Schröder zur Sappho hat, wird diese moderr Antike gar bald auf die Seite legen müssen;' and (II, p. 225, April 24, 1835): 'Ohne Schrödersch Begeisterung fällt die Grillparzersche Griechin in nichts. Ist das Antike? Goethes Iphigen kann man sich gar nicht anders vorstellen, als in griechischem Costüme; aber unsere Sapph kann man recht gut als Wiener Modehändlerin und Melitta als eine hübsche Putzjungf denken'—expressions supporting v. Weilen's view regarding the true character of Grillparzer 'classical' piece.

ng' through love, that motive which dates back to 'Spartakus' and constantly reappears (notably in 'Des Meeres und der Liebe Wellen'), Grillparzer's hitherto unobserved indebtedness to 'Romeo and Juliet' is worth noting. The language and metre of 'Sappho', though not as uniformly exalted, smooth-flowing, and polished as that of Goethe's 'Iphigenie' and 'Tasso', which Grillparzer apparently sought to emulate, comprise many passages of the highest order of expression. Of the not infrequent 'lapses' into Viennese colloquialisms it may be held, from the dramatic point of view, that these approximations to natural speech (found also in the mature 'Libussa') are praiseworthy, and introduced by design, as by Lessing in 'Nathan der Weise'. There are in addition, it is true, those perhaps somewhat infelicitous figures of speech, such as Phaon's:

> 'Da meiner Wünsche winterliche Raupen
> Als goldne Schmetterlinge mich umspielen' (ll. 493 f.)[1],

and the comparison of Melitta to a snail, so apt is she, in her *liebevolle Innigkeit*, to withdraw into her shell, and like the snail again,

> 'Nur zaudernd waget, Fremdes zu berühren,
> Doch fest sich saugt, wenn es einmal ergriffen,
> Und sterbend das Ergriffene nur verläßt.' (ll. 760 ff.)

They remind us of Grillparzer's incongruous allegory of himself, the poet as the oyster, which secretes its pearls only after sickness, prolonged suffering, and anguish—in his 1818 poem entitled 'Abschied von Gastein'. These metaphors suggest that the young poet carried home from his imaginative expeditions, at this time, but poor poetical prey. Like Goethe in Leipzig, who would go out 'hunting images' (emulating Ewald v. Kleist), Grillparzer seems to have been equally constrained, lacking objects of beauty or grandeur for his purposes, to direct his attention to 'das Kleinleben der Natur'; but it is perhaps regrettable that he thought fit to include the not so 'dainty proceedings' of caterpillars, snails, and oysters from that sphere.

Yet 'Sappho' succeeded; even the critics were impressed; and this success would appear to have encouraged Grillparzer to continue with his portrayals of women characters. He was probably in part

[1] The passage in which Tasso (ll. 3083–91) compares the process of poetic creation to the silkworm's own, through self-immolation in the chrysalis stage to metamorphosis and enviable freedom and release, is related to this of Grillparzer's (more closely than the 'armes Muscheltier' in 'Abschied von Gastein', cf. 'Wke.' I, 10, p. 273 Anm.). Grillparzer's figure probably derives from this poetic source, but how debased it is in Grillparzer's formulation by comparison!

influenced in this direction, especially (in the first place) with Sophie Schröder as an ally of his art, to choose a woman, Medea, for the heroine of his next work for the stage. The grim tragedy of that work 'Wie das Gemüt im eigenen Abgrund endet', provides a still more striking example than 'Sappho' of Grillparzer's tendency to draw on his personal experience and observation for his dramatic purposes.

The author of 'Sappho' was a famous man, but not a happy one. He was graciously received in audience by Prince Metternich; he received a gift of one thousand gulden in silver from a 'Gesellschaft dramatischer Kunstfreunde'. Moreover, the Minister of Finance, Graf Stadion, a generous benefactor, appointed him Hoftheaterdichter on May 1, 1818, with a salary of 2,000 florins, and transferred him to the department of the Hofkammer that was concerned with the management of court theatre affairs. The friendly intention here was to relieve the young poet of irksome duties, provide him with an activity that was an activity only in name, and give him leisure for his literary work. But it miscarried, in that the person to whom Grillparzer was now answerable as his chief, v. Fuljod, resented the manoeuvre and, failing in a malicious attempt to estrange Schreyvogel and Grillparzer, bore him bitter hatred and contrived to injure him in the estimation of his fellow officials as an indolent and conceited *protégé* of Count Stadion.

Schreyvogel and many others of Grillparzer's acquaintance, judging by the outward evidences of his popularity and success, considered him a happy man. With the exception of Caroline Pichler, as her understanding critique of 'Sappho' best shows, they quite failed to realize how seriously Grillparzer now took the already familiar romantic view of his poetic destiny, the loneliness and burden of his lot. He thought of this destiny as inescapable now that he had acquiesced in his official appointment to an exalted function; thus pre-occupation with his natural misgivings about being able to fulfil his obligations and satisfy his own exacting standards became the central thing in his life, depressed his spirit and obsessed his mind. The poems 'Bescheidenes Los' (G. 92) und 'Abschied von Gastein' (G. 11) express moods deriving from this feeling of oppressive responsibility. The first represents the poet as willing to renounce life (Saitenspiel, Amor, Glück, Ruhm) and longing only to possess (what is also denied him) his own personal independence and rights. The second poem, which is better known, is the one written for the visitors' book of Bad Gastein, expressing gratitude to this place which had brought him physical and spiritual healing:

> 'Was Gott mir gab, worum sie mich beneiden,
> Und was der Quell doch ist von meiner Pein,
> Der Qualen Grund, die wenige ermessen,
> Du ließest michs auf kurze Zeit vergessen'.

Grillparzer's distress at this time was due to his initial struggles with 'Das Goldene Vlies'. The theme of the whole poem, with its figures of the blazing splendour of a noble tree when rent by lightning (paralleled in Byron), the oyster's coveted 'sad pearl' (this figure too much elaborated), the rainbowed water-fall (mercilessly battered by the rocks), is summed up in the lines:

> 'Was ihr für Lieder haltet; es sind Klagen,
> Gesprochen in ein freudenloses All'.

If we are tempted to reject the implications of this romantic confession it is well to recall that Grillparzer found almost universal sanction for it in his day, that it is expressed in 'Tasso', and that it also reflects an attitude to poetic art which, like Goethe's, bases artistic work on personal experience and on a genuine sense of responsibility in the poet's endeavours to fulfil his artistic mission. This shows us a man of high seriousness of purpose. The fact that his works grew out of his great struggle to maintain and fulfil that purpose gives them their fundamental value for us. And conversely it holds true that we must seek an apt interpretation of Grillparzer's works by relating them as far as possible to his experience, thus enabling us to place ourselves at his point of view when he was creating them. No poet's work of high order can ever lose by being thus investigated and re-lived. The student of the affinity between Grillparzer's works and his actual experiences must be prepared for startling correlations, be it said. It is at times almost as if the parallels were too detailed and too sensational to be believed. 'Da und dort lassen sich Erlebnis und Gestaltung bei Grillparzer geradezu verblüffend weit verfolgen'.[1] It is well that it should be so; for it was a sound instinct that prompted Grillparzer to express in his dramas those feelings and problems and experiences of life which were his own, thus fulfilling a primary

[1] O. Zausmer: 'Grillparzers Lyrik als Ausdruck seines Wesens,' Paderborn, 1930, p. 141; he is not referring to the poems alone.

condition in all great dramatic poetry: in so doing he divested his human experience of its personal quality and gave it a universal one, raised it on to a general human plane. All art springs from significant experience—from imaginative (by no means merely imaginary) personal experience; its permanent value depends upon the degree to which that experience has been universalized.

CHAPTER III

'DAS GOLDENE VLIES'

I. UNDERLYING THEME OR PERSONAL CONTENT

AT first sight Grillparzer's 'Goldenes Vlies' seems to have no bearing whatsoever on the universal problem of the contrast between duty and desire, or 'art and life'. Yet an examination of Grillparzer's original intention in the work, and a consideration of his actual experience in relation to it, will show that this problem nevertheless plays a very important part. As a result of his achievement in portraying his Sappho Grillparzer felt not merely encouraged to develop his powers in the direction of portraying women characters, choosing Medea for his new heroine, but implies also that he took certain deliberate steps to ensure a truthful representation of woman's nature in the character of this heroine. In his relations and behaviour towards Charlotte v. Paumgartten, the 'tragic muse' of Medea, Grillparzer was influenced ultimately by the attitude of mind with regard to his art which had been induced by the success of his previous work. He now places the realization of his poetic mission or ambition before any other consideration. He feels that he must deny himself participation in the joys of life and that no sacrifice to his art is too great, no conduct undertaken on its behalf inexcusable. As long as the conviction of the exalted nature of his destiny, his confidence in the possibility of realizing his mission and vindicating the trust that had been publicly and officially reposed in him retains the upper hand, this attitude remains. The pessimism of 'Das Goldene Vlies' is to be accounted for by the fact that Grillparzer failed to achieve what he set himself to do in this work, and that this failure gave rise to a state of mind comparable to that which had prevailed at the time of beginning to write 'Sappho'. The circumstances of this renewed change of attitude and its effect upon the choice of his next theme, 'König Ottokars Glück und Ende' will be discussed.

After Grillparzer had finished his 'Golden Fleece' trilogy he attempted to explain to himself in his diary for the early part of the year 1820 (T. 645) the tendency of his works to prove failures when they were more extensively planned and were therefore incapable of completion in a single sustained effort. He found that the cause lay in his susceptible and inconstant nature and in his changing feeling and attitude of mind. It has been seen how, in his view, the unity even of his so rapidly finished 'Sappho' suffered from this supposed defect. It was not that he lost sight of what he intended, he writes, but that he unconsciously carried over to his chief characters as much as possible of his ever-changing interests in different aspects of human life, so bringing about an inequality of tone in his work. It is thus that he misjudges at this time the process that gives his works their value for us. Later on he writes again (T. 725):

> 'Daß ich bei länger dauernden Arbeiten leicht dem ersten Plan untreu werde, liegt auch mit darin, dass ich Lieblings-Themata und -Ansichten in mir herum trage, die sich mir unbewußt einmischen, wo es immer möglich ist'.

Suitable for consideration as coming under the heading of such 'Lieblings-Themata und -Ansichten' there appear interwoven with the action of 'Das Goldene Vlies' quite a number of problems and views which are variously hailed as central ideas in the work. Grillparzer himself claims pre-eminence at various times for the idea of the Contrast between Civilization and Barbarism, and for the idea of the Fleece itself as a symbol of 'property wrongfully acquired'; another writer claims that 'Das Goldene Vlies' preaches the Gospel of Renunciation; another that it teaches the Vanity of Fame and Ambition; another authority holds that it is in some respects the Tragedy of the Will to Live, and in other respects the Tragedy of the Will; another that it represents the struggle between 'Natur' and 'Kultur'; yet another, that it is a Fate-tragedy after all. The trilogy may in fact be all of these things at once, but none of them is an ultimate formula for its interpretation. Nor shall we propose one; to investigate its underlying purport is a different thing.

Stated in less general terms, as Grillparzer would most characteristically have insisted it should be, the tragedy of the Golden Fleece trilogy —corresponding with its author's experience—is that Medea should become Jason's wife, a woman of her character the wife of a man of Jason's personality. The passion of love conquers Medea, the austere virgin huntress of the expository scenes, and delivers her into Jason's hands. But Jason does not love Medea, and he has not the courage to throw in his lot with hers. In the struggle to free himself from his wife after she has served his purpose in enabling him to secure the Fleece, he wins. Medea, who has stood alone against Jason and the whole world of Greece, stranded by his final desertion of her in favour of Kreusa, asserts herself for the last time in her act of terrible revenge. At the end, Jason and Medea are left, the merest wrecks of their former selves, consumed with sorrow and remorse.

The formulation in these concrete terms of what forms the basis of Grillparzer's trilogy—but avoiding any allusion to its *personal* content—is such as we can indeed suppose that he himself would not have rejected. The tendency of criticism in his day was opposed to this pragmatism (and it has generally been so since). This tendency was one (deriving from Schiller's fallacious discrimination as between 'naive' and 'sentimentive'[1] poetry) that disappointed and provoked Grillparzer even more than malicious critical attacks, which he knew he could afford to ignore. The reason for this was that he knew it was unsound, being aware of the nature of his own dramatic procedure and of the fact that he did not set out with the desire to express abstract and pre-conceived ideas in his works. There is evidence in a score of Grillparzer's utterances throughout his career that he resented attempts at critical appraisement of poetical creations as if they could be interpreted in such terms. During his study of Schlegel's 'Vorlesungen' in 1817 he expressed his decided opinion on this subject, and it is one that he retained (T. 200):

> 'Das Generalisiren in Geschmackssachen scheint mir eben so lächerlich als es mir widerlich ist. Wenn Schlegel sagt: Äschylos wollte im Prometheus Dieß und Das schildern, so erhellt sehr deutlich, daß Schlegel gar nicht weiß, was produktives Genie und dessen Walten für ein Ding ist. Äschylos wollte im Prometheus den Prometheus schildern und weiter nichts. Kein *Dichter* in der Welt ist wohl je bei Schöpfung eines Meisterwerkes von einer allgemeinen Idee ausgegangen. Das kommt von der beliebten Einmischung der Philosophie in die Kunst. Mir kömmt ein solches Assert eben so vor, als ob jemand glaubte, der Natur lägen *wirklich* die anziehende und abstoßende Kraft zu Grunde. Die Körper sind schwer, sie fallen, sie verbinden sich, sie werden bewegt, aber von einem allgemeinen ist da nirgends eine Rede, als im Geiste des Beobachters. Weh dem Menschen, der von selbst oder durch Anleitung auf solches Generalisiren verfällt! Als Philosoph mag er villeicht etwas leisten, zum Dichter ist er verdorben ewiglich!

In his poem 'Jugenderinnerungen im Grünen' Grillparzer is complaining of the manner in which his first works had been received, and (as Backmann rightly points out) it is Schlegel's kind of criticism that he resents—as again in the 1827 poem 'Rechtfertigung'—the

[1] 'Sentimentive' as pertaining to the sentiments.

kind of criticism that attempted to reduce the life and truth of hi
creations to vague and incommensurable formulae:

> 'Doch kann die Formel Leben je bereiten?
> Was ungeheuer ist darum nicht groß;
> Ein Mögliches ragt über alle Weiten . . .'

These vast 'ideas' have nothing in common with great poetry and th
plastic forms of faithful dramatic art (such as Grillparzer knew hi
own to be):

> 'Das Wirkliche zeigt sich im Raume bloß'.

Though Backman not unfairly describes these lines as very obscure,
yet when considered in conjunction with the following five strophes, al
of which (in spite of their extravagant invective) are aimed at the well-
meaning critics, they do lend support to the view that it is a mistake t
attempt to interpret Grillparzer's works in general and abstract terms
as has happened with so many of them, including, as we have seen
his 'Das Goldene Vlies'.

2. THE CENTRAL 'TASK' UNDERTAKEN

The real interest of the trilogy centres in the relation of Jason an
Medea to one another. Yet there is evidence enough in the wor
itself that Grillparzer was to a great extent concerned with the actua
psychological motivation of Medea's crime, and Backmann's studies[2]
indicate beyond all doubt that it was Medea's character and fate i
which Grillparzer was primarily interested, and for which he principally turned to his numerous sources for suggestions when his powe
to continue the work gave out. He was interested from the firs
chiefly in the character of Medea. This was so even before he ha
made up his mind to write a trilogy and felt inclined (temporarily)
to utilize the Fleece as an agent of Fate. His first intention was to writ
a single piece entitled 'Medea', as is shown by his first diary note on th
subject written, according to Backmann, in the Autumn of the yea
1817. When Grillparzer was reading A. W. Schlegel's 'Vorlesungen'
through which he had been led to read Euripides' 'Medea' for himsel
and to formulate plans for a more thorough-going representatio

[1] Jb. ['Jahrbücher der Grillparzer-Gesellschaft'], Vol. XXXII, p. 38.

[2] Reinhold Backmann, 'Die ersten Anfänge der Grillparzerschen Medeadichtung', Disserta-
tion, Leipzig, 1910; Einleitung zum 'Goldenen Vließ' in 'Wke.' I, 2; and Vom Werdegang de
'Goldenen Vließes' in O. Katann, 'Grillparzer-Studien', Wien, 1924.

of the barbarian character of the heroine, he wrote the following words:

> 'Wenn ich, was ich wohl Lust hätte, ein Trauerspiel *Medea* schreiben sollte, würde ich in Medeen Haß gegen ihre Kinder durch deren Anhänglichkeit an den milderen Vater zu erregen suchen' (T. 274).

This statement indicates that the problem which Grillparzer originally set himself had but remote bearing on the relations of Jason and Medea to one another, whether as found in Euripides or as eventually portrayed by him. It indicates that the central task of the intended work was, for him, to motivate Medea's dreadful crime in murdering her own children.

Grillparzer wrote for the modern world, and the problem he set himself was to show how it was possible for a woman to become the murderess of her own children and yet herself live on. If Medea had remained fundamentally and by nature, not merely by origin, a barbarian in Grillparzer's work, the task would have been easier. But this was not desirable, for such a Medea would have failed to win the sympathy or the understanding of a modern audience, and her deed must have appeared a wild, unreasonable, and unpardonable act of violence and inhumanity. Grillparzer was attracted to the idea of making a genuine heroine of his Medea and of showing her to be morally superior to her enemies, until she should finally give vent to her wild longing for a terrible revenge on those who had so illtreated her.

His principal object, namely that of motivating psychologically Medea's crime, remains unaltered throughout. As Schwering puts it: 'Grillparzer war der erste, der in Medea die Verbrecherin hat *werden lassen*'.[1] It is clear that Grillparzer must have been attracted towards a dramatization of Medea chiefly on account of her crime, even if he had not himself indicated as much. Since Euripides she had existed traditionally as the supreme child-murderess of tragedy. But the problem which Grillparzer set himself was an immeasurably more difficult one than that of Euripides, for whom it was easy to impute such a crime to the non-Grecian Medea of his play. Moreover, the crime itself must have seemed less terrible to a people like the Greeks, among whom the practice of exposing children went unpunished. Euripides was also free to make use of, or made free to use, dramatic devices forbidden to a modern author; and he could even go so far as to depict the murder of the children as a redeeming act.

[1] Julius Schwering, 'Franz Grillparzers hellenische Trauerspiele auf ihre literarischen Quellen und Vorbilder geprüft', Paderborn, 1891, p. 49.

But for Grillparzer, if his Medea were to act 'reasonably' in committing her crime, it was necessary to provide a human and convincing motivation for what had come to be regarded in modern civilization as an absolutely inhuman act. The worst difficulty of all was created by the fact that Medea herself had to continue to live after the act. With such a problem looming ahead of him it is not to be wondered at that Grillparzer was constantly brought to a despairing halt during the composition of his 'monstrosity',[1] as he called it. He was compelled to return frequently to his many sources for help, which, however, only made matters worse by destroying the unity and harmony of his work.

3. GRILLPARZER'S 'TRAGIC MUSE' FOR MEDEA

Another source of inspiration to which Grillparzer instinctively turned on account of the difficulties which confronted him in the satisfactory portrayal of his Medea was one which lay very near to hand in the person of Charlotte Paumgartten. This is the primary aspect of his relation to her, as we shall see below, and it establishes the connection between Charlotte Paumgartten and Medea herself. Grillparzer accused himself of having wronged Charlotte by making a psychological study of her with a view to furthering his dramatic purpose. In this respect there is also a connection between Grillparzer and Jason, for the latter, too, makes love in the interests of his own ambition. The subsequent aspect of Grillparzer's relation to Charlotte reflected in the work consists in his desertion of her, like Jason's desertion of Medea, when she has served his purpose and seems to represent nothing more than an obstacle to his freedom.

Out of his own immediate experience Grillparzer thus came to supply material which, being presented in the universal figures of his work, takes on an aspect of tragedy far grimmer, because more plausible, actual, and truer to human life, than any that belonged to his subject-matter by tradition. Therefore it becomes for us a source of admittedly unavailing regret to reflect that Medea still had to commit her traditional inhuman crime—a concrete example, perhaps (or else perhaps not), of the so-called 'Tyranny of Greece over Germany'. For this crime, however well motivated, could only tend to rob her of our understanding and sympathy, as in this horrible act she was equally robbed of the author's own. The poem entitled 'Die tragische Muse', which contains evidence of this, was written probably towards the end of October, 1819, before the

[1] 'Monstrum', 'Wke.' I. 16, p. 159.

completion of the work. It gives an allegorical account of the difficulties with which the poet wrestled because of Medea's dreadful guilt. But his tragic Muse, none other than Charlotte, causes him to continue and complete his work, beckons to him and smiles in token of his reward—and the poet concludes: 'Mein Wesen hat kein Schild gen solche Waffen'.

It is as a result of attendant circumstances then, that Grillparzer, contrary to his original intention of depicting Jason as the gentler parent, came to lay particular stress upon the behaviour of Jason towards Medea. In so doing he is, however, by no means guilty of that inconstancy of purpose of which he accuses himself. For though he carries over in this way to the characters of Jason and Medea elements of a human problem of the greatest personal interest and concern to himself, as he himself implies, he does not in this way prove 'faithless to his original plan' and weaken his motivation of Medea's crime. On the contrary, the treatment of Medea by Jason, having its parallel no less in Grillparzer's treatment of Charlotte Paumgartten than (as we shall see) in Euripides' work, actually has the effect of rendering Medea's act of revenge more probable than it would otherwise have appeared—though still utterly unforgivable by a modern audience.

During the time of his composition of 'Das Goldene Vlies', Grillparzer's relations with Charlotte, the wife of his cousin Ferdinand v. Paumgartten, passed through their most critical stage. The trilogy itself is dedicated to her in unquestionable terms of gratitude and tenderness.[1] Grillparzer speaks of her as 'die wahre Muse' of his Medea. There is, moreover, reason to suspect that this relationship with Charlotte Paumgartten, 'trüb ein mißgeschlungnes Band', as Grillparzer speaks of it,[2] so disturbed the poet's peace of mind that it was perhaps the most important contributory cause for his inability to continue uninterruptedly with his work. The necessity for breaking with Charlotte is referred to in the poem 'Reiselust' as one of his motives for seeking his escape to Italy at that time. Before this time, during the prolonged interruption of his work, perhaps in January, 1819, previous to the death of his mother on January 23rd, the poem entitled 'Ständchen: Brim, blim, klang, kling' was written on a sheet of his Fleece manuscript. One reads it with almost a shock when viewing it in this light. Its false and strident gaiety seems to provide

[1] Cf.'Wke.' I. 16, No. 2, p. 39: Zueignung an Desdemona (Widmung des Dramatischen Gedichtes 'Das goldene Vließ' an Charlotte von Paumgartten).

[2] In the poem entitled 'Reiselust', G. 84, 4.

most striking evidence of Grillparzer's distracted and unsettled state of mind.

His relations with Charlotte gradually became a source of grave anxiety to him, perhaps partly because of the moral aspect of this forbidden passion. He was certainly not unmindful of his cousin's situation. There is diary-evidence (important in connection with a later work) of a contemporary pre-occupation on Grillparzer's part with the motive of friendship's betrayal through adultery: 'Lies' die Sage von Walter von Aquitanien wegen seiner Liebe zu Hildegunden, und seinem Verhältniß zu Etzel, dem er diese entführt' (T. 738), he exhorts himself in an entry following closely upon that of May 29th, the first of two highly significant Charlotte dates in 1820; and he makes a detailed study of this legend. He is also much concerned with the motive of jealousy, as his re-readings of 'Othello' and his style of 'Desdemona' for Charlotte indicate. But this matter has no place or portion in the tragedy before us, and an arrangement of all the available material on this particular question of his relations to Charlotte leads one to the conclusion that Grillparzer was here, as elsewhere, chiefly concerned with the necessity of holding himself free and unfettered in the interests of his art. It is to this categorical necessity that he is referring in his dedication of 'Das goldene Vlies' to Charlotte, when he speaks of being separated by a 'gebieterische Notwendigkeit' from this woman so deeply attached to him.

The poem entitled 'Der Bann', written either in the spring of 1819, before Grillparzer's escape to Italy, as Backmann suggests, or in the late autumn, before his second flight from Vienna for the purpose of trying to complete his work, refers to his experience with Charlotte Paumgartten. It was written as a leave-taking. Grillparzer describes this parting as inevitable because he has previously rashly pledged himself to another, to his art, which holds him in bondage:

> 'Im Mondenglanz, auf flüchtgem Fuße
> Schlang ich mit ihr den Geisterreihn,
> Und alles Wirklichen Genusse
> Entsagt' ich um den holden Schein'.

As a result of this, Love—or Life ('die Fürstin, der die Welt zu eigen') utters her ban over him, prophesying for him a life of restlessness and dissatisfaction:

> 'Er peitsche rastlos dich durch's Leben,
> Der wilde Dämon *Phantasie*!'

condemning him to pursue the shadow instead of the substance for the rest of his life:

> 'Zieh hin, um all dein Glück betrogen,
> Und buhl um meiner Schwester Gunst,
> Sieh, was das *Leben* dir entzogen,
> Ob dir's ersetzen kann die *Kunst*!'

and Grillparzer concludes:

> 'Seitdem irr' ich verbannt, alleine,
> Betrüge Andre so wie mich:
> Du aber, armes Weib, beweine,
> Den du verloren, ewiglich!'

This poem, which is so characteristic of Grillparzer's life-problem, does more than emphasize the tragedy of the poet's lot in being compelled to forswear happiness and peace; it also contains evidence of Grillparzer's conviction that the sacrifice was being required of him in vain. It reflects his feeling of despair at the task he had set himself in 'Das goldene Vlies', the pessimism which the conclusion to that work itself reflects.

A passage from the 'Selbstbiographie' may here be cited in support of the statement made above that Grillparzer always strove to hold himself free and unfettered in favour of his art. Speaking of his 'love-affairs' in retrospect, he writes:

> '... ich fand mich tief verwickelt, während ich noch glaubte, in der ersten Annäherung zu sein. Das gab nun Glück und Unglück in nächster Nähe, obwohl letzteres in verstärktem Maße, da mein eigentliches Streben doch immer dahin ging, mich in jenem ungetrübten Zustande zu erhalten, der meiner eigentlichen Göttin, der Kunst, die Annäherung nicht erschwerte oder wohl gar ummöglich machte'.[1]

What remains to be said of Grillparzer's relations to Charlotte Paumgartten is important, not only for the interpretation of 'Das goldene Vlies', but also for an understanding of his general attitude towards women, of whom he loved not one better than his art. In this he was not unlike, only more outspoken than, many another great man who, living in and for an exalted end, has only felt free when in whole-hearted pursuit of and progress towards that end, to the exclusion of every other temptation or distraction.

Grillparzer not only loved his art best, but was (he would have us believe) even capable of making love to women in its interests; that is to say, with an eye to making psychological observations for the

[1] 'Wke.', I. 16, p. 181.

depicting of women characters in his work. It is interesting to note in this connection that in his unfinished satirical piece entitled 'Le poète sifflé' Grillparzer causes Adele to speak the truth about himself, the object of the satire, in the words:

> 'Ich kann mir einen solchen [Dichter] denken, der ein Liebesverhältnis anknüpft, um Ausbeute zu brauchen für sein nächstes Trauerspiel, der psychologische Experimente macht mit den Zuckungen eines durch ihn zerfleischten Herzens. (Mit der Faust drohend) O, ich, wollte einen solchen!'[1]

That Grillparzer believed himself to be capable of the heartlessness and callousness which is implied by the above statement will be borne out in what follows, though it is almost certain that his psychological studies of woman's nature were pursued in spite of himself and were a necessary consequence of his analytical nature and guiding artistic impulse. Observation such as his is practised involuntarily. It is so deeply ingrained in the personality of the genuine specialist that he goes on observing—if he is, for example, a lyrist like Joh. Trojan[2]—the plants that line his death-way to the scaffold. Grillparzer was not wilfully heartless and callous in his love affairs; this was an unjust self-accusation which rather does him credit. He was at first, indeed, often a very passionate lover, but never for long. And his diaries show that he pitied his victims, as he pitied himself, because of his unconquerable propensity for psychological study, or because of the strength of his poetic urge and aspiration, which forced him rather to act the part of a lover than to give way to love. It was his nature which exercised a constraint over his intentions, his instinct to remain faithful to, and to further, his art against his conscious will, which prevented him from completely surrendering to love. Grillparzer's conviction of his poetic destiny enabled him, compelled him even, to subordinate everything else in life to it; to sacrifice his own happiness and that of others, if necessary, to its mandate; it prevented him from ever letting himself go, so that he became incapable of falling whole-heartedly in love at any time; and it led him to watch over his own nature, to keep it in check and to observe it in a detached introspective manner, for the sake of lending life to the characters of his imagination; just as

[1] Cotta^{V}, XVIII, p. 85. The words which immediately precede this passage are also of great interest to the student of Grillparzer: 'Und nun vollends die Dichter, die heutigen nämlich. Lassen Sie uns wieder auf unser Pfui zurückkommen! Es gibt ein Schamgefühl des Gemüts, das noch heiliger sein sollte, als das des Körpers. Das Gebet gehört ins Kämmerlein, aber auch die Empfindung. Diese Menschen aber, wenn sie nicht bloß äußerlich sind, und also verächtlich an sich, stören in den besondersten Geheimnissen ihres Innern und legen ihr Selbst dem Pöbel dar — für Geld'.

[2] Instance cited by O. Hinrichsen in his authoritative article indicated below, p. 114 fn.

t led him to practise his observation of human nature on those with whom he came into intimate contact with an eye to present or future work.

4. THE POET'S MODEL FOR JASON

In the summer of the year 1827 Grillparzer visited Charlotte Paumgartten on her deathbed. She accused him of being the cause of her approaching death. Grillparzer reports in his diary (T. 1613) that he did not feel particularly impressed, but felt disgusted with himself for his own heartlessness, just as he had done on the occasion of Marie Piquot's death. At that time he had gone to church to attend the funeral service in order to put himself to the test as to how heartless he really was. He had tried to be sorry, but had failed even then.[1] Another person in like case would perhaps have thought no more about it. Grillparzer had accepted the result of this experiment as a new proof of the fact that he was becoming selfishly obsessed in the cause of his art, an 'Ideen-Egoist, wie es Egoisten des Vorteils gibt' (T. 1109). He depicted his Jason as an egoist of this type (Voll Selbstheit, nicht des Nutzens, doch des Sinns), whose heartlessness towards Medea, like his own towards Charlotte, wrought such havoc in the lives of both.

There can be little doubt as to whom Grillparzer has in mind when he makes Medea say of Jason:

> 'Du kennst ihn nicht, ich aber kenn' ihn ganz,
> Nur er ist da, Er in der weiten Welt,
> Und alles Andre, nichts als Stoff zu Taten.
> Voll Selbstheit, nicht des Nutzens, doch des Sinns,
> Spielt er mit seinem und der andern Glück'

Grillparzer is accusing himself. He goes on relentlessly to make her say:

> 'Lockt's ihn nach Ruhm, so schlägt er Einen tot,
> Will er ein Weib, so holt er Eine sich,
> Was auch darüber bricht, was kümmert's ihn!
> Er tut nur recht, doch recht ist was er will.
> Du kennst ihn nicht, ich aber kenn' ihn ganz,
> Und denk' ich an die Dinge, die geschehn,
> Ich könnt' ihn sterben sehn und lachen drob!'
>
> ('Medea', ll. 629 ff.)

[1] It is true, Grillparzer did not yet know at that time that Marie P. in her last will and testament had declared herself, as it were, in Viola's case for love of him:

> 'She never told her love,
> But let concealment, like a worm i' the bud,
> Feed on her damask cheek'.

See Grillparzer's account of this circumstance in T. 1109.

If ever Grillparzer was repentant of his treatment of Charlotte Paumgartten it was at the time of writing this and his following wor
He felt that he had behaved selfishly towards her, and his youthf
sense of justice, as Mell puts it in his 'Versuch über das Lebensgefü
in Grillparzer's Dramen',[1] accounts for his extreme harshness towar
himself. There is, moreover, reason to suspect that, like Mede
Charlotte herself was not sparing in active reproaches of this kind.

A little further on in the previously mentioned passage in his diar
referring to the visit to the dying Charlotte, Grillparzer writes:

> 'Himmel! kann man dahin kommen, die Menschen nur als Figure
> einer Komödie zu betrachten ... ohne Rücksicht darauf, daß sie ei
> lebendes Selbst sind, mit Leiden und Freuden, mit Willen und Gemüt
> 'Für mich gab es nie eine andre Wahrheit als die Dichtkunst. In il
> habe ich mir nie den kleinsten Betrug, die kleinste Abwesenheit vo
> Stoffe erlaubt. Sie war meine Philosophie, meine Physik, Geschicht
> und Rechtslehre, Liebe und Neigung, Denken und Fühlen (T. 1613-4

Mell says (p. 22) that Grillparzer's first treatment of the great huma
problem, which here as elsewhere occupies his mind: how to conque
Desire (Wollen) and proceed beyond it to willing and furthering th
general good of humanity by self-denying activity or Duty (di
Pflicht zu wirken), even when the happiness or the life of a woma
is at stake, is contained in 'Das goldene Vlies' and is reflected in th
characters of Jason and Medea. This statement unfortunately migh
seem to imply that Jason is, in Grillparzer's representation, a kind o
tragic hero, a victim of the conflict between duty and desire, a
Grillparzer was of the conflict between art and life; actually it is to b
interpreted in a different sense. At this stage of Grillparzer's life it i
truer to speak of his (conscious) conception of art as an ambition rathe
than as a duty. Jason is impelled by his ambition to act as he doe
towards Medea; the parallel to Grillparzer in his treatment o
Charlotte Paumgartten lies in this representation—though we shoul
do Grillparzer a wrong if we supposed that he dealt impartial justic
to himself in such 'confession'. Mell considers (p. 19) that Grillparze
ruined practically all his love affairs through treating the objects o
his affection as useful studies for his dramatic work. That Grillparze
did accuse himself of this conduct is shown by the words from hi
diary quoted above and in the example of the famous wooing scene
where Jason's words do not proceed from his heart, but from hi
head. 'Grillparzer hatte—wie Jason um Medea—gedankenlos un

[1] Cf. Jb. xviii, p. 9.

Charlotte v. Paumgartten . . . geworben', as Stefan Hock more guardedly declares:

'auch er hatte seine Liebe wie ein Abenteuer getrieben, ohne eigene Hingebung ihre Liebe empfangen wie ein strahlender Held von einer Frau, die ihm innerlich nichts war . . .'.[1]

In his well-known letter to Altmütter about Kathi Fröhlich (B. 223) Grillparzer writes again of his 'inability to love', explaining it to himself as follows, as if it were an abnormal aspect of human nature, which of course it is not:

'—ich weiß nicht soll ich es höchste Selbstheit nennen, wenn nicht noch schlimmer; oder ist es blos die Folge eines unbegränzten Strebens nach Kunst und was zur Kunst gehört . . . —Mit einem Wort, ich bin der Liebe nicht fähig . . . Das Bewußtseyn dieser unglücklichen Eigenheit meines Wesens hat auch bewirkt, daß ich von jeher allen eigentlichen Verbindungen mit Weibern, zu denen mich übrigens mein Physisches ziemlich geneigt macht, nach Möglichkeit ausgewichen bin. Jedesmal aber, daß ich mich einließ, bestätigte sich jene traurige Erfahrung; was um so natürlicher ist, da ich mich gerade zu solchen, oder vielmehr ausschließlich hingezogen fühle, die eigentlich am wenigsten für mich passen: zu denen nämlich von entschiedenen Charakterzügen, die meinem Hang zu psychologischer Forschung und dem Stoff-umbildenden Dichtersinn in der Idee die meiste Nahrung geben; auf der anderen Seite aber durch ihr Sprödes und Abgeschlossenes im Wirklichen jedes Zusammenschmelzen nur noch unmöglicher machen'.

Here Grillparzer is clearly thinking of Charlotte Paumgartten and his previous love affair with her. Jason had felt incited to woo Medea, not because he loved her or because she seemed suited to him, but because she was the very type of woman encountered by Grillparzer in Charlotte Paumgartten and was like everything else in life for him, 'nichts als Stoff zu Taten'. A remarkable resemblance between Jason and Grillparzer lies in the fact that both of them in making love are either consciously or unconsciously smoothing the way towards the realization of their respective ambitions. For the rest, the words describing Charlotte Paumgartten in this letter describe just as surely the nature of Medea herself, who was nothing if not of 'decided character'. Just as Grillparzer had behaved selfishly towards Charlotte Paumgartten, and he does not cease to reproach himself for this, so does Jason behave towards Medea. Both women recognize too late the selfishness of their lovers; both men discover that they have incautiously let themselves go too far, and have become almost

[1] Intro. to 'Grillparzers Wke.' in 16 Tln., Berlin, bei Bong (Goldene Klassiker) n. d.

inextricably involved. For Grillparzer it was possible to tear himse
free and, as it seemed, to escape the direct consequences of his guil
But this did not happen without a struggle. We feel that Medea
like Charlotte Paumgartten in her pride and assertiveness, and th
like her she refused to be shaken off by her lover as if she were
creature of no further use to him. But though he was free, Gril
parzer's conscience did not cease to torture him. It is disturbing t
reflect that after all his mental agony and after visiting poetic justic
or bitter symbolical punishment on himself in the figure of Jasor
Grillparzer should have been reproached eight years later by Charlott
Paumgartten with being responsible for her death.

5. THE FULFILMENT OF 'DER BANN'

Such, then, is the parallel between Grillparzer and Charlotte o
the one hand and Jason and Medea in the 'Fleece' on the other. Th
work depicts the tragedy and the curse of their ill-starred relationshi
and their common guilt.

Medea's 'guilt', even in its extremest manifestation, consists in he
becoming a victim of her passions, as Charlotte herself appears t
have done. In one place Grillparzer refers to his 'Fleece'—with i
treatment of this aspect of his experience, we perceive—as exemplify
ing, 'Wie das Gemüt im eigenen Abgrund endet'.[1] He regard
the character and fate of his model for Medea as typical; in his judge
ment Charlotte's passionate nature was her doom.

If this view be taken as indeed embodying the essential dramati
conception of Grillparzer's tragedy a very strong case can be mad
out for equating it with Euripides' 'Medea' on the basis of Kitto's
analysis: 'Euripides' Medea is tragic in that her passions are stronge
than her reason' (p. 193); the tragedy is 'that such a character shoul
exist at all. She is bound to be a torment to herself and others; tha
is why Euripides shows her blazing her way through life leavin
wreckage behind her' (p. 193). The point of Euripides' tragedy
'that passion can be stronger than reason'—destructive 'to Medea'
peace—but not to her life; in short, destructive to society at larg
(p. 194). And another thought common to both dramatists: 'Love'
the Chorus sings, 'when it comes in too great strength has neve
brought renown or virtue to mortals' (p. 194). 'Medea and thos
around her are to be regarded as the victims of Medea's disastrou

[1] Jugenderinnerungen im Grünen (G. 84, 15) l. 123.
[2] Kitto, H. D. F.: 'Greek Tragedy', London, 1939.

emperament. Unless we feel Medea in this way, a tragic victim ather than a tragic agent, we shall try to sympathize with her in he wrong way, and waste valuable time working up emotions about he poor children' (p. 195). But there is one important difference in espect to this dramatic conception. *Medea* 'is contrived by Euripides, deliberately, as the final revelation of his thought'; his heroine is 'the mpersonation of one of the blind and irrational forces in human nature' (p. 199): 'Euripides remains a little detached' (p. 200). This can never be said of Grillparzer's heroine; she represented part of his experience of life as an artist and was identified both in his thought and in his conscience with his tragic muse Charlotte. The poet also felt himself to be, like Jason, an offender and passed judgement on himself with the harshness already referred to. Jason is made to uffer and repent. Again we recall a judgement from Kitto's convincing analysis—though here again there is no suggestion that Euripides' tragedy is like Grillparzer's a 'confession': 'What matters is that we should clearly see the utter baseness of Jason: this is one of the chief ingredients of the tragedy' (p. 269).

The end of Grillparzer's trilogy betrays a supreme desire to atone, in that he endows Medea, or Charlotte Paumgartten, Mell says, with greatness, and leaves Jason, that is, himself, unable to do other than return to his former untrammelled state in accordance with the dictates of his nature and destiny, deserted and alone.[1]

Jason's vanity and ambition had never been worth while. And now Grillparzer's sacrifice to his art, to his poetic ambition, seems to have been in vain. At the end of his trilogy he is by no means satisfied with his work, so that both the happiness of *life* (Glück) and the reward of *art* (Ruhm) seem lost to him:

> 'Was ist der Erde Glück?—Ein Schatten!
> Was ist der Erde Ruhm?—Ein Traum!'

It is the fulfilment of 'Der Bann' for him. At the end of 'Sappho' the poet had renounced all claim to 'life' in his elation at the achievement of his art. After the weary trials of writing 'Das goldene Vlies', his art seems a poor substitute to him for what he has been denied. He feels that he is not only unfitted for life by his nature and calling, but also, in spite of his self-sacrifice, by his inadequate natural endowment for art.

[1] Mell, loc. cit., Jb., xviii, p. 9.

6. THE LESSON LEARNED

Grillparzer's failure to achieve the impossible that he set himself to perform in 'Das goldene Vlies' did him ultimately, however, no harm as a dramatist. He had to learn the lesson that this failure taught. The difficulty of the task undertaken came to be recognized by him as having been his original incentive, and a mistaken one—as is revealed in a passage from his 'Anfang einer Selbstbiographie, 1834–5':

> 'Durch eine Eigenheit seiner Natur zur Lösung von Schwierigkeiten getrieben, führte ihn ein ungünstiges Geschick auf den Stoff seiner dritten dramatischen Arbeit, die mit dem Titel: das goldene Vließ.'

That it is useless for a poet to set himself to work in this manner is obvious; something, it is true, will come of his efforts, but only the sort of thing that we should expect, an artificial and unconvincing fabrication. And this description would have applied to the whole of 'Das goldene Vlies' but for Grillparzer's unintentional but salutary 'change of plan', and it would have applied to the results of any similar efforts which the poet might have undertaken, if work of this kind had been able to satisfy him. It is painful to contemplate the possibility that Grillparzer too might have figured, somewhat like Hebbel, as a creator of dramas 'aus literarisch-psychologischer Wollust'—in a spirit corresponding to that in which this, his most ambitious work, was conceived. Gundolf's strictures, in which he further accuses Grillparzer of deliberately choosing for the setting of his would-be classical drama 'a region of barbaric terrors in the legendary past, harbouring dragons, homeless strangers who wander about and are slain, and where death, destruction, and spectres belong to the ordinary run of things—as if the world of poetry were a shadow world of non-committal make-believe, dreams, and the unreal, a picture-book for grown-up children'[1] would be justified, if it were true that Grillparzer's trilogy were not only conceived but also executed in this manner. But the initial conception of it as a dramatic task or exercise, unrelated to experience, was contrary to Grillparzer's—if not to Euripides'—genius. Commenced in this vein, the work continues unconvincingly until, significantly enough, an *impasse* is reached—in the famous wooing scene; there the poet's own experience eventually inspires its continuance, and from that point the whole character of the work is changed, and it lives as tragedy.

Grillparzer had thus by no means given up the treatment of different aspects of experience in favour of theatrical make-believe—

[1] Gundolf, loc. cit., p. 41 f.

as Gundolf's hasty judgment of this trilogy would imply. Indeed, Gundolf's criticism of Grillparzer's dramas as a whole would not lead us to suspect that the poet had ever even started on a different basis. It is characteristic of this critic's work on Grillparzer, as of his work on Shakespeare, that he leaves out of account the mirroring in their dramatic work of the problems that beset them as men and poets.

In his first great play Grillparzer had concluded by declaring himself reconciled to the necessity for renunciation of the common joys of life. Here the attitude was a different one. Art is depicted by implication in the 'Golden Fleece' as a personal ambition, in the interests of which the poet accuses himself of having heartlessly sacrificed, by his desertion of her, the happiness of the deeply emotional woman who loved him. In this work Grillparzer's artistic striving and poetic ambition are reflected in Jason's egoistical struggle for fame and recognition. In the next work to be discussed a king becomes involved, like Jason, in guilty conduct, as a result of his unbounded strivings and selfish ambitions. The contrast between Art and Life finds ever more general application to different walks of human life. It is important to remember that Grillparzer's interest in this problem—though primarily personal—is for the dramatist a general one. Just where he appears to be treating of characters which stand out as exceptions, as in 'König Ottokar' and 'Ein treuer Diener' for instance, there will he most likely be found to be treating problems and experiences which affected him most nearly, and which he was impelled to recognize and reveal as characteristic of human life and universal. For it is in the nature of his art and genius that he should give such general utterance in his dramatic work to his own problems and convictions, experiences and feelings.

CHAPTER IV

'KÖNIG OTTOKARS GLÜCK UND ENDE'

I. PRINCIPLES OF HISTORICAL DRAMA

'KÖNIG Ottokars Glück und Ende' was Grillparzer's next work
It was written in 1823 and was, moreover, his first historica
drama. Apart from 'Blanca' there existed, however, not les
than ten earlier fragments of his which deal with historical character
and events. An examination of these fragments led us to the conclusio
that Grillparzer's principal motive for choosing these materials wa
that they enabled him to portray elements of his own character an
experience. And this is true of 'König Ottokar' as well. In his 'Selbstbiographie' Grillparzer wrote in connection with this work the following significant words:

> '*Der Dichter wählt historische Stoffe weil er darin den Keim zu seine eigenen Entwicklungen findet*, vor allem aber um seinen Ereignissen un Personen eine Konsistenz, einen Schwerpunkt der Realität zu geben damit auch der Anteil aus dem Reich des Traumes in das der Wirklichkei übergehe'.[1]

He chooses his historical material, in fact, for the same personal reasor
that Goethe chose that of 'Egmont', and in pursuance, as it were
of the principle laid down by Lessing in his 'Hamburgische Drama-
turgie', where he devotes several numbers to discussing Aristotle's
rulings on this topic:

> 'Die Tragödie ist keine dialogierte Geschichte; die Geschichte ist für di Tragödie nichts als ein Repetorium von Namen' (xxiv). Or again, translating Aristotle: "Man hält sich an die schon vorhandenen Namen, aus Ursache, weil das Mögliche glaubwürdig ist, und wir nicht möglich glauben, was nie geschehen" (lxxxix). 'Der tragische Dichter hat sich nicht weiter um die historische Wahrheit zu bekümmern, als sie einer wohleingerichteten Fabel ähnlich ist, *mit der er seine Absichten verbinden kann*. Er braucht eine Geschichte nicht darum, weil sie geschehen ist, sondern darum, weil sie so geschehen ist, daß er sie schwer *zu seinem gegenwärtigen Zweck* besser erdichten könnte . . . Auf dem Theater sollen wir nicht lernen, was dieser oder jener einzelne Mensch getan hat, sondern was ein jeder Mensch von einem gewissen Charakter unter gewissen gegebenen Umständen tun werde' (xix).

[1] 'Wke.' I. 16, p. 116 f.

We only need to associate the words here italicized with those which we have similarly emphasized in Grillparzer's passage to feel justified in assuming that Grillparzer recognized in the character and fate of Ottokar certain universal traits which linked up with his own experience and attendant thought upon life.

It has become clear to us from our examination of the previous work that Grillparzer was at this time obsessed with the idea of having behaved towards Charlotte Paumgartten in a selfish and heartless manner, 'als Folge eines unbegränzten Strebens nach Kunst und was zur Kunst gehört'. We shall see in what follows to how great an extent 'König Ottokar' may also be regarded as a treatment of the moral issue involved in this relationship. But this new material also spontaneously associated itself later with another love-experience, until then entirely absent from Grillparzer's life; much as was the case with Goethe's 'Werther' in 1774, it was not until the beginning of 1823 that a new disturbance precipitated Grillparzer's tragedy of 'Ottokar'.[1] For more than three years a laborious process of detailed preparation preceded this trigger-incident—almost as if the author were subconsciously aware of the necessity he was under to make ready for this development. 'Ottokar' is like the majority of Grillparzer's works in that respect: it ripened out of a previous experience in his emotional life towards a new crisis in it, as if under precognitive stimulus and subconscious urge.[2]

The fact that the work was not written until 1823 might otherwise make it appear surprising that it should here be represented as fundamentally associated with Charlotte and a personal problem of the author's which was by this time in a sense no longer actual. But the conception of 'Ottokar' belongs to the year 1819, before 'Medea' was completed; and Grillparzer's association with Charlotte von Paumgartten persisted until 1822. With its historical theme, moreover, it was a work requiring different treatment and technique from a drama based on legend, so that internal considerations alone would almost suffice to explain the nearly four years' delay. Eighteen years of history had to be compressed and actualized within the unity of a dramatic action, a process involving infinitely studious preparation if the work was not to travesty historical truth. Grillparzer was far too conscientious and faithful an artist to devote less than his utmost endeavour to this task. The dramatic principles he sought to

[1] This suggestion is discussed in Sec. 5 of this chapter.

[2] Perhaps it is in profound recognition of this mysterious process that Grillparzer employs the term *Entwicklung* in the passage quoted above.

observe in attempting this task are admirably stated in that memorable passage of the 'Selbstbiographie' which we have already cited, dealing with historical drama in general and 'Ottokar' in particular, when Grillparzer further observes:

> 'Ich hatte es nämlich mit einer Form zu tun die mir durchaus nicht empfehlenswert schien: dem historischen Drama. . . . Die Form des Dramas ist die Gegenwart. Die Nichtunterbrechung ist daher das wesentliche Merkmal derselben'.

The first acts reveal Grillparzer's consummate powers in the direction of effecting this active continuity and present actuality on the stage; it is all the more regrettable that the material of this work resisted dramatic compression and actualization in the later phases, where an epic or chronicle effect prevails. Grillparzer was constrained to relax in this historical drama the unity of time as never previously in his whole dramatic practice. Yet it seemed to him that the historically recorded events were 'peculiarly adapted to his intentions', as if (he declares, echoing Lessing again) they had been 'invented for that end'; he therefore adopted them, despite their past (historic) flavour and epic drag.

> 'Diese meine Bedenken und diesen meinen Trost', he adds with finality to these reflexions, 'werden freilich diejenigen lächerlich finden, für welche die Geschichte der sich selbst realisierende Begriff ist. Ich muß mir ihr Lachen gefallen lassen, oder vielmehr ich bin so frei, ihnen dieses Lachen im verstärkten Maße zurückzugeben'.

To himself as a poet he reserved in fine the right to present, motivate, and interpret the known facts and events of history as he would; that is to say, in accordance with the insight which his own knowledge of human nature, his own experience of it afforded, subject to incidental dramatic and poetic needs.

The general theme of this work is neither purely historical nor purely personal; it is essentially a perennial and universal one, and it was so conceived by Grillparzer. But he had only, like Thomas Mann, to 'write about himself' in order to loose the tongues of life in general: as a poet he knew this. The only reason we could have for suspecting that he was not, indeed, in this historical drama still actuated by his earlier personal experience (the same which had already informed his Fleece tragedy) would be if, ignoring obvious internal evidence and the contemporary inception of the two works, we thought we had reason to suppose that the effect of that earlier experience had become obliterated by subsequent developments of an essentially different ind. Yet neither Grillparzer's progress in his art, nor the condition f his relations to Charlotte, nor his love affair with Katharina Fröhlich which in spite of its promising beginning soon became a source of nisgiving, annoyance, and anxiety) had been such as to bring about a adical change in his outlook.

2. 'THE AFFAIR WITH THE POPE'

Grillparzer's material circumstances and prospects had also not mproved. In November, 1819, he had published a series of lyrical oems inspired by his journey to Italy in that year, among them one e had written in Rome, *Die Ruinen des Campo Vaccino*. In this he gave xpression to his poetic regret over the downfall of antiquity, symolized by the ruins of the *Forum Romanum* and of the *Colosseum*, and ommiserated the noble ruin for the added insult of being made to bear the Cross' which was the symbol of its distress and martyrdom. The poem was banned after publication in the *Aglaja*, Grillparzer being lenounced as a heretic—probably at the instigation of Zacharias Werner, whose religiosity he so despised (and in this poem implicitly ttacked); and the emperor demanded, through Sedlnitzky, the chief ensor, a written defence and apology. This the author prepared, in ssociation with Schreyvogel, who, as editor of the *Aglaja*, was also xposed to blame. It was a humiliating consequence of their temerity, vhich Schreyvogel had anticipated, as Grillparzer should also have lone. The matter was then officially at an end; but from now on Grillparzer had been continually under suspicion; his popularity in ristocratic circles had waned, his requests for advancement in office nad been refused, and he long continued in general disfavour because of this notorious 'Geschichte mit dem Papst'. 'Die Gehässigkeit', he wrote as late as 1838 in this same connection, 'und ihre weite Verbreitung kränkt mich ins Innerste der Seele. Ich bin ein inoffensives Wesen' (T. 3327).

Vienna in those days was hardly worthy of its son. Gossip, scandal, and intrigue were rife. Grillparzer's autobiography contains a formidable arraignment of his contemporaries for the humiliations, indignities, and misunderstandings to which he was subjected. Numberless circumstances seemed to conspire to blight his hopes and ruin his prospects. He does not appear himself to have exercised great circumspection. He overstayed leaves of absence from duty with amazing obstinacy; the reason for this was his perhaps not unnatural presumption, for those times, that, being a leading poet in the state, he was entitled not merely to fair treatment, but to privilege, patronage, and preferment. Then there was, during the Italian journey, his imprudent dallying in the Imperial retinue, giving rise to the rumour of his appointment to the post of private secretary to the empress (which belonged to none other than his cousin Ferdinand Paumgartten, Charlotte's husband). These and other acts militated against him.

3. GRILLPARZER THE PATRIOT

Whether it is justifiable to speak of these setbacks with regret, in any but a superficial sense, is questionable. It is in fact difficult to imagine that Grillparzer's contribution to poetry would have been enriched if he had been able to live on better terms with life. And as regards what would have been the inevitable consequences for his art—in Austria—of anything approaching preferment or royal patronage, Grillparzer's own words afford the aptest commentary:

> 'Jede Annäherung oder irgend ausgesprochene Gunst hätte mir bei meinen künftigen Arbeiten die Rücksicht aufgedrungen, ob ich damit nicht gegen die Ansichten hoher Gönner verstieße'.

His work would be the poorer, not the richer, if it were more strongly influenced by that noble frailty of patriotic feeling which intruded into 'Ottokar', for example, those traces of flattery (however sincerely meant) for Austria's ruling house. As Hormayr, the contemporary Austrian historian, points out, however, Grillparzer's ungenerous treatment at the hands of the authorities for his efforts as patriotic chronicler in the concluding acts of 'Ottokar'—'er hat über die ganze Hapsburgische Vorzeit von Rudolf bis auf Franz II ein wahrhaft Shakespeare'sches Netz gespannt' [1]—effectively discouraged any ambitions Grillparzer might have had to persist in these loyalist endeavours. After this experiment he was able the better to keep in mind the principle evolved by Lessing from Aristotle:

> 'Die Absicht der Tragödie ist weit philosophischer als die Absicht der Geschichte, und es heißt, sie von ihrer wahren Würde herabsetzen, wenn man sie zu einem bloßen Panegyrikus berühmter Männer macht oder sie gar, den Nationalstolz zu nähren, mißbraucht' (xix).

We see from the very beginning of the play that Ottokar, though the central figure, is not destined to become its hero, if by this we understand the figure who is to enjoy the sympathy of the audience. Ottokar is no more the hero of this play, in the accepted sense of the

[1] Jos. v. Hormayr: 'Anemonen . .', Jena, 1845, p. 59.

word, than Jason is of the 'Golden Fleece'; but he is portrayed (and this is especially observable in the last two acts) with greater pity than Jason. In making Ottokar come to see the error of his ways Grillparzer succeeds in winning for him the pity of the audience too, though this of itself in tragedy is not enough.

The 'hero' of the play, we are often reminded, is Rudolf of Hapsburg. And indeed all might be well if only this were a play about him, and not primarily the tragedy of Ottokar. As Emil Reich puts it:

> Im Drama wurde Rudolf zum vornehmen Vertreter des guten Prinzips, aber diese milde Abgeklärtheit erscheint . . . als Frucht eignen Ringens mit der wilden, heissen Natur, als Sieg festentschlossenen Willens über widerstrebende Kräfte der Charakteranlage. Weise läßt Grillparzer seinen Rudolf bekennen, auch er blicke auf eine von bloß persönlicher unruhiger Ruhmsucht bewegte Jugend zurück, wo 'der eitle Drang der Ehre' ihn verführt, 'der raschen Tatkraft jungen Arm' unbedacht 'an Fremden und Verwandten' zu üben,
>
> 'Als wär' die Welt ein weiter Schauplatz nur
> Für Rudolf und sein Schwert'.[1]

These words remind us of Medea's judgement of Jason: 'Nur Er ist da, Er in der weiten Welt, Und alles Andre, nichts als Stoff zu Taten', and in this again we recognize the autobiographical descent of another of this author's characters. In Rudolf is portrayed Grillparzer's ideal of manhood and kingship. As early as 1808 he had written a panegyric on him. Rudolf is allied to those ideal foils of his, the 'Gegenfiguren' of his youthful fragments.

4. OTTOKAR'S SUBJECTIVE PORTRAYAL

In Ottokar he portrays the danger and tragedy of unbounded ambition—and unsuitable endowment—which he believed he experienced in his own person. Sauer describes Ottokar as

> 'ein zielbewußter tatkräftiger Emporkömmling, der im vermessenen Übermute die ihm von der himmlischen Vorsehung wie von den irdischen Gewalten gesetzten Grenzen überspringt, und sein inneres wie sein äußeres Glück dabei einbüßt'.[2]

Unbounded and selfish ambition in Ottokar involves him in guilty conduct. It had impelled him to seek a marital alliance with Margareta in the first place, and it now impels him to banish her from his side—just as Grillparzer's corresponding behaviour towards Charlotte, and

[1] Reich, E.: 'Franz Grillparzers Dramen', Dresden, 1909[3], p. 128.
[2] Einltg. z. 5. Ausg., Cotta[v], I, p. 50.

Jason's towards Medea, was influenced by ambition. Like Charlotte in the poem, 'Der Bann', and like Medea too, Margareta prophesies that disaster will follow upon this act:

> 'Er soll vor Unrecht sorglich sich bewahren;
> Denn auch das kleinste rächt sich!'

and Rudolf too says in the great scene of Ottokar's humiliation:

> 'Mit ihr habt ihr das Glück von Euch verbannt'.

In history there is no authority for this bodeful impeachment. Ottokar did not reach the height of his power and thereafter commence to incur misfortune and to decline until ten years after the dissolution by Papal dispensation of his unfortunate and dishonourable marriage to Margareta of Austria, and four years after her death. Grillparzer introduces the motive (as a poet, even of 'historical' drama, he was justified in so doing) from his own feeling and experience; for all that it is historically unrecorded, the feature is significant and not inherently untrue, as he would interpose: 'Was ist denn Geschichte? . . . Der Geschichtschreiber weiß wenig; der Dichter aber muß alles wissen.'[1] It is the poet's own personal experience and conscience that teaches him aright, he claims; it is his thought and experience, not history, nor psychological speculation, that is fundamental and central in this tragedy. Rollett in the critical edition stops just short of this conclusion; he tries to interpret Grillparzer's admission, 'Der Dichter wählt historische Stoffe, weil er darin den Keim zu seinen eigenen Entwicklungen findet', as meaning 'daß Überzeugung und Weltbild des Dichters, die Entwicklungen seiner persönlichen Gedanken innerhalb der historischen Stoffe möglich sein müssen'.[2] This is lame. At the same time, he does reject the naïve hypothesis that Ottokar is, as it were, Napoleon in disguise, and admits only a *general* resemblance (which is incontestable). The particular similarity between Ottokar's and Napoleon's circumstances which Grillparzer alleges in his autobiography, however, when he remarks, 'daß der Wendepunkt von beider Schicksal die Trennung ihrer ersten Ehe, und eine zweite Heirat gebildet hatte', so far from being true, is evidence of an inaccurate and 'subjective' judgement. It can only be appreciated therefore if we are satisfied on this important point: in supplying this motive of Ottokar's downfall as attendant upon his banishment of Margareta when it seemed that she could no longer further his interests, Grillparzer may possibly have believed that it was true of Ottokar as of Napoleon; but what is more essential is that it shows

[1] 'Wke.', I. 16, p. 168. [2] ibid., I. 3, Einltg., p. 324.

him to have felt, as in the Fleece tragedy, that his action in separating from Charlotte had brought unhappiness to him and to her; also that in misusing her for the furtherance of his art, and then discarding her, so sinning against the sincerity and sanctity of their relations, he had incurred a guilt which, like Ottokar's (and Napoleon's), avenged itself on him in his failure to realize his own ambition and destiny. Ottokar, whose guilt, like Jason's, must be requited and brought home to him, is not represented as becoming involved in misfortune (as Reich would have it, and the title seems to imply),[1] but as atoning in full for the inhumanity he displayed particularly towards Margareta when in pursuit of his own selfish ends. He recognizes in the end, too, that he has sinned and he is full of remorse; and when he says:

> 'Geblendet war ich, so hab' ich gefehlt!
> Mit Willen hab' ich Unrecht nicht getan.
> Doch einmal ja! und noch einmal! O Gott
> Ich hab mit Willen Unrecht auch getan',

we realize that Grillparzer again, as in his Fleece, is accusing himself, again perhaps unjustly, or with that youthful sense of justice of which Mell speaks.[2]

This presumption that Grillparzer was accusing himself *unjustly* carries with it a damaging implication regarding his representation in this work of the nature of Ottokar's tragic guilt; we feel and know it to be subjectively interpreted, implying our judgement of it as unconvincing, that is, 'not likely to be true' of Ottokar; in our feeling, that is, not true to life at all.

It would be wrong to pretend that the work contains no other elements than those indicated above, or that it is not an historical drama in a valid sense of the word—as long as poetical considerations are held to be paramount in such an undertaking. Nor need we underestimate the fact that the figure of Napoleon bore certain 'distant resemblances' to that of Ottokar, because this contributed to Grillparzer's interest in the work, as perhaps it does to ours. Possibly we do not feel the force of this resemblance with the same conviction as Grillparzer's contemporaries did. One cause for the delay by the censorship during 1823–24 in sanctioning this work lay in the parallel to the relationship between Zawisch and Ottokar's second wife which was afforded by the notorious relationship between Count Neipperg and Marie Louise. Costenoble wrote in his diary after the first performance of Grill-

[1] Cf. also Grillparzer's (subjective) formulation of 'Ottokar's' theme in 'Jugenderinnerungen im Grünen' (G. 84, 15, l. 124): 'Der Erdengröße schnellverwelktes Glück'!

[2] Jb. xviii, p. 9.

parzer's tragedy: 'Ottokar ist recht glücklich Napoleon nachgebildet'; but he adds: 'am Schluß versinkt der Held in erbärmliche Schwäche'.[1] Costenoble could not be expected to condone, mitigate, or explain this crudely-stated circumstance on the grounds that we advance, namely that Ottokar was Grillparzer himself, and was, in the sense indicated, subjectively portrayed. The advantage of so doing is that it enables us to perceive the root cause of what we also judge to be a dramaturgical defect in Ottokar's portrayal. Costenoble, like everybody else not concerned with Grillparzer's personal problems, was justified in assuming that Ottokar is intended for a tragic hero of the Napoleonic type and therefore also in criticizing him in his fall as too feeble and broken and abject for this. Grillparzer did not observe in 'Ottokar' what Shakespeare demonstrates so triumphantly in 'Hamlet' for example: that it is important for a hero to end with spirit and dignity, 'claiming the admiration of the sleeping hero in us all,' even though the poet may be 'confessing' (in transmuted terms) his own suffering through him. Literary confessions in tragic form need to be self-vindications too. That is what is chiefly wrong with Ottokar as with Jason before him: both lack fighting strength and become too contrite and remorseful for tragic rôles.

The case for placing these 'subjective' tragic heroes thus side by side is well put by Reich:

> 'Es führt eine gerade Linie vom Thema des "Goldenen Vließ" zu jenem des "Ottokar". Der Böhmenkönig ist ein kühner Fürstensohn wie Jason. . . Auch er strebt unbekümmert um jede sittliche Schranke nur nach Ruhm, Macht und Glanz der Größe, worin er sein Glück zu finden meint. . . Ottokar lernt seiner eigensüchtigen Weltanschauung entsagen'.[2]

If we also bear in mind, as in the case of Jason, that Ottokar's ambition and the guilty conduct in which it involved him, his punishment and his desire to atone, are parallel to Grillparzer's, we shall realize that here again the author is visiting poetic justice on himself, and that there is indeed a general similarity between his Ottokar's failure to reconcile ambition with happiness and peace of mind, and Grillparzer's failure to overcome a like contrast in his own experience.

In the light of this observation affecting Ottokar's relationship to Grillparzer, we may now judge how credulous it is to attach overriding significance to the poet's studied references regarding Ottokar's resemblance to Napoleon. Equally unwarrantable does it seem to emphasize unduly that attendant outward circumstance, even though it is historical, the fact that Ottokar, like Napoleon, is placed between

[1] Costenoble, loc. cit., I, p. 340, Feb. 19, 1825. [2] Reich, loc. cit., 3rd ed., p. 120.

two women, the one older than the other, as Reich does[1]—referring to the similar situation in the cases of Phaon, Jason, Rustan, König Alfonso, (Ahasver)—because the circumstance in itself is not, in any of these examples, of primary importance. Even 'Sappho (we saw) is not genetically a 'Situationstragödie', and like Melitta in that work or Kreusa in 'Medea', so may Kunigunde here be said to owe her place in this work to the mere demands of dramatic economy. To provide occasion for Phaon's inevitable defection Melitta had to be invented; Kreusa and Kunigunde would have had to be so too, if they had not been conveniently present in the respective legendary and historical materials which the poet used. All these figures are obvious pegs on which to hang the outward motivation of an action which is in each instance inevitable and inwardly accounted for by the very characters of Phaon, Jason, and Ottokar. The all-important action of the last-named, his divorce of Margareta, is by no means to be explained merely by referring to the presence of the younger woman, and Phaon and Jason too would have acted more or less as they did even if Melitta and Kreusa had not been introduced into the plays where they appear. To argue otherwise is to say that Grillparzer was not a tragic poet but a plot-playwright. The same also applies to the works 'Der Traum ein Leben', 'Die Jüdin', and 'Esther', where infinitely more profound issues are involved than that of solving the eternal triangle. In 'Ottokar' it is permissible to discount the situation motive almost entirely. In a passage which modifies significantly the representation of the king as actuated by personal ambition and selfish impulses, one which prepares us for the reflection in Grillparzer's subsequent works of a modified judgement of his own attitude, Ottokar declares to the assembled citizens in words that are unmistakably sincere:

> 'Auch das noch, das noch, seht, um euretwillen!
> Was einem jeden Mann das Teuerste,
> Die Ruh' im eignen Haus, hab' ich gestört
> Um eure Ruh', um eurer Kinder Ruhe,
> Damit nach meinem Tod mein Reich nicht erblos,
> Mein Werk das Spiel nicht werde innern Zwists,
> Hab' ich von Margareta mich getrennt,
> Die keines Erbens Hoffnung mehr gewährt,
> Und neuer Bande Wechsel mich gefügt'.

The importance of this passage in its ultimate reflection of Grillparzer's judgement of his own conduct is profound. The only difference in himself was that, renouncing Charlotte because of a 'gebietherische

[1] ibid., p. 120.

Notwendigkeit', he did so without as yet 'submitting to new ties'. T
Margareta too the king attests:

> 'Es ist ja nicht der Jugend wilder Kitzel,
> Der gärend feur'ge Drang nach Neuerung,
> Was mich Euch meiden heißt: es ist mein Land,
> Das in mir Ehen schließt und Ehen scheidet'.

We are forced to admit the altruistic implications of this, and are b
that the less inclined to assign to Kunigunde anything but a secondar
rôle.

5. THE TRIGGER-INCIDENT OF 'OTTOKAR'

At the same time, the fact remains to be discussed that in the Kuni-
gunde-Zawisch intrigue a kind of side-issue is developed which goe
far beyond the original demands of dramatic economy, as well as o
historical tradition. During the year 1822 or early in the following year
before writing 'Ottokar', Grillparzer conceived an interest in Mari
von Smolenitz, but was destined to witness, and to reproach himsel
for, her conquest by a bolder suitor, whom he had long envied for hi
success with women and his love of life. Herein further lies th
nucleus and clue, the leading motive of several of the poet's late
works. In the wooing of Kunigunde by one who has been describe
as one of the most perfect scoundrels in German literature, th
interloper Zawisch, a significant parallel is afforded to the bearin
of Otto von Meran in the 'Treuer Diener'. Oginsky in 'Das Kloste
bei Sendomir', Naukleros in 'Des Meeres und der Liebe Wellen'
Don Garceran in 'Die Jüdin', and Belgiojoso (as well as Leopold) i
'Der Bruderzwist' derive from the same real source. Of Nauklero
it has rightly been said that he is modelled on Daffinger, whos
acquaintance we have made as the callow youth in 'Sappho'; there i
reason to suspect that the same is true of Zawisch and the others. The
all embody Grillparzer's early ideal of the confident and successfu
wooer, but with concrete satirical traits superadded of the kin
observed in Daffinger, the artist and libertine. His likeness is develope
most fully in Otto von Meran.

When we reflect how much care is devoted to the delineation of th
originally non-essential Kunigunde, and what interest attaches to he
intrigue with Zawisch, matters which history all but ignores, we fin
ourselves on the track of a fruitful investigation. Zawisch an
Kunigunde can be recognized as characters associated with th
historical Ottokar which perhaps could not, or at all events did not

ake shape in the poet's imagination until they, too, like Ottokar and Margareta themselves, came to occupy a corresponding place in his own experience of life. During the years of 'Ottokar's' preparation they were obstacles to progress, because for Grillparzer himself they were not vital, living. Then unexpectedly figures like them entered his own life, completing the analogy between the poet's situation and that of Ottokar. Time, in a phrase of Th. Mann's, 'of grace and in quiet the poet's ally', afforded at last the 'daimonic intervention'.[1] Once more the way was clear for poetic creation, and Kunigunde and Zawisch could be drawn from life; that is why they appeal to us as so convincing and original. As with all his best creations, these beings had their living prototypes in the author's emotional and real experience as an imaginative poet.

His first renewed stirrings of the love-passion, with which—as so often for Goethe too—are soon associated the stirrings of poetic courage and resolve, are reflected in the poem 'Todeswund', belonging to the beginning of 1823. This remarkable poem precedes the five 'Huldigungen' for Marie von Smolenitz, though these had been commenced perhaps before the end of 1822, as Backmann suggests.[2] Backmann's recognition of Marie as the object of some, at least, of the 'Huldigungen' (actually they all seemed to be addressed to her) indicates the proper interpretation of 'Todeswund' and points the way to the solution of a problem of long standing. When did Grillparzer first know Marie? Sauer had misgivings even about accepting such an early date as 1825. But since Grillparzer's acquaintance with Marie is inevitably associated with his residence in the Ballgasse it was possible to go back still further (with significant results) to the year 1823, as being the probable date of his change to that address.[3] There is apparent evidence in Grillparzer's autobiography that 'Ottokar' was finished (by March 9, 1823) in the Dorotheergasse, his former abode.[4] This thirty years' old recollection of Grillparzer's is however misleading; both 'Ottokar' and the 'Huldigungen' point to an earlier removal to Marie's neighbourhood. The probability is that this important change took

[1] Cf. 'Lotte in Weimar', Stockholm, 1939, p. 290. A striking instance of this phenomenon occurs while these pages are being set up in type. Mr. L. A. G. Strong in a broadcast (27 May, 1946), speaking of his latest work, as yet unwritten, declares that it has been preparing itself for the past four years. Two years ago he had a unique experience, indispensable to the maturing of the work. 'I knew nothing of this development when the book started itself,' Mr. Strong concludes; 'but the book knew! It bided its time!'

[2] Cf. G. 169, Anm.; also Jb. xxix, pp. 51 f.; Jb. xxxi, p. 33 f.

[3] Cf. 'Der Kontrast zwischen Kunst und Leben bei Grillparzer', p. 97, and fn. The assumption that Grillparzer was still living at the Dorotheergasse address in 1823 is made in the 'Wohnungsliste' there referred to; it is based on the autobiographical evidence which I now describe as misleading.

[4] Cf. T. 1103 Anm.

place in the spring of 1822 and is the impending change of addres
referred to in T. 1103. The five 'Huldigungen' preserved seem t
represent a selection from a number of such poems belonging to th
1822 period leading up to 'Todeswund' (and 'Ottokar'). This latte
poem can only be understood if we picture the dramatist exhorting
his despondent self to stretch out its pinions, as it were, and rise up t
drink from the poet's source of inspiration and vitality, which—a
with Shakespeare's Romeo, and his own Spartakus, Jaromir, Phaon
Jason, and particularly Leander—is experience of love.

'Schwing dich auf, Adler, zu Mimers Born,
Und bring mir zwei Tropfen, daß ich mich labe!
Sonst war ich kräftig und stark,
In den vordersten Reihen stand ich,
Trat auch wohl vor, als Einzelner,
Zum ringsbewunderten Kampf:
Nun aber lieg' ich, matt und lechzend,
Verwundet vom eignen Schwert,
Und nagender Durst zehrt an meiner Seele;
Schwing dich auf, Adler, zu Mimers Born,
Und bring mir zwei Tropfen, daß ich mich labe!' (G. 48).

Leander was cured of his sickness when Hero, who bore *two* pitcher
from the holy spring of Hymen, gave him (as of nectar, like Hebe) t
drink. The imagery of this poem recalls that of an earlier one, whic
also celebrates a love-experience—either with Charlotte or Theres
Heberle (his 'Hebe' in G. 34)—the poem 'Wunderbrunnen' of 182
(G. 36):

'Seit ich von dir gekostet,
Du labend heller Born!
Dünkt jedes Naß mir trübe
Und leer der Freude Horn.
Zu dir geht meine Liebe
Von dir aus all mein Zorn;
O daß du immer flössest,
Du leichtversiegter Born!'

Shortly before writing these lines Grillparzer read Scheller's 'Mythologie der nordischen Völker' (cf. T. 745),[1] where he found most o
the symbolical material of both poems, Mimer's Spring ('Born'
'Dichterbrunnen', p. 22) and the horn Giöll, from which wisdom an
'songship' is drunk (cf. frontispiece), the repeated draughts of mead (o
which Grillparzer appropriately desires but two, that is, from the jar

[1] Scheller, F. J.: 'Mythologie der nord. u. and. teutschen Völker', Regensburg, 1816.

Sôn and Boðn, p. 24), all in this 'handbook' of the Prose Edda; he found the concept of mortal combat (p. 16 ff., Valhalla) and the eagle of 'Todeswund' there too (p. 27), but not in its somewhat incongruous rôle of messenger; on the contrary this feature derives from a remote source in classical mythology. (There is no occasion to invoke with Backmann the legends of Prometheus and Ganymede.) Grillparzer's diary for 1820–21 shows (T. 836) that he read Böttiger's essay: 'Amalthea oder der Cretensische Zeus als Säugling'[1] which refers to the eagle that with its beak extracted nectar for the infant Zeus from the rocks (p. 47). This unfamiliar classical source for the eagle-metaphor in 'Todeswund' is more satisfying from the philological than the poetical point of view: Grillparzer's opposition to Scheller's (and Herder's) advocacy of native Germanic instead of Greek mythology in modern poetry exacted from him the appropriate penalty: it is only fair to add, however, that in the diary-note on Scheller a place for the Nordic conceptions in lyrical creations, as opposed to epic and dramatic, is conceded by Grillparzer. The poems 'Wunderbrunnen' and 'Todeswund', in so far as they illustrate this usage, may be said to attest his insight.

There can in fact be little doubt that the later poem marks an early phase of Grillparzer's attraction towards Marie. It represents at the same time, or is the prelude to, a new inspiration, insight, and resolve, to push on with his 'Ottokar'. Marie, the beautiful daughter of a Greek merchant, Smolk von Smolenitz and his Viennese wife (apparently by now an invalid), a girl of little more than Juliet's age, of surpassing charm, revealed to the poet, by her attitude to himself and the interloper Daffinger, the clue to Kunigunde's attitude towards Ottokar and Zawisch—and more especially, of course, enabled him to realize the king's attitude to both of them.

What has already been said about the problem in 'Ottokar', denying that the king is placed between two women, still holds good. Grillparzer himself was in no such position either. The impression we get from the play is that Ottokar is so taken up with affairs of state that he neglects his young queen, is early aware of her intrigue with Zawisch, yet fails to interfere in any effective way. The thought of being so much older than Kunigunde disables him in part; he shows towards her unwonted indulgence and uncalled-for understanding of her youthful impulses. Perhaps he suspects that she has already acquired, through experience of love, an emotional appetite which he cannot satisfy. Grillparzer represents this as true of her in Acts II and IV, when

[1] In C. A. Böttiger's periodical 'Amalthea', Vol. I, p. 1 ff., Leipzig, 1820.

she gives an account of her earlier life as a highly temperamental Hungarian princess and of her relations to a bold 'Kumanenführer', a worthy predecessor of the dashing Zawisch. At the moment when the latter deposits his 'minneliet' for Kunigunde at the foot of Cytherea's statue a pointed allusion is made to that goddess's infidelity to Hephæstus. We find this apposition in a contemporaneous poem to Marie von Smolenitz, the fifth 'Huldigung', elaborated in a sense that establishes the parallelism which we are noting (G. 169, 5):

'Wenn du die Liebe schon gekannt,
Gefühlt schon ihren Kuß,
Wer tadelt dich in seinem Wahn
Und darbet, weil er muß?
Jedes treibt wozu es ward,
So wills ein ew'ger Schluß:
Hephästen steht die Arbeit wohl,
Cytheren der Genuß'.

Ottokar himself, or rather Grillparzer, like Hephæstus in the Odyssey, felt that he must labour while his Cytherea enjoyed life in her own manner. At the time of writing this poem Grillparzer clearly believed Marie to be so disposed. He believed her no longer innocent, and considered himself at fault in expecting her to heed the same code of renunciation as himself. Let Marie confer her favours on Daffinger, as—with Ottokar's tacit connivance—Kunigunde did on Zawisch; the earnest man who has a task or mission to perform must put away desire.

Our final word on 'Ottokar', taught us by our discovery of the bearing of this experience on the work (the experience itself 'develops' further and is discussed below) must be to lend emphasis to the view already expressed: Ottokar was not (as Reich and others hold) merely a selfishly ambitious king who learns atonement; he was also altruistic. He was not merely an impious upstart tyrant; he was (unlike Jason) a man of duty and destiny as well.

CHAPTER V

'TRISTIA EX PONTO'

I. POETRY (AND TRUTH)

THE events in Grillparzer's life were not so much the things that happened to him as the works that grew out of these 'developments'. This is but natural in one whose life was so exclusively subordinated to his art; but it is true of any artistic genius. Grillparzer had quite early rejected the implication of his 'Sappho' and of the *malheur d'être poète*—the idea that poetry might be possible in divorcement from life. His Fleece trilogy soon disillusioned him about the resources of speculative imagination, 'engpsychologisches Anreihen und Anfädeln' (T. 1400), and the value of 'sources'; it drove him back on his experience. In the 1821 poem 'Incubus' his works are his 'eigenes Selbst, vom Geiste des Alls und des Bildners belebt' (G. 43), and the first of the 'Tristia ex Ponto' poems, 'Böse Stunde' (1826), invokes Inspiration ('Glut vom Himmel', the conception or genius—not the subject-matter—of a work of art based on experience), as follows (G. 84, 1):

'Wärst du das Wie und brauchst ein Was?
Nur Was durch ein Warum?
Wer Wasser schöpft ohn' Unterlaß
Und schöpft ins Danaidenfaß
Treibt wohl sich fruchtlos um.

Drum auf ins Leben, mutbewährt!
Gestrebt, geliebt, gehaßt!
Ist dir der Stoff erst, der sie nährt,
Fällt Glut vom Himmel auf den Herd,
Und lodert ohne Rast'.

The 1827 conclusion to 'Jugenderinnerungen im Grünen' includes those lines in which the poet, his life so full of thwarted effort that he is tempted to turn away from it in horror, reminds himself: 'Mocht ich's nicht leben, konnt ich's nicht beschreiben'—and twice he admitted by word of mouth (to Kuh and Rizy) that his works were his biography. There is also the epigram 'Selbstbekenntnis' (G. 698):

'Du nennst mich Dichter? Ich verdien' es nicht,
Ein Andrer sitzt, ich fühls, und schreibt mein Leben,
Und soll die Poesie den Namen geben,
Statt Dichter, fühl' ich höchstens mich Gedicht'.

Evidence of this could be multiplied a hundredfold, as the editor of the historical and critical edition of Grillparzer's works, that unique undertaking to which he has devoted so many years of his life confirms (Jb. 29, p. 27):

> 'Die Jugendschriften, die Tagebücher, die Briefe und Dokumente, die Aktenstücke, nicht zuletzt die Reihe der Dramen, auch die Prosawerke nebst den Erzählungen und der Selbstbiographie, . . . sie alle sind Teile einer großen Konfession, einer Lebensbeichte mit erschütternden Momenten'.

He then goes on to say:

> 'Was aber in ihnen, ob gewollt oder ungewollt, noch Geheimnis bleibt, die mannigfaltigen Liebesbeziehungen, eine große Zahl anderer unaufgelöster Dissonnanzen, ungenauer Angaben über Schwierigkeiten im Amte, über innere Nöte und Leiden unter dem qualvoll lastenden Druck der Zensur und dem lähmenden Einfluß der zeitgenössischen Kritik, die das allmähliche Erlahmen und Verstummen des Dichters in viel katastrophalerer Weise auf dem Gewissen haben, als noch heutzutage die Mehrheit der Forscher zuzugeben geneigt ist: alles das wird aus den Gedichten offenbar, wenn diese in die gehörige zeitliche Abfolge gebracht werden. Aus ihnen erst erwächst die ganze furchtbare Tragik dieses wahrhaft gottbegnadeten und durch menschliche Einflüsse so jammervoll zerstörten Dichterlebens'.

In a later essay (Jb. 31) Backmann discusses the *Tristia* poems:

> 'Die Entstehungsgeschichte und die Erlebnisgrundlage des größten Gedicht-Zyklus, den wir von Grillparzers Hand besitzen, der unsagbare Qualen dunkelster Jahre mit nur dann und wann einem Restchen aufblitzenden Sonnenscheins zu gestalten sucht und noch jetzt in seiner schweren Rätselsprache wie ein Buch mit sieben Siegeln, allerdings ein heiliges, den eindringenden Leser unablässig beschäftigendes und gar nicht wieder freilassendes Buch mitten in seinen Werken steht, schonender Aufhellung der inneren Zusammenhänge mehr bedürftig als jedes andere Werk dieses von seiner Zeit und von seiner Umwelt so schlecht verstandenen und so arg geschädigten Dichters, dessen Zeit auch heute noch nicht gekommen scheint'.

But Grillparzer's time will come, and it is brought sensibly nearer by affirmations such as the above and interpretation in the right spirit of the circumstances in Grillparzer's life which his writings reflect.

Some readers, unfamiliar with the material involved, might be disposed to reply that the poet's experiences do not greatly matter, and that the works, to be adequate, ought to be capable of speaking for themselves; but these would be readers content to speak as members of an audience; the true critical impulse is the one which induces the critic to imagine himself in the poet's place—writing for that audience. Or it is better perhaps to describe this impulse as the one which induces the critic to estimate the artistic adequacy (technical efficacy) of the poet's interpretation of life—in a given work—in the light of a sympathetic and imaginative understanding of his intention, and of the experience and insight from which it derives. A literary work that matters is never self-sufficient; it is not an object for superficial appraisement, as something noteworthy merely in itself or of its kind; it is also never truly perfect, nor perfectly true—but is the work of human hands, a more or less adequate extract of life's truth—infinitely important to understand for what it represents.

If this is true of those works that seem to be complete and self-contained, and are artistically and technically, in conception and execution, to all appearances invulnerable to criticism, like 'Hamlet', 'The Tempest', 'Egmont', 'Tasso', 'Des Meeres und der Liebe Wellen', or (to take a poem) Goethe's 'An den Mond'—our understanding of which is immeasurably intensified by being directed to them as reflecting their author's experience—how much more do significant works, like certain of Grillparzer's *Tristia* poems, for instance, that are less obviously satisfying and not immune to critical reproach, stand in need of sympathetic understanding and biographical reference! The way Grillparzer thought about this may be gleaned from a passage in his diary which comments on Mayrhofer's poems in words which have a specific bearing upon the draft of a poem of his own on the same page, 'Versäumt' (G. 47 a), a poem to which (if he had published it) the same criticism would have applied:

> 'Diese Gedichte hätten nie gedruckt werden sollen! Sie erklären den Verfasser und der Verfasser erklärt sie; Freunde mochten ihnen im Manuskript vielseitiges Interesse abgewinnen: aber für den Fremden sind sie Räthsel, schwer zu lösen, und nach der Lösung oft kaum der Mühe werth, die es gekostet (T. 1322)'.

'Versäumt', it is true, though imperfect as a sonnet, has a quality that puts it in a higher class than Mayrhofer's disguised confessions; yet it too needs readers who know their author, it needs a commentary. To know a good author's work is, as a rule, to feel that we know him as a man. Conversely, there is nearly always something unsatisfactory about not fully understanding a given work because we have not yet discovered the personal clue that would set free its innate force. 'Versäumt', we feel (without as yet perceiving its bearing on Grill-

parzer), is curiously incomplete. The *Tristia ex Ponto* also are in lik
case: those poems which Grillparzer held back so long, editing an
re-editing them, arranging them, adding to them, rearranging an
subtracting from them again, in an ever frustrated attempt to preser
them as an artistic whole in the form of a cycle covering an authenti
chapter in his experience, and yet escaping the Mayrhofer criticisn
Backmann decides 'Sie könnten recht wohl den Untertitel "Marie
tragen' (Jb. 31, p. 32); and poems among them, like 'Verwünschung
and 'Trennung,' to name the most familiar examples, are in highe
degree personal and stimulative of our desire for biographical clues.

Grillparzer did not actually withhold the clues; his works were hi
biography; and these include, we saw, his diaries, his autobiography
his letters, as well as his other writings, above all the dramatic work
Such evidence as these contain is critically indispensable and vitall
interesting too.

We are not permitted to discover this evidence easily. The bearin
of 'Todeswund' on Grillparzer's central experience of life was by n
means obvious, as is indeed natural in view of the intimate relationshi
between truth and poetry. In Shakespeare's 'Tempest' too, thoug
Alonso said to Shakespeare-Prospero: 'I long to hear the story of you
life, which must take the ear strangely', that engrossing story—
covering the most tragic period of Shakespeare's life, giving rise t
the recurring theme of jealousy, betrayal, ingratitude, inconstancy
vengeance, and forgiveness, in his works from 'Hamlet' to the end—
that story, alas, was never told: it has to be surmised, or else deduce
from internal evidence collated from the various works. Eve
Goethe's ambitious project and professed object of throwing mor
light on the relation between his own experience and his imaginativ
creations, between truth and poetry, is also tactfully and prudentl
evaded in respect to intimate facts; 'Dichtung und Wahrheit' als
ends prematurely. Grillparzer in his 'Selbstbiographie' sometime
even denies the existence of the corresponding relation between hi
own life and his works, especially when 'other people's secrets' are in
volved. He does so in regard to the first of two masterpieces which
growing out of his *Tristia* period, appeared during that most intensel
tragic chapter of his life. Hero in 'Des Meeres und der Liebe Wellen
he admits to be related to Marie; but of his 'Treuer Diener', the stil
more intimate work (if possible), he states that it 'satisfied no inne
need' in him. If we examine evidence from the period itself, however
in particular the year 1826, we shall perhaps understand the motiv
for, and condone, this later prevarication of his.

The pursuit of this necessary investigation is attended by almost lisheartening difficulties; yet it is needful to attempt it in the cause of interpreting the poet's works—and more especially their genesis, which is, with some of them, a matter of still deeper psychological nterest. Very little of the evidence is direct, as is also true in Goethe's case. Grillparzer was often at most elaborate pains to conceal the bearing of a diary note, an epigram, or a poem on his experience (and therefore often on his major works). If we ask ourselves why, n these circumstances, he should have recorded and preserved them—since they are little in themselves—the answer again resides in the nature and relationship of truth and poetic creation; for him these open secrets meant much and were not intended to be taken trivially nor lightly understood by the casual reader. For let us take Goethe's lines:

> 'Was ich leugnend gestehe und offenbarend verberge,
> Ist mir das einzige Wohl, bleibt mir ein reichlicher Schatz';

the reason for this satisfaction on the part of the poet is not (as Gundolf suggests) because he takes pleasure in 'offenbare Geheimnisse' and gratuitous mystification of an already unperceiving public; the reason is revealed in the implications of the concluding couplet in this pregnant quatrain of Goethe's, written for the Hermannsteiner Höhle, where he carves a cryptic 'S' in the rock to commemorate a tryst there in 1776:

> 'Ich vertrau' es dem Felsen, damit der Einsame rate,
> Was in der Höhle mich einst, was in der Welt mich beglückt'.

2. DRAMA IN THE MAKING

Clues to some of Grillparzer's 'open secrets', already recognized as existing, have led to numerous inspired and uninspired guesses, and the completion of the historical and critical edition will precipitate many more. Few investigators, however, have so far perceived the important connection—which will nevertheless be seen to be on record—between Grillparzer's 'Treuer Diener' and his experience at the time he wrote it. This is due less, perhaps, to Grillparzer's apparent denial of any such connection[1] than to the fact that his relations with Marie were presumed by his biographers to belong to a period after the work's completion. This presumption (taking into account her tender age) was not in itself unreasonable. But in fact it must

[1] Cf. Wedel-Parlow, L. v.; 'Grillparzer', Wertheim a/M, 1932, p. 95.

be recognized that these relations existed, along with thos of both Grillparzer and Marie to Daffinger, as early as 1822–23 and therefore influenced even 'Ottokar'. Daffinger himself wa formerly presumed to have been a friend of Grillparzer's only fron about 1825 onwards, whereas he had actually been a confidan of his since the 'Ahnfrau' days; by 1825 he had ceased to enjoy Grill parzer's confidence and soon became, not without cause (afte Daffinger's 'Polizeigeschichte'), a secret and despised enemy. Not i 1825, as Backmann suggests, but in 1822 or early in 1823, Daffinger ha approached Marie at Grillparzer's suggestion—and taken possessio of her for himself. The indication of this 'interloper's' rôle for Daffinge is contained, we saw, in that of Zawisch; it recurs in Oginsky and i Otto von Meran; Daffinger's nature is reflected in Naukleros in 'De Meeres und der Liebe Wellen'[1] and especially in Garceran, confidan of Alfonso (in 'Die Jüdin'), who even warns this practised wooer an gay Lothario against making bold advances on his own behalf, an later takes instructions from this lover-friend and plies him for hints Grillparzer's actual situation is best revealed and circumscribed in a indirect confession occurring in his diary for the spring of 1823 shortly after the poems 'Huldigungen', which contain suggestive an inverted compliments for Marie: 'Welche Wahrheit in dem Ver- hältnis zwischen Antonio und Bassanio (Kaufmann von Venedig)! he writes extravagantly, because thinking of Antonio as himself:[2]

> 'Antonio durch Karaktereigenthümlichkeit, villeicht auch früh Verluste und Täuschungen, oder Versäumen des rechten Augenblick unter Geschäften, für seine eigene Person vom eigentlichen Genusse de Lebens abgehalten, genießt es in der Person Bassanios. Er liebt, wirbt hofft und leidet mit ihm und ist so besorgt, ihn den Kelch, der ihm selbs versagt war ja ganz ohne Hefen trinken zu lassen, daß er, ganz in Wider- spruch mit seiner sonstigen umsichtigen Denkungsart, die leichtsinnige Sorglosigkeit Bassanios vielmehr bestärkt. I think, he only loves the world for him, sagt Salanio Act II Scen. 8.' (T. 1309).

This is not proof, of course, but evidence of the triangular situation arising early in this chapter of Grillparzer's life as revealed in the 'Briefe an Marie' to be discussed below. The fifth stanza of the earlier 'Huldigungen'[3] has been already cited, because of its bearing on

[1] Cf. Backmann, Jb. xxxi, p. 35.

[2] While recognizing that the author Shakespeare did so too and that this was the origin of the motive described.

[3] All five 'Huldigungen' seem to have been addressed (but not sent, of course) to Marie; they have hitherto been assumed to allude also to a second person, cf. Backmann, Jb. 29, pp. 9 f.,

'Ottokar'; it concludes the poems with a characteristic renunciation of Marie by Grillparzer. All five 'Huldigungen' were written at this time of his earliest infatuation for her, probably for the most part in 1822, when he was already living opposite to her home in the Ballgasse. He was to remain there under Marie's spell until his 'flight' in 1826, when (but for a fatal obstacle) she so nearly conquered him at last. Even in the spring of 1827 the issue was not yet decided. These first poems about her impute to this girl previous experience in seduction—because she was successfully exercising her charms on him in such favourable circumstances, their windows being separated by the width only of a *very* narrow street. We are familiar with Grillparzer's predisposition to impute to women who seemed to threaten his integrity of purpose or encroach upon his peace of mind baser attributes and unworthier motives than were necessarily justifiable. Even in the first months of his ill-starred engagement to Kathi Fröhlich, whose charm is extolled in 'Allgegenwart' and 'Als sie, zuhörend, am Klavier saß,' he had written in 'Incubus', describing this evil genius of his (G. 43):

> 'Flücht' ich zu ihr, die mein Glück,
> Tadellos jeglichem Blick;
> Er findet Tadel mir auf,
> Wärs aus der Hölle herauf;
>
> Und auf den Punkt, den er meint,
> Hält er die Lichter vereint,
> Daß es dem Aug' nicht entging',
> Wenn es auch Blindheit umfing':
>
> Lacht sie—so nennt er sie leicht;
> Weint sie—von Schuld wohl erweicht!
> Spricht sie—in heuchelndem Mut,
> Schweigt sie—voll anderer Glut'.

The change of residence in 1822 from the Dorotheergasse to the remoter 'beobachtende Ferne' of the Ballgasse is a token of the estrangement that had developed between them, Grillparzer being unable and unwilling to submit to the friction which frequent meetings had caused. Kathi had not retained his love. The one person who might have done so, Marie Smolk von Smolenitz, is from the start inevitably regarded by the poet with suspicion, again at the promptings

presumably on account of the *fair* hair and blue (?) eyes in Nos. 3 and 4; but this may be a familiar device or ready disguise; it conforms incidentally to the practice observed by Grillparzer in Petrarch's usage, T. 902.

of his *daimon*—his 'incubus' or predisposition, or ruling life-impulse. It would have been different if he could have loved her without perhaps even being noticed by herself in return. He might then have experienced undisturbed that creative impulse which is the poet's need—what Keats described with amazing insight and detachment as the 'faëry power of unreflecting love'. But Marie had doubtless set her cap at him. She is hardly to be more reproached for that than Grillparzer was for responding. What is surprising is that the commentators are so jealous for him that they seem to conspire to blacken and melodramatize Marie's character on insufficient and inadmissible evidence, and to remain entirely oblivious of the questionableness of Grillparzer's own conduct. He was, in fact, not only maturer and already betrothed to another, but was just as much exposed to the (superficial) reproach of unchivalry and egotism as Marie was to that of being a hussy ('Luder') or a 'grande amoureuse'.[1] These at any rate can hardly have been the qualities in Marie that cast such a spell over the man who married her, as the result of an acquaintanceship to which he had been instigated by Grillparzer. Daffinger boasted openly scores of gallant conquests; he would hardly have been likely to relish easy prey. Grillparzer, in turn, had cast a spell over Marie, as he later realized. Who shall say with what specious misrepresentation of himself as a loyal friend of the poet's Daffinger first waylaid Marie's confidence? The truth he could not have told. Did Grillparzer ever recall his own 'betrayal' of this girl (who was still below the age of consent), when subjecting her to his recriminations? The answer is, he did! He saw deeper, too. Those works of his that are a tribute to Marie, particularly his 'Treuer Diener', are evidence of his utmost honesty, his more than usual insight and impartial justice in this respect.

3. THE 'LETTERS TO MARIE'

Grillparzer's 'Briefe an Marie,' first made known as his 'Geheimschriften' in 1922, have since been published as copied by him into his diary for 1827.[2] At that time a new crisis in Grillparzer's life, Marie's impending marriage to Daffinger, gave rise to an overmastering urge in him to express and vindicate himself; and he recorded among other things these letters,[3] not necessarily exactly as they were written and probably sent in 1825—Sauer described their diary version

[1] Hock, S.: 'Grillparzers Wke.' in 16 Teilen, bei Bong, Berlin, n.d., Vol. I., p. lxxxiv.
[2] T. 1635-1640
[3] Perhaps in the late summer of the year 1827, cf. Backmann, Jb. xxxi, p. 40; hardly later, as Backmann has elsewhere suggested.

cautiously as 'Dichtung auf erlebter Grundlage'—yet in the same order essentially, as will now be shown.

The first letter is the most enigmatic of all. Sauer's guess at the meaning of the 'S', leading to the unwarrantable assumption that Grillparzer's suspicions about Wertheimstein or another were justified, is most regrettable. Marie's own explanation and denial, alluded to in the opening passage of the second letter, imply that the 'S' was not an initial at all. This first letter reads as follows:

> 'Zu alle dem, was, wie du wohl weißt, so schwer auf mir liegt, kommt nun noch, daß ich dich untreu glauben muß. Du maltest neulich als wir, Karten in her Hand, scheinbar spielend, einander gegenüber saßen, und dein Knie solange zögerte, den gewohnten Gruß zurückzugeben, du maltest ein großes lateinisches S auf das neben dir liegende schwarze Täfelchen; und zugleich sprach dein Mund denselben Buchstab aus. Ich kenne den Namen, dessen Anfangsbuchstabe dieses S ist! Oder wolltest du mich nur quälen, indem du den falschen Verdacht mir in die Seele schleuderst? O du bist boshaft, boshaft; ich habe das oft erfahren'.

At the time of writing this letter, Grillparzer was in the midst of his 'erste, wirklich ungemein reizende Liebesperiode' with Marie, as he spoke of it in 1832, adding: 'Aber dasselbe was anfangs an sie zieht, stößt unendlich zurück. Ihre Vorzüge und Fehler vereinigen sich in einer Eigenschaft: sie ist ein Kind' (T. 2020). It was a childish or at any rate unreflecting act on her part to test on Grillparzer the effect of communicating 'le chiffre d'amour'[1] to him, the serpentine 'Linie der Liebe' (for this it probably was), a free-love token familiar to the circles in which Daffinger as well as her father (an 'Illuminat' and versed in the lore of SS and Roses) moved. Grillparzer promptly imagined the S to be the initial of a name, and his jealous, suspicious bent found (or made him pretend to have found) the bearer of such a name. In her reply Marie would seem to have rejected and dispelled his suspicions, and to have interpreted the temptress-symbol; and this enables us to surmise the date of this exchange as February–March, 1825. For immediately following upon the March revision of the famous quatrain to Marie (G. 449):

> 'Allmacht ist deine Macht, o Schönheit, mächtige Herrin!
> Was dein Szepter berührt, ändert das Wesen, die Art.
> Als ich am Fenster sie sah, in papiernen Wickeln die Locken,
> Glaubt ich die Charis zu sehn, milchfarbe (weißliche: 1831)
> Rosen im Haar',

[1] The true title of a famous painting by Fragonard; cf. the present author's account of this in 'Publications of the English Goethe Society', N.S., Vol. IX, Cambridge, 1933, 'Goethe's (and Grillparzer's) Cryptic S'.

the epigram 'Nomen et Omen' is suggested by the serpent-symbol which Marie had invoked; it reads as follows (G. 450):

'Fehlt, um Charis zu sein, deinem Namen ein einziger Buchstab,
Ruft, wer dich sieht, ihn doch aus; heißest somit was du bist.'

Now, the 'only letter missing' from *Charis* in the name of *Marie-chen* is S; whoever utters this sound (as Marie did), gives her out with serpent's hiss for what she is—according to her infatuated and misdoubting lover—herself a 'Schlange'. This (indifferently) ominous epigram precedes, perhaps, the second letter, which explains itself:

'Schilt mich nicht, daß ich argwöhnisch bin! Ich habe ein Recht zum Argwohn. Du bist das schönste Weib; nie hat mein Aug eine Schönere gesehn! Ich aber? Wer mich nicht abschreckend findet, thut mir viel Ehre an. Bist jung! Ich könnte, dem Verhältniß der Jahre nach, zwar nicht dein, wohl aber der Vater deiner Schwester seyn, die fünf Jahre jünger ist, als du. Du blühst in Fülle und Gesundheit, denn dieß Herzklopfen und dieser Kopfschmerz, die du für Krankheit hältst, sind eher ein Übermaß des Guten, als dessen Mangel. Ich habe dagegen nichts aufzuweisen, als ein Bischen Ruhm, erkauft um den Glanz und die Freuden der Jugend; ein Bischen Ruhm, das noch dazu weniger im Aufnehmen ist, als im Verblühn. Sollte ich da nicht mißtrauisch seyn? Ich mißtraue mir selbst, nicht dir!'

The third letter, too, contains only one passage for commentary: the 'immerwährender Streit' refers to the countless trials besetting Grillparzer since his first successes; in part it refers to the differences between himself and Kathi (which were known to have had the 'nerve-racking' effect alluded to),[1] but in particular to the recent difficulties over 'Ottokar' with the censorship, which had stood in the way of its production—for no known reason—till about this time:

'Liebe Marie! Fast thut es mir leid, daß du mir gut bist. Du liebe, liebe, liebe! Ja, wenn ich noch der wäre, der ich einst gewesen bin. Als noch tausend Entwürfe in meiner Seele keimten, als noch tausend Gefühle meine Brust belebten, als noch mein ganzes Daseyn ein seliger Traum war von einer bessern, geahnten Welt. Ich sage dir: nie war ein männliches Wesen der Neigung eines begabten Weibes würdiger, als damals ich. Aber nun? Marie! Die Kämpfe des Lebens haben mich müde gemacht. Wohl fühlend, daß immerwährender Streit mich aufreiben müsse, beschloß ich geschehen zu lassen, und in beobachtender Ferne abzuwarten. Aber die Spannkräfte der Seele wollen geübt seyn, wie die des Körpers, und indem ich dem Übermaß entfliehen wollte, fiel ich dem Mangel

[1] Cf. B. 251, 'Wke.' III, 1, p. 296. See ref. above to Grillparzer's removal in 1822 to the Ballgasse (pp. 87 f. and 97).

in die Hände. Du bist zu gut für die Reste. Und doch, da die Sonnen so selten sind, laß dir den Mond gefallen! Ich habe noch genug, einen kleinen Kreis zu erleuchten, ja zu erwärmen, wenn ein ungestörtes Vertrauen mich erst wieder mir selber gibt'.

If Grillparzer was earnestly concerned to retain Marie's affection and save her from Daffinger (as the next letter with its reference to his rival's 'Gemeinheit' shows), then the mood expressed in this third letter was calculated to defeat his purpose. Though she was only half his age, it was unnecessary for him who, at thirty-four, still had his best work to perform, notably his fresh and youthful 'Hero und Leander,' to speak of himself in terms contrasting himself unfavourably with his unworthy still older rival as regards vigour and self-confidence. His fourth letter remedies this, though it does not do so of set purpose—its sincerity is unmistakable:

'Und du hast Recht, dich mir zu entziehen! Wie die Irrlichter in Göthes Märchen würde ich nur das Gold aus deiner Mischung aufzehren, mich dadurch für einen Augenblick wesenhafter fühlen; doch sobald der vorübergehende Zuwachs vergeudet, unwiderstehlich zu neuer Nahrung fortgetrieben, und dein edler Selbst in verworrener Zerstücklung, dir selbst unkenntlich und Andern, zurückgelassen. Da ist keine Befriedigung zu geben und zu empfangen. Nur in Einem könnte ich dir nützen: Du bist an die Gemeinheit verkauft und sie streckt immer näher ihren Arm nach dir. Diese Besitzergreifung hätte ich ewiglich verhindert. Doch hierin kann auch der Entfernte wirken. Marie! so lange du meiner gedenkst, wirst du nie werden wie der, der dich umringt. Und gäbest du nach, würdest du abtrünnig von dem Edlen, dessen Abglanz deine Züge verschönt; nach zehn und zwanzig Jahren würde mein Anblick hinreichen dir die Erinnerung dessen zurückzuführen was du warst, und Verzweiflung zöge ein in dein Herz mit Thränen bejammernd den ungeheuren Fall'.

The situation becomes explicit in the next letter. The period he there refers to, that of Marie's 'erste Jugendblüthe, halb Kind und halb Mädchen' (she was now, in 1825, no longer inexperienced) is when he first lived opposite to her in 1822 and the days of 'Ottokar's' completion: the 'Huldigungen' of that time were apparently misjudged. He has learned better since—that he should have kept the treasure for himself (and this is where the sonnet 'Versäumt', or 'Versäumter Augenblick' (G47a–b and Anm.) of 1824 comes in!): 'Thor der ich war! Betrogner um das schönste Glück!' In July, 1823, he had at last been promoted to the position of a chief clerk to the Minister of Finance, Graf Stadion, whom we have spoken of as an admirer of Grillparzer's poetic work. Grillparzer's duties took him away from

the Ballgasse in the summer and autumn to Stadion's country seat a
Jamnitz for repeated periods of several weeks; during these absence
from Vienna those letters of his to Kathi were written, the later one
of which afford evidence of his genuine affection for her—whe
parted from her for a time. It was in the interval between thes
visits, perhaps, that the encounter took place when Marie was wit
Daffinger at the theatre and gave Grillparzer that look, never to b
forgotten, the same look that Erny gives to Otto, and Hero to Leander
This encounter *must* antedate the diary note T. 1372 of December, 1824.
It was actually in the late autumn of 1823 that the first meeting of Grill
parzer and Marie took place in Döbling, when Marie gave tangibl
proof that Daffinger meant little to her. If, as seems probable, it wa
Grillparzer she was really in love with, she may have felt intuitivel
quite early that modesty would effect little with him, since he himsel
appeared to betray this attribute to excess. It is true that the implication
of such remarks as these transcend our everyday morality, and avai
little perhaps to vindicate Marie; they may not be misplaced, however
if they throw some light on the woman's tragedy—for Marie, it mus
not be forgotten, suffered deeply too.

The place where this is revealed on a universal human plane, wher
Grillparzer grappled with and interpreted the problem (Shakespeare'
greatest problem too) of 'unfaithfulness', dissimulation, and seemin
contradictions in woman's loving nature, is in his dramatic works
The fifth letter concludes with an allied reflection—'Ich habe dich ni
verstanden . .'—the tragic keynote in Grillparzer's relations to Mari
and the genesis of his greatest tragedies:

> 'Ich habe mich getäuscht! Du bist noch, wie du warst, du denks
> meiner noch, hältst noch fest an der Empfindung, die ich dir entwunden
> die ich von dir losgelassen glaubte. Du Liebe, Einfache, Gute! warum
> kann ich dich nie verstehen! Aufrichtig! Nie habe ich dich verstanden
> Als du in deiner ersten Jugendblüthe, halb Kind und halb Mädchen, mi
> bestimmt warst, mir, durch den ersten Eindruck meiner armen Wesenhei
> auf dein unschuldiges Herz, und du oft lange am Fenster stehend, eili
> zurückwichst, so oft ich in das meinige trat, glaubte ich in diesem Aus
> weichen ein Merkmal des Widerwillens zu erblicken, Thor der ich war
> Betrogner um das schönste Glück! Als ich dich, schon halb an eine
> Andern gekettet, in der Loge im Theater wiedersah, und du mir bein
> Scheiden jenen langen, tiefen Blick in die Brust senktest,—ja, was glaubt
> ich nur da? Ich weiß es nicht mehr ganz; zum Theil aber: ich hätte mic
> getäuscht. Als wir, wieder in Gesellschaft jenes Andern, dem du damal

[1] See below, p. 129.

schon ganz gehörtest, von Döbling im Mondschein zurückfuhren, du uns beide Männer zwangst, die Plätze im Grund des Wagens einzunehmen, und du dich allein auf den Rücksitz setztest; als du da dem Körperlichwerden meiner Empfindung so rücksichtslos entgegen—, ja zuvorkamst; in der Folge meiner Besuche jede Annäherung so freudig ertrugst,—Marie ich schäme mich! Ich war in Gefahr dich für leichtfertig zu halten. Und selbst das standhafte Ablehnen des ersten Kusses, als pflichtwidrig, konnte mich von meiner Blindheit nicht heilen. Ich habe dich nie verstanden. Doch ist es nicht natürlich? Der Mensch versteht alles, nur das Völlig-Einfache nicht, und—Marie!—das Unerhört-Künstliche!'

This contradiction confronting Grillparzer in the person of Marie was also in himself. That is why this woman's nature appeared to him as virtuous and vicious, naïve and designing, when ordinary mortals might have taken only the one (probably the more uncharitable) view. In certain characters modelled on Marie—Erny, Hero, and Esther—a natural balance, as it were, is struck. Marie's 'steadfast refusal of the first kiss' (because she imagined herself plighted to Daffinger—betraying to Grillparzer, but for his 'blindness', her true inexperience and naïveté) is a motive far more closely reproduced in Act III of 'Hero' than is that other well-known motive drawn from his own experience, that of Charlotte setting down the lamp in order to have her arms free for a passionate embrace. Yet the same modest Hero—who (so unlike Charlotte) says 'Die Lampe soll's nicht sehen'—has already uttered the words 'Komm morgen denn!'—and gives herself wholly to Leander at the end of the Act.

With like 'contradictoriness' did Marie behave, though not with such 'dramatic continuity' as Hero. The occasion of the first kiss referred to in this letter Grillparzer promptly commemorates—we may assume—in an interesting diary entry (T. 1328) of early 1824, significantly near the earliest plan for 'Die Jüdin' (T. 1330) with its circumstantial and obviously first-hand grasp of the young prince's infatuation. The Rahel of the finished work and Marie herself are known to be akin. We shall see that they were so from the very beginning. The earlier entry—an elaborately disguised 'confession' too (and perhaps contemporary with, as it is related to, 'Versäumt')—takes the form of a poem in Spanish. (This was the time of Grillparzer's intensest Lope studies.) The poem is described ingeniously, though disingenuously, as having been 'communicated by a South American'—this to account for its unfamiliarity, for its curious character, and for inequalities in the language—'Gedanken eines

Frauenzimmers aus Panama, deren Liebhaber einen erhaltenen Kuß ausgeplaudert hatte' it is styled and runs as follows:

'Dicha si no fuese dicha,	
Dicha si (no) fuese callada,	(?)
No te basto ser lograda,	
Si no ser lograda y dicha?	ohne Zweifel verstümmelt,
Ay que notable desdicha!	der Gedanke aber schön.
Sean los hombres poco sabios,	
Pues convierten beneficios en agravios,	(Pues convierten en agravios).
Y es gran mengua,	Beneficios y es gran mengua
Tenga desdichada lengua	Tener desdichada lengua.
Quien tuvo dichosos labios!'[1]	

(Von einem Südamerikaner mitgetheilt).

Small wonder that nothing is known, nor likely to be learned (despite Backmann's optimism[2]) of the original. The probability is—we feel tempted to suggest—that Grillparzer imitated some passage of Lope that he had before him, borrowing from it the characteristic antitheses, turns of phrase, etc., and adapting them to his own use. On the basis of this hypothesis we should have to assume that the 'howlers' in line 4 ('Si no' for 'Sin', perpetrated perhaps in order to eke out the octosyllabic line) and line 6 ('Sean' for 'Son') are at best Grillparzer's deliberate corruptions. They are incidentally *not* Central or South American in character. But even if Grillparzer could be supposed to be quoting from a genuine Peruvian-Spanish text—as previous investigators have taken for granted—and the entry could be regarded as a curiously corrupt version of an original (not very original) Spanish poem, presumed to have been actually 'communicated' by some disinterested South American, the poet's own experience of its motive would still have to be presupposed, to explain sufficiently his citing and conscientious 'editing' of it in his diary. These comments and queries in the margin of the poem denote Grillparzer's (justified) misgivings at the style and syntax of this

[1] These lines might be rendered as follows:

Not-sad, had it been not-said,
Not-sa[i]d, had it been kept silent;
Couldst thou still be discontent,
Wouldst success were ever said?
'Tis so, 'tis indeed most sad!
Men in this much folly show,
Converting all their joys to woe;
And it was a grievous wrong
So to let your blurting tongue
Destroy the joy our lips did know.

[2] Cf. 'Wke.' I, 15, p. 272, Anm. 36.

outlandish effusion. The whole is, however, as will now be shown, unquestionably a fiction, and it is manifestly a device for confessing poetically his personal experience. With this love-experience is associated a natural feeling of exultation, refusing to be entirely (and prudently) repressed.

At this particular time Grillparzer was using the editions of Lope that were available in the National-Bibliothek of Vienna and, having read the first seven volumes of the comedies consecutively, he turned to the first volume of the *Obras sueltas* in the 1777 edition, as the evidence of 'Wke.' I, 15, Anm. 37 f., testifies. He only needed to turn over the pages of this volume in order to perceive a poem of Lope's (occurring in the story of 'El Desdichado por la Honra' (!) which deals with a situation exactly corresponding to his own. This poem's identity of theme, as also of metre and rhyme, no less than its general similarity of thought, style, and expression makes it apparent that it served Grillparzer as the 'source' or trigger of his own confession: even the difficult rhyme for *lengua* (the archaic *mengua*) occurs in Lope's fourth stanza. The coincidences are too striking to make any other explanation probable.

Lope de Vega's first stanza apostrophizes the 'sweet silence of love', adding that if he who loves is granted such joy by keeping his love-affair secret from the world, he will seek none greater:

'Dulce silencio de amor,
si tanta gloria callando
consigue quien sirve amando,
no la pretendo mayor. . . .'

The second stanza still more clearly develops the motive of the lover's self-defeating impulse to give utterance to his feeling of exultation, the very impulse which Grillparzer's 'Peruvian maid' deplores, because her lover has given way to it. 'To love without daring to proclaim one's love' is cowardly, Lope's lover reflects, adding, however, that to be otherwise than cowardly is fatal; 'but I will suffer the disquiet to which my respect (for her honour) condemns me and will fear no change (in her disposition towards me), for I do not lose expectation of love as long as I do not lose my disquiet':

'Amar, sin osar decir
tanto amor, es cobardia,
mas perder el bien seria
determinarse a morir:
pero yo quiero sufrir

la pena, a que me condena
fuerza de respetos llena;
y no temer su mudanza,
pues no pierdo la esperanza,
mientras no pierdo la pena'.

The engaging feature of this poem is the subtle way in which i affords the poet an outlet for the very impulse he felt constrained tc repress. In the third stanza he actually says: 'I should like to be under- stood, though I do not make my meaning clear':

'Quisiera ser entendido,
quando a entender no me doy'.

We can only add that it remained for Grillparzer to surpass this devic of Lope's with the elaborate subterfuge of his pseudo-philologica variation in 'Peruvian'-Spanish on the same theme. 'Was ich leugnen gestehe und offenbarend verberge'; again we recall Goethe's word relating to a similar concealed but also revealed confession, that of hi own and Charlotte von Stein's secret.

Grillparzer's procedure in his dramatic works constitutes (quit legitimately) a parallel to what we observe in this example; but it i instructive to examine the procedure in such simple isolation as here If it seems complex and curious, perhaps this is due to unfamiliarity or our part with the psychological processes of artists as normal huma beings—in which case the study of Grillparzer may profit us indeed In reality such masked treatment of intimate experience in literatur is usual and in itself perhaps of minor interest. Our profounde interest in perceiving what is effected and how it comes to be effecte occurs when the poet's creation is itself an attempt,[1] sometimes for u a triumphantly successful one, to solve one of life's contradictions.

The Troilus-and-Cressid motive, for example, cannot indeed—leas of all by Shakespeare-Troilus—be humorously dismissed, as Goeth dismisses one aspect of woman's wooing in his 'Mummenschanz':

'Doch das Naturell der Frauen
Ist so nah mit Kunst verwandt'!

When the poet's innermost feelings are involved, and partly becaus of instinctive counter-stress in himself, he may experience this seemin

[1] Cf. Zausmer, O.: 'Grillparzer's Lyrik as Ausdruck seines Wesens', Vienna, 1933, p. 141 'Grillparzer dichtet nicht reflexiv, sondern er reflektiert dichtend'. Cf. also G. 439, a favourit distich of Grillparzer's:

Nimm erst, Kummer, Gestalt! Nur das Formlose martert und ängstet,
Hat sich der Feind uns gestellt, halb ist gewonnen der Sieg.

contradiction in woman's loving nature as a tragic human problem and insufficiency—'Der Mensch versteht alles, nur das Völlig-Einfache nicht und—Marie!—das Unerhört-Künstliche'—and his only resource is to 'confess' in his works his apprehension of these contrasting aspects of the same reality, ranging from triumphant vindication of female constancy and truth (as Shakespeare does in 'The Winter's Tale') to bitter exposure of female perfidy. Shakespeare's and Grillparzer's works afford sufficient examples of these extremes, as well as of associated and intermediate reflexions of the same experience. How often were both poets—racked by inner conflict and distracted by seemingly contradictory reality—in the very mood which this sixth and final letter reflects!—

> 'Ich bin ein Thor, Marie! Wie viel Ursache habe ich, dir zu mißtrauen, und wie oft und sehr habe ich dir mißtraut; doch, da ist kein Zweifel, der der Gewalt deines Anblicks widerstehen könnte, ich habe keine Waffen gegen dich! Was ist es denn auch? Daß dein glattgescheiteltes, lockenloses Haar sich wie ein schwarzer Höllenfluß um die für einen Himmel viel zu wenig lichte Stirn hinschlängelt, um eine Stirn, die vielleicht zu niedrig ist, und die du—Falsche! Kokette!—durch ein quer darüber hin laufendes schwarzes Schnürchen theilst, um sicherer zu berücken? Daß diese deine lohbraunen Augen, mit denen du mir zu freigebig bist (freigebig gegen jedermann), und an denen mir einmal der Schnitt und die Lage der inneren Augenwinkel mißfiel, daß diese Augen so fromm thun können und so warm? Daß diese deine unschuldigen Wangen!—Ja, Marie, das alles ist's,—und ist's nicht; und wenn nicht, so ist keine Treue in der Welt, und Gott und Natur hat gelogen. Dort, inmitten der niedern Stirn, ober den beiden Augen, eingefaßt von den schwarzglänzenden Haaren, dort inmitten sitzt die Wahrheit, und macht mich zum Sklaven deines kindisch plaudernden Selbst. Ich sehe sie diese Wahrheit. Sie ist ein lichter Punkt, zusammengeronnen aus den Strahlen ihrer himmlischen Umgebung. Dort sitzt sie, dort; und ich glaube, und bin selig'.

What a remarkable document this is! Reading it, we cannot doubt the intensity and depth of the writer's experience, of this great mind's apprehension of the relation between beauty and truth as life's ultimate problem. If we thought of him as a victim of ambition when he grappled with the unreal psychological problem of Medea, how shall we think of him now—beyond ambition, in the grip of this vital passion and vision, the tortured poet victim who knocks—hopefully, despairingly, pitiably—at the door of certainty and spiritual peace? He will get no answer, assuredly, and will find no peace, except such as his poet's pen provides. The contrasting figures of Erny, Elga, Hero, Rahel,[1] Esther, Lucretia rise up at the suggestion of phrases in this letter, and above all those matchless portraits by Daffinger of their living prototype, 'Marie in all ihrer damals wirklich himmlischen Schönheit', appear before us. Like Daffinger's paintings, Grillparzer's dramatic heroines too are contrasting portraits, akin psychologically, though outwardly differentiated, of the same life model. They too are experimental probings, aspects, reflexions of the one reality—each masterpiece more estimable and true than that reality; more real than the original—or indeed than life itself, with its baffling complexity and irreconcilable contradictions—life, that is, in our distorted view of it, which art alone can right, because it can select.

4. GRILLPARZER'S 'SECRET MARRIAGE'

The 'Briefe an Marie' were written, then, in 1825, though (as we saw) the early part of the previous year marked the beginning of Grillparzer's secret intimacy with her. His first attraction towards her occurred more than a year before that, as the letters confirm. Apart from the Spanish poem and the evidence of the 'Jüdin' plan, Grillparzer seems to have kept his diaries for the years 1822–4 free from readily traceable allusions to Marie. It is true that the passage of doggerel from Byron's 'Don Juan' (T. 1341)—'that love and marriage scarcely can combine . . .'—quoted in the summer of 1824, is far more likely to point to her than to Kathi Fröhlich, if for no other reason than that his relations with Kathi, so far from being wine-like, were already vinegary—without being soured by matrimony. Towards the end of the year he read Choderlos de Laclos' 'Liaisons Dangereuses'. A passage from it (T. 1367) which has an obvious bearing on his portrayal of the villainous Otto von Meran (ll. 15 f.) is referred to by Grillparzer himself, as also is one having a bearing on his Erny (ll. 22 f.); and both of them indicate personal experience. From the same book he quotes (T. 1372) a passage which reminds him of that searching look of Marie's, recalled in his fifth letter to her, as well as repeatedly in his works. But it is in his poems and epigrams that we find more conclusive evidence.

The title of the work by Laclos anticipates in character that given by Grillparzer to a series of epigrammatic verses, mainly distichs, begun soon after, in January–February, 1825, those of the 'Matrimonio

[1] Most significant is the parallel between the passage in the letter referring to a physiognomical peculiarity of Marie's eyes and Alfonso's similar observation about the dead Rahel at the close of 'Die Jüdin'. He decides that Rahel was not beautiful, but sinister and strange. This is a drastic declension from the theme of this sixth letter to Marie.

Secreto' (!). The following interpretation of these epigrams may not seem very convincing at first. It can hardly, however, be doubted that they must have an esoteric significance and that the names in them are substitutions ('Decknamen'). As epigrams these verses are not good, Grillparzer being apparently content that for the time being they should retain their hidden significance for himself alone; in fact they are not really epigrams at all, but idiograms, yet very significant ones. They are ostensibly addressed to Dardanelli, Lablache, Fodor of the Italian opera (Catalani's from Naples) in Vienna, actors who were appearing in Cimarosa's 'Il Matrimonio Segreto' and other pieces at that time; but they refer in fact, as will be seen, to Marie, Daffinger, and Grillparzer respectively—a characteristic and almost undetectable subterfuge required by the circumstances. Nowhere else is there the slightest indication that Grillparzer actually knew or was interested in any of these performers personally, a circumstance which in itself suggests that we ought not to take these 'epigrams' at their face value. The first of them is a single hexameter (G. 437, 1), inspired perhaps by Daffinger's having attributed 'gracefulness' to Marie:

> 'Grazie hättest du? Nein! Du *hast* sie nicht, Holde, du *bist* sie!'

Very soon this hexameter, with its inner association (Grazie—Charis), 'inspires' the famous Charis quatrain (first occurring conjointly here with the 'Dardanelli' tributes in three preliminary versions, G. 438, 1–3). In Grillparzer's later arrangements of these epigrams this hexameter is indeed the more clearly recognizable as being in reality addressed to Marie by the fact that it is brought into juxtaposition with the Charis quatrain. Following the hexameter we read (G. 437, 2):

> 'Schimmernd in rosigem Kleid, mit Rosen bekränzet die Scheitel
> Sonst schon sah ich dich so, nur warst du damals zu drei'.

The roses were part of a modish coiffure of contemporary Vienna in the fashionable circles in which Marie moved. The 'rosiges Kleid' recalls the second of the 1822–3 'Huldigungen' (Daß dein Kleid rosenrot/Find ich recht fein'), where it was, however, hardly a going-out dress.[1] But the clue to this distich is to be found in the contemporary poem, 'Rangstreit' (G. 178, ll. 20 f.), in which the triple rose-symbol is rendered, making it almost certain that Marie is meant in both cases. By March Grillparzer's 'Matrimonio Secreto', proving a good vein, has assimilated new elements and is arranged in his diary (G. 448–9) with apt allusions to (1) *Daffinger* [one distich: Lablache], (2) *Grillparzer*

[1] Marie is probably attired in this *déshabillé* for our frontispiece portrait!

[two distichs: Fodor], (3) *Marie* [one new distich and G. 437 trans posed: (Dardanelli), and the Charis quatrain with 'Nomen et Omen' Marie Smolk von Smolenitz]. With all but the first four distichs alluding ostensibly to members of the opera troupe, we are alread familiar. The first of these four would protest that Lablache [Daffinger is a hypocrite, an actor, and not as the public have always said of him a *faithful* artist:

> 'Wahrheit nennt ihr sein Spiel? Er lügt, der Heuchler, belügt euch!
> Wie er Geronimo scheint, ist er Barbier und Assur'.

If this meant what it says, it would not flatter Grillparzer's sense of th theatre. On other occasions Lablache had certainly also appeared a the Barber of Seville, and as Semiramide's dusky paramour Assur though it would have been preposterous to hold that against him a Geronimo in 'Il matrimonio segreto'. But Grillparzer had contrivec an (almost) perfect alibi: the notorious Daffinger was the 'factotun del bel mondo' and dark-skinned *amoroso* he warned against. Daffin ger's handsome half-blood appearance in his self-portraits—'lächerlich und lodernd schön, wie ein Violin-Zigeuner' (Costenoble called him *Caraibe*!)[1]—and his boasted intimacies and offices with the Viennese fashionable world stamp him inevitably as Barbier and Assur— though Marie herself, like those who praised the 'Wahrheit' of his art apparently thought more highly of him.[2]

The couplets addressed to Madame Fodor (though how inaptly!) the *diva* whom Grillparzer had first heard in her prime at Venice in 1819:

> 'Kennt ihr die Sängrin des Hains? grau sitzt sie in graulichten Ästen,
> Und die unscheinbare Brust schmettert dein Brautlied, Natur!
>
> Nachtigall flöte nicht mehr! du gibst deine Seele den Tönen,
> All dein Leben dem Lied! Was bleibt dir? daß du lebst.

are in reality allusions to himself. He is the nightingale, as in his *Cantate* to Stadion (G. 172, Lied), who, living for his art, is constrained to press the thorn of suffering into his own breast. The expression of 'nature's nuptial-song' for 'art', a metaphysical metaphor which recurs

[1] Loc. cit., I, p. 57, Sept. 22, 1819. Karaibe = a Caribean or 'Cannibal' Islander, typical (dusky) 'barbarian' since the Age of Discovery. It would be interesting to know whom Shakespeare intended to 'expose' and ridicule, castigate as an oaf, lout, and brutish 'barbarian' in the person of his Caliban (for 'Cannibal'). A like inquiry regarding Grillparzer's 'dumme Galomir' in 'Weh dem, der lügt' is more readily answered.

[2] Grillparzer obviously infers—perhaps justly—that an *unworthy* man could not be a *worthy* artist. Posterity in its judgement of Daffinger's specific accomplishment as miniaturist tends to corroborate Grillparzer's verdict: Spiel! Lüge! !

later, throws a revealing light on Grillparzer's aesthetics: it implies, perhaps, that in artistic creations nature exults in consummation towards the realization of her purposes.

Grillparzer would like to be able to partake of happiness—and espouse Marie, as he now conveys ruefully, and at the same time sardonically, in the one new Dardanelli inscription:

'Sorgsam beschaut dich und prüft. und wählet dich doch nicht der *Conte*?
Doch ich besinne mich erst; ist er der Tor nicht des Stücks?'

in which he is the hesitating *Conte* of this 'Matrimonio Secreto', though warier than the one in Cimarosa's piece. The remainder of this cryptic composition of Grillparzer's: the Rose motive, the Grazie verse, the Charis quatrain, and the S riddle, are familiar already—the whole enabling us to surmise, in some detail, the time and nature of a relationship that was to prove the major crisis in Grillparzer's emotional and artistic life.

Two fragments and the poem 'Rangstreit' belonging to 1825 (Sauer's dating, G. 177–9) reveal corroborative evidence. They contain nothing to establish that they are in the wrong order and place (cp. Anm. and Jb. 31, p. 36 f.). The first (which we find *re-enacted* in ll. 849–54 of 'Bancban'!):

'Und diese Sieger-Augen
Hab ich besiegt gesehn,
Hoch über sich geschlagen
Feucht um Erbarmung flehn'

suggests a jealous, inquisitional scene between the poet and Marie, not inconsistent with the implications of the 'Matrimonio Secreto' and the two remaining poems ('Rangstreit' and G. 179), which may well bespeak intimacy, despite Backmann's view.

5. DAFFINGER'S 'POLICE-AFFAIR' AND THE 'LUDLAMSHÖHLE'

Was it jealousy in turn on Daffinger's part, as well as innate unworthiness—'Gemeinheit' (a frequent epithet now), that prompted Daffinger in difficulties to betray Grillparzer, his whilom boon companion, to the police? In his diary for March, 1826, Grillparzer recalls the outward causes of his inactivity since the production of 'Ottokar' (February 19, 1825); he still smarts with anger over the preceding struggle with the censorship and annoyance at the failure of 'Ottokar' to impress the discriminating in Germany; his bodily robustness, contrasting with an inner feeling of listlessness and helplessness, so little suggestive of that [other] 'incubation' period from his eighteenth to twenty-fifth years, have been causing him distress; his relations to

'Luzie' (Kathi), which were nearing a breach, have given him no peace; and then 'throughout the winter Daffinger's Polizeigeschichte and his own implication in it'! (T. 1426).

According to the account contained in Sauer's 'Aus dem alten Österreich',[1] Sedlnitzky, as Chief of State Police, issued to the Viennese police authority on December 10, 1825, a decree granting their application to imprison Daffinger for three days. This was to be the punishment for his abuse of a military policeman on an occasion in November when he was in the company of Grillparzer and certain members of the 'Ludlams Höhle', a non-political club. The decree also instructs the police to warn Grillparzer officially (how gladly did Sedlnitzky add this warning!)—*if the present allegation against him were established as true*—of the serious consequences for him, a civil servant, of any future allegations of like nature—it having been asserted that he had not only applauded Daffinger's insubordinate sentiments, but also himself given voice to presumptuous comments on the same occasion.

But why should there have been any doubt on Sedlnitzky's part about the truth of the allegation? Clearly because it was only reported, as being alleged against Grillparzer in the communication he had received about Daffinger from the police authority. Consequently we are tempted to conclude that Daffinger himself, when summoned to appear for trial or at some earlier time, had made the allegation. The actual communication reporting any such mean and cowardly deposition of Daffinger's is 'missing' (p. 29)! But a further application and report respecting an appeal by Daffinger against the three days' sentence, pleading among other things his artistic temperament and intoxicated condition, contains an allusion to Daffinger's *unmännliches Betragen vor Gericht* as a factor apparently reported on previously; it therefore looks as if Grillparzer may have owed the humiliating admonishment he duly received to the unfriendly offices of the wretched Daffinger himself. Who, reading the following lines, can doubt, at any rate, that Grillparzer believed this to be so? And believed perhaps also that Marie abetted his rival in this betrayal. An 'exposure' of the circumstances by the poet occurs at the climax of the Don Cäsar underplot, which Grillparzer introduced into 'der Bruderzwist' to effect this end:

DON CÄSAR. Laßt mich erkennen Euch, nur deshalb kam ich:
Zu wissen, was Ihr seid, nicht, was Ihr scheint.
Denn wie's nur eine Tugend gibt: die Wahrheit,

[1] Sauer, A.: 'Aus dem alten Österreich', Prague, 1895, als Hs. gedruckt.

Gibt's auch ein Laster nur: die Heuchelei . . .
Als ich, nun lang', zum erstenmal Euch sah,
Da schien mir alle Reinheit, Unschuld, Tugend
Vereint in Eurem jungfräulichen Selbst;
Zeigt wieder Euch mir also, laßt mich glauben!
Und wie der Mann, der abends schlafen geht,
Von eines holden Eindrucks Macht umfangen,
Er träumt davon die selig lange Nacht,
Und beim Erwachen tritt dasselbe Bild
Ihm mit dem Sonnenstrahl zugleich vors Auge:
So gebt mir Euch, Euch selber auf die Reise,
Von der zurück der Wandrer nimmer kehrt.
Kein Weib, ein Engel; nicht geliebt, verehrt.

LUCRETIA. Wie ohne Grund Ihr mich zu hoch gestellt,
So stellt Ihr mich zu tief nun ohne Grund.

DON CÄSAR. Nicht doch, nicht doch!—Ihr stießet mich zurück,
Ich mußt' es dulden, manchen Fehls bewußt.
Doch seht, da war ein Mann, Belgiojoso hieß er,
Ein Heuchler und ein Schurk'—

LUCRETIA. Er war es nicht.

DON CÄSAR. Verteidigt Ihr ihn denn?

LUCRETIA. Wer klagt ihn an?

DON CÄSAR. Ich, der ich ihn gekannt.—Er hielt zu mir;
In all dem Treiben, das mit Recht man tadelt,
Im wilden Toben war er mein Genoß.
Doch ging er hin und zeigt' es heimlich an
Und brachte mich um meines Vaters Liebe.

LUCRETIA. Der laute Ruf erspart' ihm diese Müh'.

DON CÄSAR. Die Welt hat Recht zum Tadel, nicht der Freund.
Doch plötzlich kehrt' er sichtlich mir den Rücken,
Zu gleicher Zeit betrat er Euer Haus.

Succinct as this passage is, it does not tell the whole story. Nobody knew that better than Grillparzer. As far as Marie's rôle is concerned, insuperable doubts and irreconcilable contradictions remain, and his portrayal of her in Lucretia is pale and unconvincing. But the author, in Don Cäsar, is positive and (at the time of writing, 1827), actively resentful about Belgiojoso's conduct, both here and in Act I: 'ein Weiber-, Pfaffendiener, Ein Heuchler und ein Schurk' '.

The circumstances in which he was involved, the imminent danger of a public scandal, must have impressed on Grillparzer the advisability of leaving the Ballgasse. He writes soon after this the moving lines, so eloquent of the true state of his feelings for Marie:

'Erst da ich dich vermisse, dein entbehre,
Empfind ich, was ich nie für dich empfand,
Und aus dem Umfang erst der rückgebliebnen Leere
Die Größe Des, was vor darinnen stand',

which Backmann justly ascribes to this time (G. 195 and Anm.). Grillparzer's summons to appear on February 14, 1826, at police headquarters (to receive his 'severe reprimand') had to be renewed the following day and directed to an address in the Spiegelgasse (B. 274–5). He had returned to Kathi, as prudence and propriety demanded, and he now even shared the Fröhlichs' roof. The fragment 'Der Scheintote' is written now (G. 188):

'Die Angel knarrt, die Pforten fallen zu
Und Dunkelheit umgibt mich, finstres Schaudern,
Die Hände rühren tastend schroffe Mauern,
Rings um mich her des Grabes stumme Ruh'.

The first period of his relations with Marie is practically at an end.

Any one reading superficially Grillparzer's diaries of this time (including his uncannily perceptive Hamlet notes, T. 1414–6) might suppose, like Decurtius, that there was some justification for regarding him as a 'depressiv-sensitiver Psychopath',[1] if such terminology applied to him were not itself too symptomatic of certain modern, highly aberrant extra-clinical endeavours to identify genius with madness. Grillparzer was a creative artist and at all times predisposed to take himself to task and grow depressed because of his recurrent unproductivity. F. H. Bradley has said that 'to do good work a man must no doubt be industrious; to do great work he must certainly be idle as well'. Grillparzer could hardly be expected to know and appreciate this fact himself, however, especially at the time of his greatest apparent idleness; because it was precisely then that he was undergoing experiences so depressing that he could not possibly have envisaged them consciously as desirable from the productive point of view; yet that is what they were, and subconsciously he did 'desire' them, as he later recognized. The first version of his epigrammatic 'Selbstbekenntnis' (G. 982) contains the second line:

'Ein andrer sitzt *und führt* und schreibt mein Leben'!

[1] Decurtius, F.: 'Grillparzer in psycho-pathol. Beleuchtung' (in Ztsch. f. d. gesamte Neurologie u. Psychiatrie, Vol. I, 148 (1933), pp. 620 ff.) Also: 'Beiträge zur Kenntnis der Persönlichkeit Fr. Grillparzers' (in Allg. Ztsch. f. Psychiatrie, 1934, pp. 313 ff.).

As a corrective see Hinrichsen O.: 'Depression u. Produktivität' (in Ztsch. f. d. gesamte Neurologie u. Psychiatrie, Vol I, 144 (1933), pp. 455 ff.).

It is not enough to say that the tragic poet must suffer to produce; like Goethe at Wetzlar, he also unconsciously begets experiences, and suffering, to that end—production: towards the satisfaction, so to speak, of the instinct urging him to create and teach.

Perhaps this is only another way of saying that these trials of Grillparzer's were necessary and genuine, were indispensable to Grillparzer the poet and the man. But in his reflections on his condition at this time Grillparzer laments the *poet* in himself (T. 1433):

> 'Was je den Menschen schwer gefallen,
> Eins ist das Bitterste von allen;
> Vermissen was schon unser war,
> Den Kranz verlieren aus dem Haar,
> Nachdem man sterben sich gesehen,
> Mit seiner eignen Leiche gehen'.

> 'Ein inneres, entsetzliches Gefühl sagt mir jetzt, es sei mit der Dichtergabe sebst zu Ende' (T. 1419).

To fulfil his poetic destiny is what he lives for:

> 'Ist einmal der Dichter über Bord, send' ich ihm den Menschen auch nach' (T. 1424).

So he confesses still; when he might have been justified in showing personal resentment enough against his poetic chains to throw the offending *poet* overboard—if the man and the poet in him, body and mind, 'Leiche und Dichter', as he puts it (though this 'corpse' of his was at the time unusually robust) had really been separable at all. In so far as this separation is thinkable, Grillparzer performed it by implication in his self-satirical work 'Ein treuer Diener seines Herrn'. He reveals in Bancban—a victim, like so many, of too unquestioning self-sacrifice—the tragedy of *excessive* loyalty, or man's instinctive selflessness. But that achievement was not yet to be.

There is more to record, more than is in the diaries, of Grillparzer's experiences, before we can adequately understand the purport of that work. Reviewing in March, 1826 (T. 1428), his efforts to write during the past winter: first 'Libussa' ('spitz, kaltwitzig'), then 'Hero und Leander' ('kalt, leblos'), and lastly 'die Geschichte des Palatins Bancbanus, dessen Frau der Bruder seiner Königin, Otto von Meran entehrt', Grillparzer betrays a very different interest from the one he admits in his 'Selbstbiographie', and it is clear from this entry what reality—associated with this plan—preoccupies him most: the psychological anatomy of a 'Libertin'! This is the 'Hirsch' his gun is loaded for (T. 1432 and G. 180, ll. 19 f.), but at present he is too stunned by what is happening to him. Marie, who seems earlier to have revealed Grillparzer's 'Charis' lines about herself to Daffinger (to judge by his contemporary portrait of her in that *négligé*),[1] appears by the early spring to be changed indeed! (G. 187 and Anm.) *Sinnpflanze*:

> 'Sieh wie sich die Blumen freun!
> Alle öffnen ihre Blätter
> In der Sonne warmen Strahl;
> Du allein nur bleibst verschlossen?
> Bist du fühllos? freust dich nicht?—
> Fühllos nun gerade nicht!
> Will mich auch wohl wieder öffnen,
> Nur hat mich, eh du gekommen,
> Tastend eine Hand berührt'

—which Backmann comments on as follows:

> 'Der bis aufs Blut gehende Kummer, den Grillparzer auf seinen damaligen Spaziergängen mit sich abzumachen suchte, war in erster Linie bittere Enttäuschung über Marie, die Entdeckung, daß ihm ein anderer bei ihr den Rang abgelaufen und sie in jedem Sinne sich zu eigen gemacht hatte. *Sinnpflanze* (auch *Noli me tangere* genannt) legt bei leisester Berührung ihre Fiederblättchen aufwärts zusammen und öffnet sie erst nach längerer Zeit wieder. Grillparzer ist der Fragende selbst, die Antwortende aber ist Marie'.

Grillparzer knows soon after this that Marie is going to have a child. But does he know by whom? Backmann thinks it inconceivable that Grillparzer could have recovered from the blow, if he had known at this stage that it was the 'traitor' Daffinger. But could he feel *assured* he was not himself the culprit, or alternatively, that he would not be involved? Marie, in a bewildering situation—when challenged by the man she truly loved—had always protested her innocence and constancy to himself alone; she had done so, no doubt, because a 'frank' confession would have misrepresented her to him far more! Grillparzer, at any rate, though at first himself bewildered and not unnaturally alarmed, perceived this truth; upon mature reflection—in Erny, Hero, Esther, and in Rahel too, he reveals this deeper insight. Of cruder interpretation, the passage from 'der Bruderzwist' itself shows also, what is evidenced elsewhere, that he partly blames himself, though yet more his rival, for what has come about. No doubt he bore well in mind, moreover, that all might have been prevented, 'if he had forborne to do what most depended on his choice originally' (T. 1339), a conception of tragic guilt embodied in his Bancban.

[1] Reproduced in our frontispiece from Grünstein, loc. cit., facing p. 50.

Meanwhile Grillparzer makes a brave effort to distract himself:

> 'Ich muß Scherz treiben oder ganz schweigen und meine innere Seelenmarter, meine Menschenscheu, meinen langweilend gelangweilten Mißmuth zur Schau tragen und das mag ich nicht, kann ich nicht, will ich nicht (T. 1421).'

He consents to join the Ludlam club, as if in defiance of the system of government which had so recently 'corrected' him again, saying that as between Bedlam and Ludlam he preferred deliberate folly (B. 276). In his diary he writes:

> '*ad vocem* Scherz treiben: gestern Abends die Ludlam[1] besucht. Was man da Spaß macht, wie viel ich da gelacht habe, und immer dabei des marternden Seelenzustandes bewußt' (T. 1422).

A few weeks later he was subjected to an early morning visitation by the police, who routed about amongst his papers, cross-examined him, and detained him until evening—they were 'cleaning-up' the harmless Ludlamites, who were suspected (perhaps because, since the Daffinger affair, Grillparzer had joined them) of treasonable machinations.

> 'Wer mir die Vernachlässigung meines Talentes zum Vorwurf macht, der sollte vorher bedenken, wie in dem ewigen Kampfe mit Dummheit und Schlechtigkeit endlich der Geist ermattet' (T. 1435).

The police decided to cover their mistake by disbanding the society as a precaution against all contingencies. Grillparzer applied in June for leave of absence for a visit to Germany; he was seriously thinking of leaving Austria; but in August he was still engaged in dealings with police-headquarters over the futile Ludlam affair. In March he had written a poem 'Vision' (G. 59) of genuine thanksgiving for the Emperor's recovery from a serious illness; it had been read out to and acclaimed by the loyal Ludlamites; publishing it, Grillparzer hoped to create an impression in high circles which might win him some measure of protection against those who seemed bent on ruining him. But the Empress was highly incensed because Grillparzer had spoken in 'Vision' of *two* women, whereas she alone (without her step-mother) had watched by the royal bedside!

[1] The name of the association, perhaps after that of its *locale*, 'die Ludlams-Höhle', appears to derive, no doubt curiously, from that of a kind of artificial grotto in England, a 'romantic' feature of Moor Park, Sir William Temple's estate, near Farnham in Surrey. It was famed in the eighteenth century and earlier as the reputed former abode of a kindly 'white' witch, after whom it was called *Mother Ludlam's Hole*. See the account of this in Grose's Antiquities, Vol. v, p. 110 ff.

The effect of these setbacks was to aggravate Grillparzer's sens of spiritual extinction. He reflects on the futility and tragedy of h emotional life. His betrothal he admits has proved but a fiasco an has undermined his faith in the existence of genuine feeling (T. 1436 37). Again he speaks of himself as having become a 'corpse', and adc these tragic words:

> 'Das Theater erregt mir Abscheu, und kömmt jemand auf das z sprechen was ich geschrieben, oder daß ich wieder etwas schreiben soll, s reißt sich ein so ungeheures Gefühl in meinem Innern los, ich sehe einen s ungeheuren Abgrund vor mir, einen so dunkeln leeren Abgrund, daß ic schaudern muß, und der Gedanke, mich selbst zu tödten, war mir scho oft nahe. Das sind nun freilich Läppereien und so etwas zu thun wir Niemanden einfallen, aber der Gedanke daran ist schon arg genug (T. 1439).

6. THE JOURNEY TO GERMANY

In his 'Selbstbiographie' Grillparzer cites as an added cause for under taking the 'curative' journey eventually embarked upon in August 1826, his 'in Verwirrung gekommene Herzensangelegenheiten' Nothing, he adds, would induce him to particularize these; bu we know enough already to appreciate his situation. In th Gallery at Dresden he was singularly impressed by Adrian van de Werf's 'Vertstoßung der Hagar'; we can appreciate, too, his perhap subconscious motive for discerning in this representation a suprem example of art, expressing with such truth its human situation (T 1515):

> 'Das Gesicht Hagars ist abgewendet und doch liest man den ganzen Gehalt des Augenblickes in jeder der reizenden Wendungen des Halses des Kopfes. Wie sie sich nach Abraham hin kehrt, klagend, vorwerfen und offenbar zugleich lauernd, ob nicht ein Wink, eine Bewegung anzeigen werde, daß er nur gezwungen handle, daß sein Herz nicht se bei seinem grausamen Ausspruch. Und Abraham hat wirklich so vie gedrücktes, die Wendung der Entfernung gebiethenden Hände hat so viel entschuldigendes, daß ohne die lauernde Sara, die Szene wohl ein andere Wendung nähme'.

Only one consideration, but it is an important one, might induce u to doubt the analogy as complete: Grillparzer's real reason for behaving like this Abraham was not so much the attitude of Kathi as the con sideration he later indicated. In his 'Selbstbiographie', where he i hinking primarily of his interrupted relations with Marie, he wrote he passage quoted in an earlier chapter:

> 'Mein eigentliches Streben ging doch immer dahin, mich in jenem ungetrübten Zustande zu erhalten, der meiner eigentlichen Göttin, der Kunst, die Annäherung nicht erschwerte, oder wohl gar unmöglich machte'.

Ie undertook the journey to Germany (like the earlier escape to taly and the later one to England) as another Shavian Don Juan unning away from woman, in order to be free for work. He asks imself in Dresden why he had left Vienna, was it for distraction? Ie was distracted already! Was it to make acquaintances among cholars and artists?

> 'Gehöre ich denn noch unter sie? Hier ist die Quelle meiner Marter, der Mittelpunkt meines Lebensüberdrußes. Daß ich nicht fähig bin zu schaffen, und ein dunkles Gefühl mir die Fratze vorhält, ich werde es nie mehr werden, das jagt mich wie ein gehetztes Wild' (T. 1508).

Only Goethe among these men, he adds, will be likely to make him eel constrained; and at Weimar, when in early October he finally rrived there, that feeling did come over him. At table next to his evered host, whose kindness so moved him, he had been self-conscious n this 'almost greatest moment of his life'. The following morning Grillparzer was requested to appear at Goethe's house to sit for the ortrait in charcoal by Schmeller and, joining Goethe in the garden, e had with him there a more personal talk. This was the occasion vhen Goethe spoke of 'Sappho' with approval. Grillparzer met with nderstanding, too, when he complained of unfriendly surroundings n Vienna—being honoured by an admission from Goethe of what he elt he owed to his former companionship with Schiller. Already, no oubt, there were signs of approaching confidences. In the course of he day Grillparzer received an invitation to sup with Goethe alone. t may have been due to an impression that he was not definitely xpected, but more probably to his natural dread of having to reveal he true nature of his poetic confessions, as well as of his desperate piritual situation at this time—at any rate, Grillparzer, in this respect truly naïve poet, without experience of 'congenial' friendship, did ot go. He always reproached himself for thus sacrificing Goethe's oodwill, but he could not help himself. Yet it was not weakness of haracter, as he supposed, that kept him away, but true knowledge of he relation between poetry and experience, added to ignorance of the world; Goethe would have encouraged, but not embarrassed him.

In his much later 'Selbstbiographie' Grillparzer declares that a stay in Munich (extended beyond the period of his leave) restored his zest for work; and that on returning home he immediately embarked upon his 'Bancban' despite its relative lack of attraction for him; he states that he thought it might be suitable for dedication to Goethe and was unlikely to cause difficulties with the censorship. Actually his 'Bancban' was none of these things; and Grillparzer's mental condition on his return and after it—he did not commence his drama till October 31st—was unchanged. In November he drew up a list of thirty tragic and eight comic subjects to work from; but that was nearly a month after his return. In the meantime Marie's child was born—a circumstance that must have affected him as final and conclusive, and possibly (in his poetic capacity) as a trigger incident. He seems to have had recourse first to his earlier repeatedly rejected *Tristia* plan and to have intended these poems to reflect his condition from the winter to the autumn of that tragic year.[1] First came the beginning of 'Böse Stunde', invoking Inspiration in vain (he fears), then 'Polarszene', then the beginning of 'Frühlings Kommen', followed by the whole of the summer poem 'Der Fischer', with its detached and tranquil feeling, and its altogether significant hint in the final strophe. Before his autumn mood defined itself, indeed, this hint of fishing in beclouded water ripened to a resolve! The memorable conclusion—earlier quoted[2]—to 'Böse Stunde' is written now (rendering this title in part invalid); Inspiration is in fact at hand—because an experience, now completed, has engendered it. Thus ends abruptly the first phase of Grillparzer's 'Tristia ex Ponto'; the dramatic plan which has so long been maturing is ripe at last.

[1] Cf. Jb. xxxi, p. 11 f. [2] See p. 91.

CHAPTER VI

'EIN TREUER DIENER SEINES HERRN'

I. DELAYED RESOLVE TO PUBLISH

THE figure of fishing in beclouded water, like that of stalking the stag (G. 180 and 60)—strictly analogous to Shakespeare's Caliban-baiting and Tempest-raising—is apposite enough as applied to the characters and situation in the 'Treuer Diener', if only because their true identity has up till now remained *obscured*. Yet, as with the characters in 'Sappho', Grillparzer must have feared at first—as was but natural—that their disguise was transparent, his 'exposure' too sensational; for months he kept this work, which had been swiftly completed before the end of 1826, securely locked up in his desk and in reserve; it would have been just as safe from detection—except perhaps by his more intimate acquaintances—if it had been released without delay. For this tragedy is an outstanding example of a drama *masking* in its prime capacity a poet's personal experience, and effectively doing so, in that this circumstance has indeed escaped disclosure, even longer than was necessary. The reason for this immunity is two-fold: the natural reluctance of critics to trespass with what they would regard as intrusive commentary and hazardous, 'irrelevant' conjecture; and the predisposition of the poet not to anticipate, but to delay—if not by prevarication to avoid, detection. The poet, after all, is at bottom far less concerned about the personal facts his works derive from, than he is with the human truth these works reveal; the secret gratification derived from 'exposing' his enemy, for example, is far outweighed by the lasting satisfaction of expounding villainy itself; so much so, in fact, that (as with Grillparzer and Daffinger) he is often thus rendered magnanimous towards his personal adversary again—the opposite effect to that observed in love entanglements. Criticism, as a rule, neglects to take account of this significant process: it fails to discriminate regarding what matters primarily in dramatic creation and what ultimately. If, on the other hand, it belittles the poet's personal involvement with his work, as is usual, the critic is more harmlessly so engaged than he would be in overstressing or oversimplifying it. This is a province for almost as much reticence and caution on the discerning critic's part as on the poet's own—

especially if they be contemporaries. The present drama affords a illustration of this.

In his dedication of the 'Wiener Grillparzer Album' in 1877, Riz (Grillparzer's cousin) explains his motive for editing the poems i includes. A small circle of intimates always knew, he declares, th experiences from which Grillparzer's lyrics ('occasional poetry in th best sense of the word') derived; recognizing that they thus hel the key to their proper understanding, they published this com mentary to the poems as a memorial and a pattern in biographic criticism for successors of theirs among the poet's friends. It woul be a mistake to under-estimate the extent of Rizy's detailed knowledg of the circumstances involved; yet by reason of his tact this commentar of his has proved somewhat unhelpful in the sense advertised. It wa too early to disclose particulars; names and facts were still withhel Nevertheless, the implications and hints conveyed by Rizy are dis tinctly worthy of notice. Speaking of the *Tristia ex Ponto*, for instanc he recalls the growing eagerness with which the appearance of 'Aglaj was awaited, as—in poems of increasing candour—the poet nurture progressive public interest in his private affairs. Then Rizy revea that Grillparzer's intimates were aware that most of these tragi confessions, which Grillparzer had at first kept under lock and ke belonged to the period ending with December, 1827. This means th Rizy was privy to the actual circumstances and situation, involvin Daffinger and Grillparzer and Marie, which gave rise to the 'Tristi poems. Among these, 'Verwünschung', 'Trennung', and 'Porträt malerin' are interconnected, as he justly comments. Bauernfeld, to may well have known as much. From among these symptoms of th poet's desperate condition at that time Rizy cites as highly significa a *short poem* (G. 192), in which Grillparzer was constrained, he states, t characterize even his current dramatic work (his 'Bancban'!) as a act of defiance and self-defence against the baseness of a hostile worl (The formulation of Rizy's comment on this poem implies tha knowing the 'source' of 'Bancban', he questioned Grillparzer's wisdo in so far admitting it as in this document.) In mid-September, 182 when Marie's intention to marry Daffinger had become know and Grillparzer—now grimly determined—at last handed over h tragedy to the Hoftheaterdirektion, he wrote in his diary, as Riz tells us:

'Es hat fast den Anschein als wollte es zu Ende gehen. *Ich will ab sterben mit den Waffen in der Hand,*' and followed this up with the sho poem mentioned (G. 192), an elaboration of the same thought—including for us, be it said, familiar allusions to (Daffinger's) *Gemeinheit* and his own (and Marie's) 'extinction'—on a separate sheet:

> 'Wohlan denn nun, nicht klaglos will ich fallen
> Dem Opfertiere gleich, das stöhnt und stirbt;
> Auf daß Gemeinheit zu den Siegen allen
> Die schon sie feiert, nicht noch Den erwirbt,
> Daß kundlos ihre Tat, daß, die sie schlachtet,—
> Wenn nun die Welt früh eh der Morgen glüht
> Die Leiche schaut und keinen Täter sieht,—
> Als Frevler an sich selber sei'n geachtet'.

Rizy need not have entertained misgivings. In spite of his assistance, the force of this poem has apparently eluded apprehension. It is difficult to see why it should. Rizy obviously had inside knowledge: he did not arbitrarily and independently merely guess the poem's date and associate it with the drama—how could he have done? Backmann erroneously supposes (G. 192 Anm.) that Rizy was thinking of Charlotte *v.* Paumgartten's death in connection with the mid-September date; as against this he points out that the paper (Rizy's separate sheet) on which the poem is written is of later origin. The answer to this is that the revised MS. of the existing poem was presumably substituted by Grillparzer for the original version.[1] The fact that it contains the metaphor of night and death, which also occurs in 'Verwandlungen' (G. 84, 7), makes Rizy's date appear the more obviously authentic.

What these lines opening with the combative expression 'Wohlan denn nun . . .' clearly express is the poet's resolve to lay now before the public his complaint and self-vindication, hitherto kept in reserve, his exposure of base treatment, virtual extinction—not of himself alone—at the hands of a vile braggart and inveterate despoiler; lest the world subsequently suspect the victims of having brought about their own downfall. He felt that in publishing his 'Treuer Diener' he was giving utterance to his own sufferings and his outraged feelings at Marie's betrayal and subjugation, in addition to justifying his own passive conduct in this affair, in which he had not been a free agent.

The diary lines that put this latter thought on record, during the work on 'Bancban' at the end of 1826, contain the epithets which

[1] Are the variants (e.g. Täter: Mörder) in the extant printed versions of this poem evidence of differing MS. versions having been used?

Bancban echoes plaintively on Erny's death: 'O Erny, o mein Kind mein gutes, frommes Kind' and read as follows (G. 189):

> 'Ich werde gut sein, fromm: das sagen ist wohl leicht,
> Das *Kind* verspricht's, der *Mann* läßt Leichtsinn walten.
> Allein geruhe mich, O Herr, beim Wort zu halten,
> Denn du sollst *leben* bis ich es erreicht'.

Marie is the child; the man is Grillparzer—he who has given his vow that of a faithful servant, to fulfil the task in hand, that art and truth may live.

But the task in hand was intimately bound up with the whole delicate situation. Grillparzer came to look upon his product with misgivings in this respect. Not until he felt driven to it ('Wohlan denn nun ...') could he bring himself to publish this self-vindication. For this is exactly what Grillparzer was doing, from his own point of view. If at the same time he proved himself, as author of this tragedy a medium for the interpretation of universal truth, not just his own that was an austere consolation for him and, ultimately, a source of inward satisfaction—because suffering was his means to poetic self-fulfilment, as Bauernfeld, in effect, at the time reminded him ('Freundeswort', G. 84, 16):

> 'Mag dein Schmerz sich roh entladen,
> Zeigst du ihn durch stummes Toben?
> Wen die Musen so begnaden,
> Fühle höher sich erhoben!
>
> Bist ja Maler, brauche Farben!
> Bist ja Dichter, brauch das Wort!
> Gram und Herz, wenn Beide starben,
> Dauern so geheiligt fort'.

This is not so much a romantic as a realistic view of the creative literary process. The 'romantic' view is the one assuming that the poet borrows or invents situations and characters, informing them with life and truth by virtue of his gift—imagination—eked out with source-material and influences by various predecessors.

2. ORIGINS OF 'BANCBAN'

These sources and influences are present, in 'Bancban' no less than in other works, and play an important, though secondary, rôle. Grillparzer came across the subject-matter of this work in the first place 'from without' when perusing the annals of Hungarian history in consequence of a request from Dietrichstein for a suitable piece to perform at the coronation ceremony of the Empress Carolina Augusta as Queen of Hungary in 1825. Sauer assumed, because of this, that Grillparzer actually wrote the work—excellent in technique and characterization—in a detached spirit, and for this reason succeeded in rendering it so noble, definite, and clear in tendency, so well calculated to appeal to his contemporaries, officials and public alike (Jb. III, 9, 29). Actually this masterpiece was none of these things: not unrelated to its author—despite appearances to the contrary; not noble, definite, and clear in tendency—at any rate not in the sense implied; and definitely not calculated to please authority.

Ein Treuer Diener Seines Herrn! Grillparzer was not thinking approvingly in the first place of a loyal subject's service to the state, but with inward wrath of the cost of his own allegiance to his art.

T. S. Eliot has justly said, and his own poetic practice bears this out, that—

> 'The only way of expressing emotion in the form of art is by finding an "objective correlative"; in other words, a set of objects, a situation, a chain of events, which shall be the formula of that *particular* emotion' (*Sacred Wood*, p. 92).

In Grillparzer's case an 'objective correlative' presented itself to him in the 'Geschichte des Palatins Bancbanus, dessen Frau der Bruder seiner Königin, Otto von Meran entehrt', undoubtedly from the start the formula, the fitting cloak, for expressing artistically his own experience.

Left in charge, with the Queen herself, of State affairs during the King's enforced absence, Bancban feels constrained to require of his young wife that she should determine her own attitude towards the Queen's brother, Otto v. Meran, who is bent upon subduing her resistance to his advances. By utterly despicable means and abuse of authority Prince Otto contrives to ensnare her, only to be cheated of his defiant victim by her desperate suicide. Bancban, ignorant of the exact circumstances of Erny's death, is stunned with grief at her cruel fate and his loss, and knowing the harm and futility of bloody vengeance, bestirs himself only to *oppose* a rebellion led by his headstrong kin, which threatens the safety of the child-heir to the throne. The Queen herself loses her life, and it is only by coercing her worthless brother into assisting him that Bancban, with the child, evades capture and is able to fulfil the burdensome trust and excessive service demanded of him till order is restored and justice done on the King's return.

In this story, as duly modified and adapted by himself, Grillparzer found his own sense of self-denying allegiance to his poetic destiny and its price translated, as it were, or aptly paralleled in the more general terms of patriotic duty and loyal self-sacrifice. In the tragic figure of Bancban, departing here significantly from history, he portrayed a man who, like himself, could not help behaving as the 'faithful servant of his master'. Bancban certainly displays loyalty 'to a fault'—this is his tragic guilt—in tolerating for even one single moment the Prince's molestation of Erny, allowing it to go unchallenged and Erny unprotected out of overweening regard for his own paramount ideal. This is the place[1] where Grillparzer was able to apply in his artistic practice his affirmation of a saying of Lichtenberg's, regarding guilt (T. 1339):

> 'Bei einem Verbrechen ist das, was die Welt das Verbrechen nennt, selten das, was die Strafe verdient, sondern da liegt es, wo unter der langen Reihe von Handlungen, womit es sich gleichsam als mit Wurzeln in unser Leben hineinerstreckt, diejenige ist, die am meisten von unserm Willen abhieng, und die wir am leichtesten nicht hätten thun können. Lichtenberg I, 192. *Herrlicher Stoff zu einem Trauerspiele*'.

He had noted this first in 1820–21 (T. 855) and then again with rueful conviction in the summer of 1824—with an eye to future work—because of its bearing on his own fatal relinquishment of Marie to Daffinger; at that time too his suffering due to this consequence of the 'contrast between art and life' was also reflected in a diary citation from Luther (T. 1344):

> 'Schweig, leid, meid und vertrag,
> Deine Noth niemand klag,
> An Gott nicht verzag,
> Sein Hilfkommt alle Tag'.

Now he portrays his Bancban, whose tragedy, as we noted earlier, might well have been averted—'if he had forborne to do what most depended on his choice originally'.

3. DRAWN FROM LIFE

It is true that Bancban's character and circumstances, like Grillparzer's own, rendered such forbearance to consult his own interests

[1] i.e. in the conduct of Bancban, not that of Erny and the rest; but cf. 'Wke.' I. 3, p. 356.

natural, if not inevitable. (Our recognition of this implies that his case is typical.) Bancban had to be represented as feeling that he lacked full claim to Erny. The characteristic lines, comprising Meran's scurrilous serenade (G. 58):

Alter Mann	Schön Erny, lieb und gut,
Der jungen Frau,	Verschläfst dein junges Blut,
Ist er klug,	Vermählest ohne Scheu
Nimmts nicht genau!	Dem Winter deinen Mai!

belong to an early phase of the work on 'Bancban'. But when Grillparzer made his hero so much older than himself, perhaps even more than three times Erny's age, he doubtless went too far. It would have been sufficient, almost, for Bancban to have *thought* himself declining. We can understand, in part, Grillparzer's reason for introducing this unhistorical feature: he not only had a weakness for the age-disparity motive, but was also most unsparing in self-portraiture: the suggestion in his letters to Marie that he felt himself ageing and almost old enough to be her father is here endorsed. A hint afforded in an early diary note, which conceivably also includes the first suggestion for the figure of Erny, because it speaks of 'die hübsche E.', the young wife of an 'old, almost repulsive' husband (T. 331), is perhaps associated with this self-satirical impulse, resulting in a resemblance (which Sauer stresses Jb. III, 24) between Bancban and Grillparzer's father. This still implies, however, satirical self-portraiture: in the diary notes, 'zu Fixlmüllners Charakteristik', Grillparzer wrote (T. 1655):

> 'Überhaupt, je älter er ward, um so ähnlicher wurde er diesem Manne, von dem er sich in seiner Jugend so verschieden gefühlt hatte, als nie ein Sohn von seinem Vater'.

Hating—like Wenzel Grillparzer—irregularity of every kind, disrespect, extravagance, untruthfulness, Bancban reveals himself qualified rather to be an official than a statesman, to be equipped for duty rather than for higher trust. That is intentional. We are to perceive that—though admirable and likeable enough, despite his household tyranny and bluster (like Grillparzer himself he affects a protective 'crust' for his tender and subconsciously self-pitying soul) Bancban is not fitted for the mission imposed upon him by the king, who is in this respect at fault. The king irresponsibly exploits Bancban's allegiance and dependability, being perhaps aware of the necessity he himself is under to observe his duty to the state and make amends for his own weakness towards the queen. Gertrude almost persuaded him to appoint her worthless brother (whom he knows for what he is) co-regent with herself; he would indeed have done so if Meran had not been absent on his nocturnal escapade. No sooner has the king appointed, instead, his 'faithful servant' Bancban, than it becomes apparent from the queen's attitude what a blunder and criminal imposition this really is. The victimization and exploitation of Bancban goes so far that his unjust monarch on his departure threatens him with ignominy and oblivion if he does not maintain the peace thus obviously endangered. So much for the faithful servant's master! Bancban's destiny, which is his tragedy—it is every man's destiny (the poet implies) to be born unfree—required him to show, not personal heroism in external action, but mute self-sacrifice, self-abnegation despite internal strife and latent qualms. He acts as in his circumstances any man might act. To feel no *pity* for Bancban, and no *fear* through him, would be to lack imaginative insight: his case (apart from accidents) might well be our own.

Bancban has literally no longer any option. In Act II it is clear to him that he must deny to Erny the protection she needs. He even looks to her for an attempt at social conduct in accordance with his station—a dignified return to the festivity she has just fled in terror! And his reply to her naïve entreaty that he should resign office for her sake:

> 'Gib sie zurück denn, dieses Amtes Bürde!
> Sei Ernys Gatte bloß, mit ihr beglückt'.

must manifestly be: 'Was fällt dir ein?'

This is followed by the remarkably realistic scene, recalling the 'besiegte Siegeraugen' lines, where Erny after her cross-examination by Otto is so searchingly questioned by Bancban—a scene in which we are intended to feel that Erny's conscience is not absolutely clear. This seems for long to have been Grillparzer's conviction regarding Marie, if we are to judge by his letters to her. In his diary he wrote of Erny's conduct (T. 1619):

> 'Wenn nicht aus dem Betragen Ernys hervorgeht, daß sie früher doch einiges, wenn gleich unschuldiges, Wohlgefallen an dem Prinzen gehabt, so handeln die ganzen 3 ersten Aufzüge *de lana caprina*.'

The portrayal of Erny in these acts is one of the most astounding revelations of woman's nature in literature. Erny in this work, which has been described as the poet's 'schärfster naturalistischer Vorstoß', is drawn with such consummate art and insight up to the very moment of her violent death as to be evidently 'drawn from life'. Progress beyond the point thus reached by critical intuition has, however, seemed almost impossible to those who accepted it:

> 'Woher der eigentümliche, so unglaublich wahre Charakter dieser Frau gekommen . . . wird wohl ein Rätsel bleiben, dem auch Vermutungen nur höchstens ein Zipfelchen seines Geheimnisses werden lüften können !'[1]

But Grillparzer's living model was, of course, Marie.

The villainous character of Otto v. Meran, too, is drawn with startling realism and subtlety. Grillparzer, taking his cue from Shakespeare perhaps, whom he understood so well, avenges himself here upon one who served him as model for a lecher. Yet Meran is not intended to appear utterly ignoble, any more than Daffinger can have appeared so under Marie's influence, and we are reminded of the passage in Grillparzer's diary in which he says:

> 'Es *gibt* keinen noch so verhärteten Bösewicht, bei dem die Gegenwart und der Anblick der Neigung eines tugendhaften Weibes nicht wenigstens für *Augenblicke* Einfluß auf die Gesinnung haben sollte' (T. 1367),

a remark which he was moved to make because he felt that the 'Liaisons dangereuses' of Choderlos de Laclos were *unreal* in implying the contrary. Another passage from this work which Grillparzer transcribed into his diary in December, 1824, (this circumstance showing how long he had grappled with these problems and emotions before discovering their artistic medium and setting) was the one describing that long, deep, searching look (of Marie's), the very kind of look we meet with again in Erny, where it is described in such detail by Otto von Meran, and again in the figure of Hero, when she sees Leander for the first time (T. 1372):

> 'Souvent meme, sans oser porter mes regards sur lui, je sentois les siens fixés sur moi: oui, mon amie, je les sentois, il sembloit qu'ils réchauffassent mon ame: et sans passer par mes yeux, ils n'en arrivoient pas moins à mon cœur'.

Apart from this look Erny betrays in other ways her unconscious desire for the Prince's attention. Bancban himself perceives and chides her exaggerated hatred and contempt for Otto. There is also no need to doubt that she had actually, though involuntarily, as it were, returned the pressure of his hand; nor that she had similarly appropriated to herself a lock of his hair on an earlier occasion; Otto had witnessed this. Grillparzer wrote twenty-four different versions of this passage: other ideas occurring in them include those of her dalliance

[1] 'Wke.' I, 3, p. 356.

with a miniature portrait of Prince Otto, and her admiration for his brilliant horsemanship. Both these ideas pertain to Daffinger, as also does the one retained, referring to his hair. Daffinger was inordinately proud of his lovelocks. (It gave satisfaction to some when the secret state-police once cut them off.) The reason why this tonsorial motive prevailed with Grillparzer was perhaps because of its implicit malice. But the horse-riding had already been used in connection with Zawisch. It is wanted too for other characters contemporary with Otto in Grillparzer's poetic creation, Prince Leopold and Don Cäsar in 'Der Bruderzwist'. The portrait motive also is wanted for that work, as well as for 'Die Jüdin' and for his short story 'Das Kloster bei Sendomir', which was already written, though as yet unpublished. Two other ideas experimented with, those of the silken scarf and a Leda gesture, reveal Erny's identity with Hero—who is also of this time.

But regarding Erny's identity with Hero (who is known to be inspired by Marie Daffinger) do not their self-same manner, bearing, and accents, so life-like and characteristic, so unmistakably akin, point to this?

Perhaps the most astounding thing in 'Bancban', one of the attainments that have put Grillparzer in the very front rank of dramatists, is the utter realism of the scene which culminates in Erny's desperate self-immolation. Grillparzer knew her personally, as he knew her assailant: nothing that they do or say is out of keeping: a literary 'source' like Hock's Neumann-Weißenthal is non-essential.[1] The stark truth of this apex-scene is so vivid and dramatic, the suspense so keen and tense, the tragic issue so terrible, that we half assume through this absorbing interest that the drama has become—not Bancban's, but Erny's! Yet Erny, like Cordelia (*pace* Dr. Johnson) another relatively blameless victim, is not *central*, and she perishes through Bancban's original 'tragic guilt'. The sensational nature of Prince Otto's conduct towards Erny, with Bancban unheeded, increases this effect of change of theme. Otto is, indeed, the perfect villain, we feel, while Bancban fails to perform the rôle of ideal hero. But we should not complain. Though it is true that Grillparzer felt strongly on the subject of lechery, 'Unsittlichkeit' (cf. ll. 1919–25), as he had occasion to do, and represented Otto's preoccupation with it, 'in Schauerhöhlen mit Molch und Natter spielend' (l. 1230), as evidence of an insidious vice and prevailing evil; still, reprehension of

[1] Hock, S., edit. cit., Vol. x, Intro. and n. Alluded to by Rollett in 'Wke.' I. 3, Intro. as 'admissible'; Anm., pp. 368 f.

mmorality in princes is not in 'Bancban'—as in Lessing's 'Emilia Galotti'—the central theme. Grillparzer's treatment of the historical ubject-matter in this tragedy of everyday life is of wider scope and ndeed perennial purport. The tragedy of 'Bancban' has its validity o-day, when countless 'loyal subjects of their masters' prove agents and victims alike of the slavery they confess. We live in times of excessive subject-loyalties, when with Simon we might challenge Bancban (ll. 1425–6);

> 'Schwachsinniger! Bewahrst du andrer Rechte,
> Und kannst die eignen nicht bewahren dir?'

As a matter of fact, the performance of the 'Treuer Diener' should trictly be proscribed in any absolutist state, where it is manifestly mpolitic to afford the individual such obvious occasion to question, even unconsciously, the ethics or the cost of 'loyalty to the state'. This work of genius exemplifies the function of tragedy at its highest: to open our eyes to aspects of human nature and conduct as interpreted by an intuitive higher morality, the poet's conscience. It is untrue o say that 'in real life there are no tragedies',[1] unless it be because we still lack the kind of insight and sympathy to perceive them there.

We feel, perhaps inevitably, a sense of defeat when the aged Bancban n Act IV declines to act. But Bancban does not know with us that Erny is guiltless. He rather thinks, being predisposed to do so (like Grillparzer of Marie, not without grounds), that she *may* be to blame:

> 'Wenn mein Weib sich
> Auch eines Fehltritts, wie es heißt, vermaß,
> Für den man sie so hart, ach, gar so hart bestraft,
> Geschahs gewiß aus Übereilung nur,
> Denn sie war ruschlich—o mein Weib! mein Weib! mein Weib!—
> Was sie versehn, und wie sie sich vergangen,
> Ob man zu streng, zu hart an ihr getan,
> Es wird sich weisen, kehrt der König wieder.
> Und das soll bald, gemeldet wards ihm schon.

This reason, combined with Bancban's anxiety to fulfil his duty (preventing civil strife and bloodshed) and his heart-rending grief, as of a stricken soul, would suffice of themselves to justify his bearing, without his being physically old and feeble. His brother Simon is not old or feeble. But Grillparzer has intensified this trait to accord with his own emotion, his own sense of seniority and moral responsibility, just as he does with other personal motives in this play.

[1] Dixon, MacN.: 'Tragedy', London, 1924, p. 5.

The end of all is most significant and moving. When Bancban learns that Erny was innocent and how she met her end—and feeling now that he can freely mourn her—he renounces the cause to which he was so cruelly constrained to sacrifice her, deeming it fulfilled. But he does not depart without performing an act symbolical of *ideal* loyalty. Kneeling[1] to the child, heir to the throne, for whose safety he has given all, Bancban—thus bowed before one whose gentleness and goodness reflect the affinity of heavenly and earthly majesty—expresses for Grillparzer and for ourselves a reverence and submission wholly befitting.

4. POLITICAL INFERENCES AND REPERCUSSIONS

On the other hand, the words of Bancban, intended to be heeded beyond the footlights, convey a criticism of the ruling monarch present, the dead Queen, and still more Meran, as representatives of kingship who failed in their own person to merit such faithful service as was Bancban's. A rejected variant of the concluding passage, ending with the words:

> 'Sei ein getreuer Herr erst deinen Dienern,
> (mit der Hand auf den König zeigend)
> Dann sind sie treue Diener ihres Herrn.'

brought out still more clearly this aspect of the work as reflecting Grillparzer's conditional loyalty to the crown. It shows that so far from being a work in which 'Grillparzer expresses servile subject-sentiments felt by him in common with millions of Austrians of his day' (Scherer), or in which he 'portrayed the narrowness and servility of Bancban with too much affection and approval' (Volkelt), or in which he embodied a 'Kantian categorical imperative' (Reich)—these are the usual views—it is a work which in its explicit allusions and personal implications respecting allegiance is tragic, two-minded, unresolved. The title of this tragedy, like its concluding line: 'I nu! Ein treuer Diener seines Herrn!' bears properly, if not a sardonic, then a rueful, chastened, ironical, or diffident, fundamentally *tragic* inflexion. As relating to the poet's sacrifice and suffering out of loyalty to his mission this was clearly warrantable. If it is true that Grillparzer was 'eine tief im Ethischen verankerte Natur und wußte um die Verantwortung des künstlerischen Schöpfers',[2] it is also true that he knew

[1] With this work, following upon his Lope studies, Grillparzer achieves the first of a series of theatrical masterpieces, in which plasticity, or memorable and significant dramatic attitude is a new ideal.

[2] Hock, E., loc. cit., p. 247.

the cost of this devotion; and also that he was realist enough—or modest enough—to question the ultimate worth of his artistic achievement as compared with that of the things sacrificed to it—things within positive reach of attainment, the values of moral integrity, 'quiet happiness', and love—humanly perhaps more estimable values.

But the subject matter of this work reflects more than a personal issue of the poet's; the tragedy of 'Bancban' projects his problem on to a political plane; and Grillparzer's doubts and distresses were in point of fact equally applicable and appropriate to this sphere, on objective as well as on personal grounds. Quite apart from the occasion which contemporary absolutisms afforded for objective criticism, even greater occasion in Grillparzer's days than in those of Lessing and Schiller, the poet had personal grounds for ranklings and resentment, as our account of the outcome of his various loyalist impulses has shown. Speier suggested—and this was doubtless a contributory motive of this tragedy—that Grillparzer was conscious of that weakness of his own, his incurable loyalty to the Habsburgs, and that 'he sought to free himself of this awareness by portraying in 'Bancban' the consequences of indulging this virtue to excess'.[1] Small wonder that the ruling member of the House of Habsburg, the cunning Kaiser Franz, having seen the work eventually produced, soon grew suspicious —and designed counter-measures.

Or if it be held that the Emperor himself was not sufficiently astute, since the actual source and origin of his amazing proposal to acquire *in perpetuo* sole rights in Grillparzer's 'Bancban' with a view to suppressing it is not known, it is quite certain that he had in his physician, Staatsrat Andreas von Stifft, an adviser alive to any subversive hidden tendency in literature—and able, if no one else was, to extract convincingly for him the seditious moral from this insidiously non-authoritarian piece.

When 'Ottokar' had been finally released by the censorship in 1824, this had happened on the same Baron von Stifft's advice, the chief censor, Sedlnitzky himself, being only belatedly informed. Kaiser Franz was apparently dissatisfied with Sedlnitzky's attempt in January, 1824, to justify the ban (as well he might be) and appealed to his 'confidant' v. Stifft for a new report. On March 28th this had been supplied; it dismissed in detail Sedlnitzky's objections as due to ill-timed and ill-founded timidity, and stressed v. Stifft's own advocacy of the piece by pointing out that the only people who, if asked, would oppose the production of such a loyal and patriotic work were the Liberals themselves![2]

[1] 'Euph.' VII, p. 541. Cf. ref. in Rollett's Intro. in 'Wke.', I. 3, also Anm., p. 364.
[2] Cf. Jb. xxvi, pp. 46–51.

Now, if we imagine v. Stifft asking himself a similar question regarding Grillparzer's next piece, his 'Bancban', there can be little doubt that his verdict would have been the exact opposite, that its production ought to be opposed by good Conservatives with all the means in their power. This situation, in fact, may well have come about. Grillparzer's tragedy (for reasons already suggested) was not handed in to the Hoftheaterdirektion until September, 1827. Before many months had passed it was in production. It is matter for small wonder that Sedlnitzky, this time, his knuckles still smarting from the previous rap, saw nothing to object to in the new work. In February, 1828, the Emperor witnessed a very successful first performance of it and professed himself very well pleased. What, then, is more likely than that an intelligence like that of his personal adviser, v. Stifft, should have opened his eyes to the hidden implications of this tragedy? For it was only a few days later that the Emperor approached Grillparzer, through Sedlnitzky, with his unusual proposal. Grillparzer in his response, a most creditable document, had the hardihood to compare the intentionally prohibitive price demanded by himself to the mess of potage for which Esau sold his birthright. This reply was communicated by Sedlnitzky, who defended his own action in previously declining to ban the tragedy; he now recommended that the Emperor should take *his* advice and inform Grillparzer accordingly that the proposal was withdrawn—advice which in due course, on further counsel from Count Kolowrat, the Emperor followed.[1]

It would be too much to say that the subsequent uncomprehending reception of 'Bancban', both on the stage and in book form, has proved Kaiser Franz's fears lest it should throw an unfavourable light on loyalty to have been groundless; from critics of liberal persuasion Grillparzer's tragedy has indeed called forth more scorn of 'servility' than any other product of its era—but the irony of the situation is that the poet himself has incurred this censure and consistently been judged by these critics to be at fault in precisely this political respect. As we have seen, this verdict is inept. The author deliberately portrayed his hero as the tragic victim of a natural, though excessive, instinct of loyalty; it follows that such political implications as can be descried in 'Bancban' were favourable perhaps least of all to the Austrian Imperial system of government under Metternich and Kaiser Franz, which Grillparzer described as a 'crime against the human race and against God' (T. 1409), because it sought only to conserve, was selfishly and stupidly unprogressive.

[1] ibid., pp. 103 ff.

But this is not to aver that Grillparzer consciously imported political tendency into his piece; what he was concerned with was human truth as lived and learnt by himself.

'Ein treuer Diener seines Herrn' is Grillparzer's greatest work so far, a genuine tragedy, not an apt subject for derision by political thinkers. How discriminatingly did Ernst von Feuchtersleben, Grillparzer's democratic friend, express his appreciation of this work! He describes it simply and eloquently as a genuine work of art:

> 'Ich weiß wenige dramatische Werke, die so ganz dramatisch sind, wie dieses: wo alles so ganz sich selbst darstellt, alles Charakter, Handlung, Wirklichkeit ist—wo, mit der kunstvollsten Ökonomie, ohne rhetorische und lyrische Behelfe der ganze, reiche und tiefe Gehalt an Verstand und Empfindung in Ereignisse umgewandelt, ganz eigentlich *verkörpert* ist. Nur das Wesentliche und Individuelle (der Kern aller dichterischen Wirkung) ist gegeben, mit einer Entsagung alles leeren Nebenschmuckes gegeben, die dem Kenner Ehrfurcht einflößt; denn dieser will die Gedanken und die Gesinnung des Dichters sich selbst aus dem Werke entwickeln; er will sie nicht in moralischen Phrasen sich wie conventionelle Münze ausbezahlt sehen. So waren alle die großen, *immer* lebenden Werke des Altertums, so werden alle sein müssen, die immer leben wollen,—denn Poesie ist nichts anderes als wahre, lebendige Darstellung und beruht auf dem, was die Menschen ewig und überall, sie mögen sprechen, denken und phantasiren wie sie wollen, ohne daß sie es wissen, ergreift und erhebt'.

CHAPTER VII

'DAS KLOSTER BEI SENDOMIR', 'MELUSINA'

BUT Grillparzer did not publish his 'Treuer Diener' yet; he may well have felt that in it he might have gone too far; and was the disguise with which he had cloaked his experience, he may have asked, not too transparent? Above all, was it true that Daffinger was the culprit; or, at any rate, was not he himself perhaps in danger of being ensnared? Grillparzer, we recall, had these grounds for hesitation. So far there had been no actual breach with Marie. Her portrait in Erny is drawn with love and deep solicitude. Even if he has long suspected and avoided her, he has suffered for her; there is as yet no ungenerosity in his mind, he loves her still, she is his inspiration.

The record of his work shows that straight from 'Bancban' Grillparzer turned in January, 1827, with ardour, yet with like secrecy and circumspection, to a long-neglected plan, his 'Hero and Leander'. When his misgivings about the model for his Hero conflicted too severely with his conception of this heroine, as we must suppose, he would turn to his old plan 'Der Traum ein Leben', or to that other portrait of Marie embodied in 'Die Jüdin', this one according better with his less favourable view of Marie's nature.

I. 'DAS KLOSTER BEI SENDOMIR'

This attitude is also reflected in a further work of the greatest interest from the point of view adopted in the present study. Written mainly in 1825, it was now summarily completed at Schreyvogel's request in the Spring of 1827 and published in his 'Aglaja' in the Autumn. The work in question is Grillparzer's short story 'Das Kloster bei Sendomir', described on the title page as 'based upon an episode reported as true'. This unique product has aroused much interest in virtue of its sensational character, and much speculation as to its actual source—some commentators even hazarding the opinion that it was intimately associated with the author's own experience. In his commentary on this work in the historical and critical edition Backmann confirms this impression, though he feels constrained—from his knowledge of its genesis—to rule out the conviction, expressed by others, hat the experience reflected in it involved Marie. Yet, if we hold, as from evidence already adduced we must hold, that Grillparzer's awareness of Marie dates back to 1822, there is no difficulty about ecognizing her in the diary plan of that year and consequently no occasion to invoke Charlotte v. Paumgartten at this stage and at later tages, as Backmann does. At an earlier period, however, Charlotte does come in.

It will be recalled that we spoke in connection with 'Medea' of Grillparzer's preoccupation with the adultery-jealousy-and-vengeance heme of 'Othello' when he gave the name of Desdemona to Charlotte and exhorted himself, in 1820, to read the story of Walter of Aquitania. He found this legend in Vol. I of Grimm's 'Altdeutsche Wälder', and it is recognizable as the earliest source of his plan for 'Das Kloster bei Sendomir'. The features which make this indisputable are to be seen in the fundamental situation—parallel to Grillparzer's own with Charlotte and her husband—and in a number of details, including the Polish setting, which reappear in the final result.

The next relevant document is the one dating from Autumn, 1822, some time after the change of dwelling alluded to in T. 1105, when Grillparzer presumably first came to live opposite to Marie in the Ballgasse. It is an extensive diary entry (T. 1245) comprising a complete sketch of the ultimate story and is probably an 'original' composition of the author's, though deriving some of its apparatus from the earlier (1820) source. In the main it runs as follows:

A Polish nobleman falls in love with a beautiful girl [encountered by night in equivocal circumstances] belonging to a distinguished family in decline. He pays off debts, secures pardon for her exiled relatives, and eventually marries the girl, retiring happily with her to his estate. After some months an old forester reluctantly informs him that he has a rival for his wife's favours. The Count subsequently convinces himself that a child born soon after is not his own. He confronts his wife with this knowledge and informs her that the only way in which she can adjust the wrong she has done him is to murder her offspring. She is on the point of doing this when he stays her hand and slays her with his sword; he would have given her an opportunity to repent at leisure in a cloister if she had refused, so he declares. The Count exiles himself into the wilderness and is never seen again.

Unavailing researches have been conducted to discover a literary source of this narrative. Yet, if we reflect on the theme, it becomes apparent that there is no need whatever for such a source to exist: tragic oblivion after a jealous crime of vengeance is the outcome of a worthy man's infatuation and betrayal at the hands of a beautiful girl, unchaste, designing, heartless enough even for child-murder. It will be seen that all the components of this familiar attitude of Grillparzer's are contained in (*a*) the 1820 situation (including, through inter-association of Charlotte and Medea, the ill-starred motive of child-murder) *plus* (*b*) the current situation in 1822, as revealed in the contemporary 'Huldigungen':

> 'Hast du die Liebe schon gekannt,
> Gefühlt schon ihren Kuß . . .',

addressed to Marie by one who sought to ward off an influence which seemed to threaten the integrity of his life and purpose. The fact that an interloper has not yet taken positive shape is revealing, since he occupies only a hypothetical place in this 1822 situation. But by the time Grillparzer came to write his full version of the story this interloper's place was well filled by Daffinger, echoing whom (in the MS. version) Oginsky is made to utter his vile boast: 'Ja, ich habe sie *genossen*'; and even the child of disputed paternity materializes, and the suggestion for the *portrait*-motive emerges, to reveal the child's parentage. We witness in all this another striking instance, it would appear, of time's 'daimonic intervention'.[1] Grillparzer's 1822 plan anticipated, as it were, these necessary developments in his future experience. The kinship of Elga to Erny has been observed by various critics (in one place in his 'Bancban' manuscript Grillparzer wrote Elga for Erny by mistake); but Rahel of 'Die Jüdin' and above all Lukretia of 'Der Bruderzwist' might be said to contribute more telling characteristics. We observe, too, that in 1825, when 'Das Kloster bei Sendomir' was elaborated, the theme from Grillparzer's contemporary 'Briefe an Marie', that of beauty combined not with truth but with *un*truth, is prominently featured in Elga's appalling hypocrisy. Starschensky himself is also easily identifiable in scores of allusions as a self-portrait of the author. Little more need be said here to establish the connection between Starschensky's fate in being so woefully imposed upon, betrayed, ill-used, and finally wrecked, and the fate which threatened Grillparzer, as he imagined, whether through the agency of Marie or another, if he did not guard against being similarly used, to the destruction of that personal integrity which he valued so highly on behalf of his art.

But Grillparzer's projection in this work of one thinkable explanation of Marie's conduct is by no means adequate and anything but

[1] See pp. 87 and 77 above.

exhaustive of her 'enigmatic' personality; like her other portraits it may be deemed experimental. It is almost certain, seeing the manner and form of its publication, that the author found his short story unsatisfactory and unconvincing. In characterizing the 'Novelle' as a genre, Grillparzer spoke of it in terms which, while implying its close relationship with drama, indicate that he regarded it as of lower literary standing.[1] In particular he stated that the essential difference between the short story and the drama was that whereas the former was 'eine gedachte Möglichkeit', the drama was 'eine gedachte Wirklichkeit', a distinction which explains no doubt why he never attempted to dramatize 'Das Kloster'—leaving this for Hauptmann to essay. If, to culminate his exploration of the *hypothesis* of great beauty masking extreme depravity, Grillparzer's inclusion of the 'possible' motive of child-murder itself in this material must be regarded as a problematical side-shoot from 'Medea', it is no more convincing and satisfactory here than it was there, where it marred so much. Perhaps it is not without ironical significance to observe that 'Das Kloster bei Sendomir', otherwise a perfect short story, proves unsatisfactory only in respect to this feature and conception, the only one not drawn from life, the only one which is speculative, 'eine gedachte Möglichkeit'.

Grillparzer's relaxation of ideal critical demands in dealing with the 'Novelle' would not satisfy the literary standards of to-day, perhaps, except possibly for purposes of presentation on the screen (and what a tense film-melodrama this MS. would afford!). We cannot acquiesce in the author's representation of Elga's conduct as something which is 'possible', which indeed might happen; in fact we feel constrained to reject it as not representing 'what would happen', and so not satisfying a standard of truth and plausibility which we do not by any means wish to see restricted to drama as the highest literary form.

2. BEETHOVEN AND 'MELUSINA'

The fact that Grillparzer allowed 'Das Kloster' to appear in its present form is thus definitely an indication that he thought not highly of it from the point of view of truth and art. It belonged to his definition of the short story that it was to be regarded as a 'Herabneigen der Poesie zur Prosa'. Numerous passages from his jottings indicate that he was out of sympathy with the intermingling of art-forms which

[1] Cf. Backmann's Intro. to 'Das Kloster' in 'Wke.'I, 13, p. 288.

romanticism advocated. In the same way as he thus thought of th
short story as an adulteration of poetry, so did he think of certai
contemporary music as 'impure'. In his 'Erinnerungen an Beethover
Grillparzer speaks of music's invasion of the sphere of poetry, an
though he does not say it in so many words, it is probable that h
thought of the mature Beethoven as sinning in this sense. Yet, despit
indications from Grillparzer that Mozart represented his ideal in music
it does appear that he was an unconscious convert to the style of musi
manifested in the later works of his great contemporary and fellov
citizen. 'Ich habe Beethoven eigentlich geliebt', he writes in th
'Erinnerungen', and speaks of his boundless grief on hearing the new
of Beethoven's death.

Beethoven died on March 26th in this tragic year of 1827. Accordin
to Grillparzer's own account, he was approached by Schindler t
prepare a funeral oration, to be spoken by the actor Anschütz. It ma
truthfully be said that Grillparzer rose to the height of this suprem
occasion. The reason for this lay as much in his understanding o
Beethoven's art and his affection for the man as in his intuitive sens
of their common destiny. His own words reveal this:

> 'Ein Künstler war er (he writes in this oration) aber auch ein Mensch
> Mensch in jedem, im höchsten Sinn. Weil er von der Welt sich abschloß
> nannten sie ihn feindselig, und weil er der Empfindung aus dem Weg
> ging, gefühllos. Ach, wer sich hart weiß, der flieht nicht! Die feinste
> Spitzen sind es, die am leichtesten sich abstumpfen und biegen ode
> brechen. Das Übermaß der Empfindung weicht der Empfindung aus
> Er floh die Welt weil er in dem ganzen Bereich seines liebenden Gemüt
> keine Waffe fand, sich ihr zu widersetzen. Er entzog sich den Menschen
> nachdem er ihnen alles gegeben und nichts dafür empfangen hatte. E
> blieb einsam, weil er kein zweites Ich fand. Aber bis an sein Grab bewahrt
> er ein menschliches Herz allen Menschen, ein väterliches den Seinen, Gu
> und Blut der ganzen Welt.
>
> 'So war er, so starb er, so wird er leben für alle Zeiten'.

These words were among those spoken at Beethoven's grave; the
following passage appears in Grillparzer's address for the unveiling of
Beethoven's tombstone in the Autumn of the same year. Again stressing what Grillparzer and Beethoven had in common, this passage also
reveals the source of Grillparzer's reverence and awe: Beethoven's
music itself had taught him that here was an artist surpassing his own
genius, one whose strength of mind and spirit had enabled him to rise
superior to tragedy, resolving or transcending in 'Begeisterung' the

dire contrast between art and life in a way which Grillparzer himself could not achieve:

> 'Selten sind sie, die Augenblicke der Begeisterung, in dieser geistesarmen Zeit. Ihr, die ihr versammelt seid an dieser Stätte, tretet näher an dies Grab. Heftet eure Blicke auf den Grund, richtet alle eure Sinne gesamt auf das, was euch wissend ist von diesem Mann, und so laßt, wie die Fröste dieser späten Jahreszeit, die Schauder der Sammlung ziehen durch euer Gebein, wie ein Fieber tragt es hin in euer Haus, wie ein wohltätiges, rettendes Fieber, und hegt's und bewahrt's. Selten sind sie, die Augenblicke der Begeisterung, in dieser geistesarmen Zeit. Heiliget euch! Der hier liegt, war ein Begeisterter. Nach Einem trachtend, um Eines sorgend, für Eines duldend, alles hingebend für Eines, so ging dieser Mann durch das Leben.—Nicht Gattin hat er gekannt, noch Kind; kaum Freude, wenig Genuß.—Ärgerte ihn ein Auge, er riß es aus und ging fort, fort, fort bis ans Ziel. Wenn noch Sinn für Ganzheit in uns ist in dieser zersplitterten Zeit, so laßt uns sammeln an seinem Grab. Darum sind ja von jeher Dichter gewesen und Helden, Sänger und Gotterleuchtete, daß an ihnen die armen zerrütteten Menschen sich aufrichten, ihres Ursprungs gedenken und ihres Ziels'.

It is clear that Grillparzer must have apprehended this from his kinship with Beethoven and from experience of Beethoven's music itself. Would not this constitute a tacit admission that the composer had for him *successfully* extended the realm of musical utterance to embrace that also of poetry? Even if, however, Grillparzer could have admitted as much, he would still have held that Beethoven had achieved his triumph without demonstrating how it was effected, that is to say, through a medium not constituted to render explicit his attainment of this life's goal. Concluding his 'Erinnerungen an Beethoven', Grillparzer's verses, which tell of an intrepid voyager and pioneer performing a veritable *salto mortale* to reach his destination, include this expression:

> 'Als Sieger steht er schon am Ziel,
> Nur hat er keinen Weg gebahnt!'

Yet the recognition of the achievement itself is a significant admission, implying that Beethoven *had* paved the way, stimulating the spiritual imagination of his hearers to triumph with him over the travail and tragedy of this life and apprehend sublimity beyond it. For Grillparzer to entertain preconceived misgivings as to the validity of music as the medium, in face of such a boon, was to be unduly rationalistic. Grillparzer forgot that even when a like service is performed for us through the medium of words, in poetry or drama, as in the sublime *finale* of 'Faust', this is equally attained *per saltum* and is a process no whit the more explicit, demonstrate, or proven. As is stated in Wilhelm Meister's 'Lehrbrief': 'Das Beste wird nicht deutlich durch Worte'. Beethoven's music, too, is infinitely more accessible to the many than 'Faust', this almost unique example of drama transcending mortality. It is only to be regretted that such music should still fail to be universally recognized as performing what Grillparzer said it performed. One would have thought that the century which has elapsed since Grillparzer's words were written would have sufficed to remedy this critical shortcoming, making possible an advance in musical criticism now long overdue. There are, however, some indications that the time is perhaps not so far distant when musical critics in general, no longer content to allude vaguely to Beethoven's crystallization (in this or that work) of 'one big idea', will venture to say what the big idea really is.

The already mentioned important difference between Grillparzer and Beethoven, in spite of their great similarity, a difference not so much of outlook and destiny as of character, consists in the inability of the former as against the ability of the latter to rise superior to his own tragic experience of life. In this lies the root explanation of the fact that Beethoven, despite his expressed intention on repeated occasions during the last years of his life, could never bring himself to set to music the opera libretto he had solicited from Grillparzer. The latter's 'Melusina', essentially characteristic of its author, an 'elegischer Dichter' (as he described himself), was thereby unsuited to the genius of one for whom it was as impossible as it was for Goethe to go down in tragedy in his own creations[1]—as Raimund[-Grillparzer] does in this 'Melusina' libretto, like Jaromir, Sappho, Jason, and Ottokar before him. Sauer implies, further, that 'Melusina' falls between two stools, presumably those of naïve allegory and abstract symbolism; but the same might be said, with equal show of justice, of much in 'Faust' Part II, including Faust's journey of terror to the realm of the Mothers; in point of fact Raimund's sojourn in Melusina's kingdom is strictly comparable: it, too, is the realm of poetic creation, and the ring here has the same symbolic value as the key there, both standing for the poet's pen. Yet, if we hold that Grillparzer's 'Melusina' is a perfectly consistent allegory throughout, its temper is not such as

[1] In J. G. Robertson's judgement this inability to 'go down in tragedy before the life mystery' denotes a falling-off in poetic power in the mature Goethe. With the example of 'Egmont' and the significance of 'Faust' before us, above all, with the attainment of Beethoven's music before us, it seems permissible to dissent from this aesthetic opinion.

could commend it to Beethoven, whose inclinations lay rather in the direction of the heroic piece.

'Melusina' can truthfully be described as an allegorical presentation of the contrast between art and life in its most characteristic form for Grillparzer. He originally intended to write it as a drama and chose it as being suitable for composition as an opera libretto from among dramatic materials he had at hand when he was approached by Dietrichstein on Beethoven's behalf in 1823. In his 'Erinnerungen an Beethoven' Grillparzer speaks of having avoided as far as possible the introduction of 'reflektierende Elemente'; yet in spite of the fact that the work was written in little over a week, from March 15th to March 23rd, 1823, it contains sufficient of such elements to indicate how closely and cogently bound up the theme was with Grillparzer's own problem in life. Everything points to the fact that Melusina's kingdom represented for Grillparzer the world of poetry, a circumstance incidentally referred to by Tibal in his 'Etudes sur Grillparzer' and endorsed by August Sauer.[1] Raimund is unconsciously but irresistibly drawn away from the world of common life towards that of poetry. But Raimund does not find complete happiness in having renounced the world to embrace his ideal. He is tortured with doubts and filled with longings for life's certainties again. Yet when urged by Bertha and the rest to return—

'Zu der Erde stillem Glück',

he recovers and reaffirms his faith. It is only when Raimund betrays Melusina, in his attempt to convince the unbelieving world of her divinity and truth (just as Grillparzer, according to the confession of the two works which preceded 'Melusina', betrayed his own muse) and then discovers that aspect of her nature which fills him with horror and distaste, it is only then that he feels disposed to embrace the world again and forswears his love. But he has already tasted of real happiness in Melusina's kingdom, and all the temptations of the world are powerless to withhold him from seeking to atone and striving to recover what he has lost. He eventually perceives—too late—that true happiness was only realizable by a complete sacrifice of self to his ideal; he and Melusina are only by death again united in the end. The concluding words, which stamp the whole work 'zu einem der tiefsten Selbstbekenntnisse des ringenden Dichters',[2]

[1] André Tibal, 'Etudes sur Grillparzer', in Annales de l'Est, publiées par la Faculté des Lettres de l'Université de Nancy, 28e année-Fascicule I, Paris, 1914, p. 64. Sauer, A.: in 'Wke.' I. 4, p. 220.

[2] Cf. 'Wke.' I, 4, p. 220.

make it clear that the moral of the piece is the same as that of 'Sappho':

> ' Wem sich höhre Mächte künden,
> Muß auf ewig sich verbünden
> Oder nahen mög' er nie,
> Halben Dienst verschmähen sie'.

'Melusina' (subsequently set to music by Kreutzer), while thus chiefly interesting for its personal content, reveals incidentally a good deal respecting Grillparzer's prevailing attitude to music: it was one to which this traditional Viennese 'Romantic Opera in Three Acts' was well adapted. Grillparzer's numerous allusions to his passionate love of music further reveal his distrust and misprision of the art; he felt it to be a drug and an opiate and disapproved of Kathi's enslavement to it as much as his own, because it was a too welcome distraction and left 'hardly a corner for poetry' (T. 1631), his serious life's vocation. 'Die Leidenschaft für die Musick' he wrote, among a series of contributions 'Zu Fixlmüllners Charackteristik', at the end of 1827, 'stieg bei ihm bis zu einem solchen Grade von Unsinn, daß er geglaubt hätte der glücklichste Mensch zu seyn, wenn er sich dem Studium des Systems derselben ausschließlich, oder doch vorzugsweise hätte hingeben können' (T. 1661).

3. MORE 'TRISTIA' POEMS

Following this we find an entry assigning the cause of his 'ruination' to his failure to break with Kathi; he considers that his intention to contrive that their feelings should gradually cool off was responsible at the same time for a cooling off of his own enthusiasm for his art.

It is well to recall that Grillparzer was still beset with this anxiety about his engagement to Kathi Fröhlich during the same period that brought to a climax his relations with Marie. The 1827 poem, 'Willst du ich soll Hütten baun?' (G. 191), which Backmann attributes to matrimonial promptings of Kathi's, is, it is true, rather more likely to refer to Marie. Grillparzer's answer:

> 'Doch kehr' abends ich zurück,
> Und du harrst noch mein,
> Wenn ich erst mein selber bin,
> Bin ich auch wohl dein'

indicates the source of his main anxiety. He entertained other explanations, too, of his failure to fulfil himself, and these in turn are advanced.

In particular, of course, Grillparzer blamed the political conditions of his native land, including the censorship, and he blamed also at great length in two poems, 'Jugenderinnerungen im Grünen' completed in 1826, and 'Rechtfertigung' in 1827, the kind of misunderstanding he met with from modern critics of the Schlegel school. These passages of overworked and extravagant invective give the impression of being outlets for distress deriving from a different, hidden source. But the real irony lies in the circumstance that, so far from their being a valid explanation of Grillparzer's unproductiveness, this unproductiveness does not in fact exist. The period round about 1827 marks on the contrary the climax of Grillparzer's poetic production, though it was attended by, or rather derived from, such acute suffering that the poet (as we saw) could not think of it as satisfying or satisfactory; especially as his efforts did not achieve immediate fulfilment, or else produced works which seemed to him at this time totally unsuitable for publication. We are already familiar with the reasons for Grillparzer's disinclination to release his 'Treuer Diener' and have seen how he turned instead to other materials, not indeed as the mood took him, but as he needs must, because his tragic problem demanded interpretation and working out.

His first 'Sketch' of 'Hero und Leander', and also a 'personal' manuscript which advanced as far as Act IV, Scene 2, bearing on its title page the description of '*Ειδιλλιον*', together with the subsequent title in its earliest formulation (likewise in Greek)—this was Grillparzer's first task in this year; and it was undertaken manifestly not with an eye to publication, but as an almost instinctive 'private' reaction and self-admonition in a period of renewed love-happiness with Marie.

Such experience was with Grillparzer always dogged by compunctions and conscientious scruples, giving rise to doubts and suspicions, or to self-justification or self-reproach. These and allied feelings proved in turn favourable to the elaboration of sections at least of 'Der Traum ein Leben', 'Die Jüdin', and 'Der Bruderzwist', in addition to more diary 'confessions' (including the 'Briefe an Marie') and more 'Tristia'. It seems likely that Marie, who upon renewed acquaintance appeared more beautiful and enchanting than ever, was able at first to lull Grillparzer's dire suspicions and was in the Spring of 1827 as near vanquishing his fear of marriage as she or any other woman was at any time. This situation, however, was inevitably short-lived. Even supposing Marie had been, and continued to be, a pattern of loyalty and integrity, Grillparzer would nevertheless have been impelled to discover or manufacture grounds for criticizing or suspecting her, as long as she entertained 'designs' on him. It was in this year, after his recovery of himself at the cost of a definite and later regretted breach with Marie, just before Charlotte von Paumgartten's death in September, that he wrote (T. 1613–4):

> 'Kann man sein ganzes Wesen zur Passivität, zur Stumpfheit verdammen, weil man eigensinning und auf *eine* Art thätig seyn will, und diese eine Art sich uns versagt? Ich brauche eine große Krankheit, oder ein großes Unglück, die bis aufs Lebendige durchdringen, und den Menschen wieder erwecken, sonst ist auch der Dichter verloren.
>
> Für mich gab es nie eine andere Wahrheit als die Dichtkunst. . . . Dagegen hatten die Dinge des wirklichen Lebens, ja seine Wahrheiten und Ideen für mich ein Zufälliges, ein Unzusammenhängendes, Schattenähnliches, das mir nur unter der Hand der Poesie zu einem Nothwendigen ward. Von dem Augenblicke als ein Stoff mich begeisterte, kam Ordnung in meine Theilvorstellungen, ich wußte alles, ich erkannte alles, ich erinnerte mich auf alles, ich fühlte, ich liebte, ich freute mich, ich war ein Mensch. Aber dieser Zustand vorüber trat wieder das alte Chaos ein. Mein ganzer Antheil blieb immer der Poesie vorbehalten, und ich schaudere über meinen Zustand als Mensch, wenn die immer seltener und schwächer werdenden Anmahnungen von Poesie endlich ganz aufhören sollten'.

Seventeen months later, suspecting that his concern and sacrifice for art had indeed been in vain, or had been misdirected, and that it had probably cost him his life's happiness, he wrote deploring his hasty judgement of the earlier time (T. 1722):

> 'Nachmittags bei Daffinger. Die Frau wunderschön. Habe mich doch gelangweilt. Eine gestörte Empfindung stellt sich bei mir nicht wieder ein. Auch sie scheint durch mein brüskes Benehmen von ihrer frühern Neigung ziemlich zurück gekommen zu seyn. Der Mann malträtirt sie im eigentlichsten Verstande. Wie weit ganz mit Unrecht, weiß ich nicht. Ich traue nicht leicht derlei unschuldigen Mienen. Diese Frau vollends ist mir ein Räthsel. Entweder ihre Unbefangenheit ist wahr, und dann hat mein vorschneller Unsinn das einzige verscherzt, was mich aus meiner gegenwärtigen widerlichen Lage villeicht noch hätte reißen können; oder es ist Lüge, und dann, dann freilich ist alles in Ordnung'.

These words recall the passage from his fifth letter, alluding to the situation in 1825, as also to the one in 1827 when (probably) the letters were transcribed or re-edited: 'ich habe dich nie verstanden. Doch ist es nicht natürlich? Der Mensch versteht alles, nur das Völlig-Einfache nicht, und—Marie!—das Unerhört-Künstliche!' In the course of this year, 1827, Grillparzer also felt prompted to translate a couplet from Calderon (G. 478 and Anm.):

> Die wahre Kunst zu lieben,
> Ist lieben ohne Kunst,

which likewise betokens a revival of Grillparzer's distrust and heralds the then approaching separation from Marie.

But the most eloquent record of this crisis in Grillparzer's career is contained in a succession of poems which found a place in his 'Tristia' cycle (Nos. 6–10). Two of them, the most famous ones, 'Verwünschung' and 'Trennung' (Nos. 6 and 9), being very outspoken, were originally not intended for inclusion in the cycle, but they seem to be arranged now in their proper psychological context and to tell with the other poems their own story.

The poem 'Verwünschung' reflects Grillparzer's apprehension, at its extremest pitch, of Marie's 'dæmonic' character as portrayed in Elga and Lukrezia, and concludes its melodramatic exorcism of her with the stanza:

> 'Und so gemischt aus Wonne und aus Grauen,
> Stehst du, ein Todesengel, neben mir,
> Ein Engel zwar, doch auch ein Tod zu schauen,
> Und wer da lebt, der hüte sich vor dir'.

The next poem is entitled 'Verwandlungen' and consists of three parts, 'Klage', 'Trost', and 'Epilog'. In the first of these Grillparzer alludes to the night and desolation that has overtaken him; the second (which includes a fleeting reference to Charlotte v. Paumgartten's death) speaks of the hope of a new sunrise; while the conclusion to the poem condemns that hope as delusive.

The poem 'Porträtmalerin' calls for more detailed commentary. Rizy (we saw) assigned it to this period, doubtless correctly. Not universal in its force, but intensely personal and occupying a cardinal place in Grillparzer's 'life-poem', it signalizes the ripening of the poet's suspicion that it is Daffinger who retains possession of Marie's being and soul: Daffinger, the portrait painter, so widely famous for his uncanny power to impart a quality of life to his portraits—an observation applying essentially to his remarkable portraits of Marie, which literally seem to breathe. The poem closes with this beautiful mournful cadence:

> 'Ach, ich kenne Malerhände,
> Die beleben ihr Gemälde

Schöpferisch mit wahrem Leben.
Doch die Seele, die sie geben,
Ward dem Urbild erst geraubt'.

This poem recalls 'Sinnpflanze'. The reason why it is entitled 'Di Porträtmalerin' is that for Grillparzer it alludes thus to her (das Urbild who had fallen a prey to Daffinger and was now to become his *wife* while at the same time disguising from others the fact that it refers t him who claimed her for a victim. If it were called 'Porträtmaler' simply, there would certainly have been less scope for the variou ingenious interpretations of the poem that have yet been offered.

In order to understand clearly the next poem, 'Trennung', it is agai only necessary to recall what we have learned of Daffinger and of hi relations to Marie. In it Grillparzer takes leave of Marie, apparentl moreover, at her request; for in the tenth stanza we find the words 'Denn wie du jetzt bemühst dich, halb vergebens/Zu malen dir die Band als schwere Last', suggesting that she was weary at last of th hopeless struggle to win Grillparzer for herself. He, on the other hand contends that there is something which constantly intrudes betwee them:

'Ob ich dies Etwas, ewig störend, kenne?
O gebe Gott, daß ich es nicht erkannt!
Denn ist es, was ich denk', obgleich nicht nenne,
So bist du, Weib, in einer furchtbarn Hand.

In einer Hand, die einmal schon die Klauen
Nach deiner Jugend Blüten ausgestreckt,
Und die, zum zweitenmal genaht in Grauen,
Ihr Opfer hält, bis es die Erde deckt'.

These lines explain themselves. A great deal of the rest of the poem applies itself—like the 'Briefe an Marie'—to insisting on the magnitude of Marie's loss, the depth of her fall, the contrast between her poet-lover's orbit and Daffinger's low and vicious world.

The concluding poem among the 'Tristia' of this sequence is entitled 'Sorgenvoll':

'Mein Kummer ist mein Eigentum,
Den geb' ich nicht heraus',

implying that Grillparzer is resisting the impulse to seek relief in poetic confession: he will cherish his grief in silence till the end.

But then must occur by contrast the poem 'Freundeswort', which is given a later place in the same cycle (No. 16) and is a reply (like 'Rechtfertigung') to Bauernfeld's lines of encouragement. Bauernfeld, it will be recalled, knowing of Grillparzer's sufferings (to judge by the first two stanzas of 'Freundeswort' already quoted)[1] had apparently exhorted him to use his gifts as *artist* and *poet* to confess them. The two remaining stanzas give Grillparzer's retort: it implies that his works of this period have been held back because they were for him veritable and ill-disguised cries from the heart:

> 'Ach, die Worte und die Bilder
> Sind für selbstgemachte Leiden!
> Wer kann Flammen, wild und wilder,
> In Gewand, verhüllend, kleiden?
>
> Drum mein Wort, es sei der Aufschrei,
> Nicht an Ton und Maß gebunden,
> Und die Farbe, die mir gut däucht,
> Hier! das Blut aus meinen Wunden'.

One would judge this poem as almost contemporary with the lines, 'Wohlan denn nun . .', when Daffinger's engagement to Marie had been announced, and Grillparzer, seeing his worst fears for her so soon realized, felt that the outrage must be avenged and the villain of his 'Treuer Diener' 'exposed':

> 'Auf daß Gemeinheit zu den Siegen allen
> Die schon sie feiert, nicht noch Den erwirbt,
> Daß kundlos ihre Tat',

We saw that in releasing his 'Treuer Diener' Grillparzer clearly felt that he was uttering in lamentation his own sufferings and expressing outraged feelings; for him to describe this tragedy and 'elegy', his greatest work so far in an ascending series, as a virtual *outcry* is illuminating and apt. It marks a climax of his development in this practice. In the diary passage written about this time, when Grillparzer says (T. 1617): 'Ich bin eine elegische Natur', he is referring, not primarily to his lyrical efforts, but to his dramatic poetry. The next entry in his diary, another contribution 'zu Fixlmüllners Charakteristik', recalls our 'motto' epigram:

> 'Er war zugleich Zuseher und Schauspiel. Aber der Zuseher konnte nicht Plan und Stoff des Stückes ändern, noch das Stück den Zuseher zum Mitspieler machen'.

The end of the year 1827 produces a series of these self-satirical commentaries, in one of which he repeats (T. 1656):

> 'Die Natur seines poetischen Talentes war durchaus *elegisch*. Es machte ihm Anfangs eine angenehme Empfindung seine Noth und was ihn

[1] See p. 124.

bedrückte den Leuten poetisch zu klagen. Je älter er aber wurde, um so widerlicher dünkte es ihn, sich vor Zusehern zu entblößen',

and the following entry affirms (T. 1657):

> 'Es war ein Gefühl in ihm, daß man die Geheimniße seines Innern nicht zur Schau tragen solle'.

That a process of poetical production so painful should be succeeded by an experience so bitter as the one we have described after 'Bancban' was performed in February, 1828, explains in his account of the proposed transaction the poet's concluding resolve (T. 1624):

> 'Ich muß meinem Vaterlande Lebewohl sagen, oder die Hoffnung auf immer aufgeben, einen Platz unter den Dichtern meiner Zeit einzunehmen. Gott! Gott! ward es denn Jedem so schwer gemacht, das zu seyn, was er könnte und sollte!'

This is the time, too, of his revised epigram (G. 485):

> 'Auszeichnung hier erwarte nie,
> Denn das System verbeuts,
> Man hängt das Kreuz nicht ans Genie,
> Nein das Genie ans Kreuz',

which, with its reassuring candour, is a characteristic example of Grillparzer's skill in this genre.

There is a genuine *dramatic* (not really 'elegiac') quality in Grillparzer's 'Treuer Diener', one which we have already referred to and which Grillparzer has in mind when he thus styles himself a genius. It is a quality observed by him as absent from the German drama in general, as the following passage records (T. 1626):

> 'Sie sind auf ihrem Theater an den prächtigen Wortschwall gewohnt; die Handlung mit unbedeckter Blöße ärgert ihr keusches Auge. Ich fühle mich aber gerade jenes Mittelding zwischen Göthe und Kotzebue wie ihn das Drama braucht. Die Deutschen könnten villeicht ein Theater bekommen, wenn mein Streben nicht ohne Erfolg bleibt'.

When we read these lines we think primarily of the 'Treuer Diener', the fragment 'Esther', and particularly of 'Hero und Leander' as vindicating Grillparzer's contention and realizing his aim. During the rest of the year 1828, and the early part of the following year, the latter work was brought to completion. It is his masterpiece.

CHAPTER VIII

'DES MEERES UND DER LIEBE WELLEN'

1. LIFE-CONTEXT OF THE WORK

'DES Meeres und der Liebe Wellen', the culminating product of Grillparzer's best period and the only love-tragedy in the German language which invites and sustains comparison with Shakespeare's 'Romeo and Juliet', is, paradoxically enough, less adequately appreciated in its dramatic quality than it should be. This fact is due to its supreme excellence in a subsidiary respect. Grillparzer's skill in the portrayal of women characters, among whom Hero holds pride of place, has given rise to a tendency (shared even by his most recent editors and critics) to dwell on this aspect of his achievement and to attempt to explain Hero's intimate and human appeal by representing her as the poet's romantic ideal of womanhood. ' "Hero" wie keine andere Dichtung ist aus unerfüllter Sehnsucht emporgewachsen,' writes Backmann in the opening of his Introduction in the standard critical edition. The objection to this tendency is that it seems to ignore not only the significant fact that Hero herself is drawn from real life, but also that the work, as a whole, is based on the author's actual experience.

The first existing reference by Grillparzer to this material occurs in the summer of 1820, after the completion of 'Das goldene Vlies', and consists simply of the words 'Hero und Leander' entered in his note-book (T. 320). There is no reason to suppose that Grillparzer had previously considered utilizing it; the natural circumstance of his including in the subsequent make-up of the principal characters certain features and motives from early plans and fragments (some traceable as far back as to his earliest adolescent yearnings and literary discoveries) is no indication of the contrary.

After an interruption of some weeks, during which Grillparzer seems to have studied and thought about his project, consulting in particular Passow's edition of the Grammarian Musaeus's 'Epyll' of Hero and Leander, he notes down the following plan (T. 322):

'Hero und Leander. Wie kein Mann sie rühren kann, und sie Priesterin der Venus wird. Dann sieht sie Leander. Beim Wasserhohlen im Hain der Göttin findet sie ihn wieder. Er schöpft ihr Wasser. Der dritte Akt schließt damit: daß Leander, zum erstenmahl nach Sestos zu dem Thurm der Hero hinüberschwimmt, zu ihr hinaufsteigt, nachdem sie ihm einen Mantel hinabgeworfen, sich damit zu bedecken. Gespräch der Liebe. Hero hört ein Geräusch außen, und indem sie die Lampe nimmt, um nachzusehen, was es sey, heißt sie unterdeß Leander in ihr Schlafgemach treten. Vierter Akt. Hero mit dem Gefühle als *Weib*. Der Priester hat etwas von dem Verständniß bemerkt, und Fischer haben ihm von der Lampe erzählt, die allnächtlich am Thurme leuchte. Er ahndet den Zusammenhang, und beschließt, streng und ernst will er das Unerlaubte im Keime ersticken. Hero, die die Nacht gewacht, ist schläfrig. Er gönnt ihr nicht Zeit zu schlafen; er beschäftigt sie unausgesetzt. Der Abend kommt. Hero zündet die Lampe an, will sich wach erhalten, schläft aber doch ein. Der Priester löscht die Lampe aus. 5Akt. Fischer finden die Leiche Leanders'.

If, in addition to Passow, we take into account the other sources that Grillparzer must surely have been acquainted with, notably Ovid's epistolary exchange between the lovers in his *Heroides*, Schiller's ballad 'Hero und Leander', and the German folksong 'Es waren zwei Königskinder',[1] the most novel feature of this plan, as in the finished work, is its implication that Hero is made to suffer because she neglects her duty and breaks her vows—shown in Grillparzer's introduction of the figure of the high-priest as an Agent of Just Retribution. This innovation is, however, characteristic of and natural to Grillparzer—quite apart from the consideration that it meets the requirement of dramatic economy. There can be little doubt that his interest in this work from the start lay in the affinity of its theme to his own life-problem—in its exemplification for him, on a general human plane, of the contrast between duty and desire.

At the time we are speaking of the poet, who had recently accepted the duties and responsibilities of *Theaterdichter*, engaged to deliver works at regular intervals to the *Hofburgtheater* of his native city, was distracted by his entanglement with Charlotte Paumgartten, whom he had styled the 'tragic muse' of his Fleece trilogy. The character of Hero in Grillparzer's 1820 plan (unlike that of the chaste, natural, and naïve heroine of the finished work) accords with that of Charlotte, as it does also with that of Medea. This early (and immature) conception of Hero, who deliberately infringes the temple rule and repeatedly breaks her vows, seems to be based in part on the poet's interpretation of Charlotte's nature and temperament. The intention was clearly to

[1] I. Erk und Böhm: 'Deutscher Liederhort', Vol. I, p. 293; Avenarius: 'Balladenbuch', p. 98. A different version in Des Knaben Wunderhorn, 'Es waren zwei Edelkönigs-Kinder'. Cf. below, p. 186, fn. 2.

create a work in which tragedy should result from a deliberate and punishable neglect of duty—a neglect analogous, incidentally, to Grillparzer's own, or what would have been his own, as he thought, if he had been disposed to behave in a manner corresponding to that of his Hero and Leander.

This presumption regarding Grillparzer's earliest intentions affords a satisfactory explanation of his failure to proceed with this plan, which implied a bias in favour of duty and too rigorous and reproving an attitude towards the lovers—however understandable in his circumstances this view of the material may have been. The difficulty of making the priest—destined of necessity to avenge duty's infringement—appear to act in a manner entirely free from personal motives was probably foreseen by the dramatist. Not to succeed in this would have spelt failure to perform his poetic task in conformity with the laws of tragedy. Even in the finished work Grillparzer only 'half-succeeded' (T. 1893) in this particular, as he himself recognized, and as is discussed below (p. 181 f.). Yet some human agency of intervention was indispensable. Unlike the legend of Romeo and Juliet, where the inter-family feud provides spontaneously for this personification of the opposing principle, the material of Hero and Leander, as it presented itself to Grillparzer, offered only the impersonal sea as a counteractive factor: the figure of the priest, supplied by Grillparzer to cover this lack, had to be retained. At one time he even thought of making him a 'Priester des Neptun', but soon abandoned this pagan notion.[1] For, as a modern poet, Grillparzer was bound to dispense with the introduction of Divine personages from antique Mythology and to exclude all the celestial machineryof Retribution present in his sources. We observe how, in the finished work, he attempted to compromise between Divine and human intervention. The priest is intended to appear, not as acting in any respect of his own free will, but as an Agent of Higher Causation. Grillparzer was himself not satisfied with the result, and he writes in his diary even as late as 1837 (T. 3247): 'Vor allem ist die Figur des Priesters zu kurz gekommen'.

Another reason why Grillparzer hesitated to proceed with the execution of his 1820 plan is likely to have been that he was unable to think of any other way of concluding the play than by causing Hero to commit suicide. We may suppose, however, that he would be disposed to reject suicide for several reasons. A suicide committed in madness or out of frustrated passion, such as seems actually to have

[1] Cf. 'Wke.' I. 4, p. xiii f.

been contemplated,[1] would have been too unedifying; and one committed by way of atonement and in recognition of guilt would have been altogether too reminiscent of Sappho's end. A suicide, on the other hand, on account of grief would scarcely have suited the character of his heroine as then conceived, if 'heroine' she was intended to be; nor would it have accorded with the trend of his original theme. Yet the character of Hero as indicated in the early plan, though it did not permit of a catastrophe by means of the obvious device of suicide, was itself better adapted to Grillparzer's original 'tendency' than the later one. But this tendency too, as we shall see, is later, in effect, reversed. The device adopted in the finished work of causing Hero to die of a broken heart may have been suggested by Marlowe, whom Grillparzer did not read until 1822 or later (T. 1293); it may also be in part due to Grillparzer's belief that Marie Piquot[2] and Charlotte Paumgartten[3] died of broken hearts. The early Hero, in any event, could not have ended so; she seems to have been intended to behave in a manner deserving of censure and punishment by practising wilful deceit and subterfuge. On the whole, considering what subsequently grew out of his original plan, we doubtless have good cause to be grateful that for one reason or another Grillparzer was unable to complete his work at this time.

Not until over five years later, the winter of 1825–6, does any further reference to work on the projected tragedy occur. It is true that Grillparzer's diary for the year 1822 contains the note referred to above, to the effect that Marlowe had written a 'Hero and Leander', and it is safe to conclude that Grillparzer soon investigated further; in point of fact, most of Grillparzer's subsequent departures in detail from his early plan might, as shown below, be ascribed to Marlowe's influence. But there was also another influence at work, parallel, as one might say, to Marlowe's, and more important: Grillparzer's own experience with Marie von Smolenitz; yet, even as late as January, 1827, this does not take positive form, and we find him on January 8th still struggling with his original conception of Hero and stressing aspects of her nature which belonged, not to Marie, but to Charlotte.

But Grillparzer had by then completed his 'Treuer Diener', and we soon have evidence, later confirmed by the poet himself, of the influence on Hero, too, of 'Marie in aller ihrer damals wirklich himmlischen Schönheit'. The first indications appear in the poet's first ('miniature') manuscript. Backmann describes this MS., which succeeds a rough 'sketch' of the whole tragedy begun on January 8,

[1] Cf. Sauer's Intro. in Cotta^{v}, p. 73. [2] Cf. T. 1109. [3] Cf. T. 1613–6.

1827, as being embarked upon by Grillparzer, not with a view to publication, but for his own private satisfaction and needs, as being of a format 'ganz intim' and inscribed on the cover with the term *Ειδιλλιον*.' The title, too, given on the inside of the cover, and corresponding literally to the title finally adopted, is expressed in Greek: *Τὰ τοῦ ἔρωτος καί τῆς θαλάσσης χύματα*.[1]

The significance of these indications invites speculation. Wedel-Parlow affirms, probably with justice, that the style: *Ειδύλλιον* as used by Grillparzer implies that the work was for him 'ein Bildchen . ., eine verschwiegene Huldigung, der "wunderschönen Frau" (Marie von Smolenitz) dargebracht'.[2] The rest of the evidence supports this interpretation. But why the secrecy? The answer, as before, is that Grillparzer could not bear to contemplate the exposure of himself and others—the scandal even—which he feared would attend the completion and publication of his poetic confessions.

'Ein Treuer Diener seines Herrn', finished, but locked up in his desk, was altogether too revealing of the triangular situation in which he was involved with Marie and the notorious miniature-portraitist, his rival. The egregious Daffinger was already celebrating Marie's great beauty in portraits and miniatures that seemed to breathe with life. And this is perhaps the reason why Grillparzer obscurely alludes to his new dramatic work, containing its own intimate and life-like portrait of Marie, as an *Εἰδύλλιον*, a 'miniature' in which he thought to equal, if not outshine, his rival for her appreciation and regard. There are indications that Marie deliberately fostered this artistic rivalry. Of nearly the same date, too, is Grillparzer's echoing of Correggio[3] in 'Jugenderinnerungen im Grünen' with the outcry, 'Doch Meister, schaut, ein Maler bin ich auch!' And, indeed, the dramatist had good cause for pride in his skill and mastery: his 'portraits' of Marie in the characters of Erny ("Treuer Diener') and Hero are truly astonishing achievements. Moreover, they have their proper place and universal value in dramatic masterpieces as larger wholes—

[1] Cf. 'Wke.' I. 4, p. xvii. [2] Cf. op. cit., p. 106.

[3] Cf. Backmann, Jb. xxxii, p. 37; also p. 11 above, 'das stolze *anch' iov*, (Hilda Schulhof). In reality it does not seem reasonable to assume that Correggio's words on seeing Raphael's 'St. Cecilia': *Anch' io sono pittore!* were uttered in self-vindication and *pride*; they appear rather to express a crestfallen mood: *And I call myself a painter!* A parallel instance occurs in Goethe's 'Italian Journey'. Off Naples on his return from Sicily, Goethe tells of the priest from Constantinople who, being invited to admire the prospect of Naples before him, as compared with Constantinople, concedes 'sehr pathetisch': *Anche questa è una citta!*

It may, indeed, be questioned on another count whether Grillparzer intended any allusion to Correggio: in order to 'echo' Correggio (as misreported?) he would have needed to say, for his part: Ein *Dichter* bin ich auch! Jealousy, we may suppose, prompts his use in this context of the term *Maler*, as indeed on other occasions about this time.

examples of great art; for the sake of these the poet, like a 'faithful servant', might well feel perforce constrained to renounce 'life' and allow Daffinger (so he told himself) to prevail over him in his wooing of Marie. After the poet's 'Trennung' (G. 84, 9; Sept., 1827) from Marie, and after it became clear that she would marry his rival, Grillparzer determined to vindicate his own attitude and bearing by publishing his 'Treuer Diener'; he also soon took up his 'Hero' again, commencing a second MS., this time in a format of 'representative size' ![1]

Any temptation we might feel rather to interpret Grillparzer's curious designation of his first MS. as indicating that he thought of it, in the specific sense of the term he used, as an 'idyll' is countered by a moment's reflection as to the true literary character of this work and as to the meaning of the title which he concurrently supplied. The fact that this title is first expressed 'exclusively' in Greek, so far from revealing its source to be discoverable in Musaeus (cf. Backmann, 'Wke.' I. 4, pp. xiv, 255), suggests rather that it had, like *Εἰδύλλιον*, in the first place a personal bearing and significance for Grillparzer himself; it denotes in what sense 'jene tief im Menschenleben wurzelnde Fabel'[2] allegorized his own lot; it meant that the tragedy of Hero and Leander was typical of his own (private) tragedy.

The tragic arises from a contrast between Necessity and Freedom which is felt as harmful.[3] These are but general terms: Necessity might in a given instance be equated with the World or *duty*, and Freedom with the Self or *desire*.[4] In normal human experience there is apparent equilibrium between these counteracting forces. But the balance may easily be disturbed, and such disturbances, which, if serious, provide the stock-in-trade of tragic poets, may occur in either direction, too much on the side of 'duty' or too much on the side of 'desire'. 'Ein treuer Diener seines Herrn' reflects an interpretation of Grillparzer's actual situation in the former sense, while 'Des Meeres und der Liebe Wellen' does so in the latter sense. If Bancban, in a moment of great emotional stress (or of insight, or liberal conviction) had acted in opposition to his duty, or forsworn it, and so betrayed the trust placed in him and sacrificed his honour and perhaps his life, the position would have been strictly comparable to that in 'Des Meeres und der Liebe Wellen'.

[1] Cf. 'Wke.' I. 4, p. xvii. According to Backmann's revised opinion (Jb. xxxi, p. 14) the main work on this manuscript was performed in the year 1828.

[2] Gottfried Keller's phrase in opening paragraph of 'Romeo und Julia auf dem Dorfe', alluding to the kindred legend of that work.

[3] In comedy the same kind of contrast in milder form is felt as harmless.

[4] In comedy the contrast—relieved of suffering, provocative of laughter rather than tears—might be between Society or convention and the Individual or liberty.

The romantic-sounding title of this work provides in a perhaps unsuspected sense a clue to Grillparzer's fundamental intention in creating it. In reference to what has already been said regarding his tendency to give a wider human meaning to problems which affected him personally, it is interesting to recall that he explains the title of this work as having been chosen to indicate the general significance of the work itself. In his 'Selbstbiographie' he writes:

> 'Der etwas prätiös klingende Titel: Des Meeres und der Liebe Wellen sollte im voraus auf die romantische[1] oder vielmehr *menschlich allgemeine Behandlung* der antiken Fabel hindeuten'.[2]

The title 'Hero und Leander' would have been suggestive, he feared, of a treatment of his subject as a simple story for its own sake and would have directed attention rather to the content than the intent of the work. Strictly speaking, the title 'Des Meeres und der Liebe Wellen' has all the force of the once popular sub-titles to novels in the days when authors strove to make their titles descriptive of their aims, and their novels really interpretative (often unfortunately too pointedly and moralizingly) of human life. A great drama, just as a great novel or any other work of art, must have a general significance for mankind, or it will fail in the long run to appeal. Great poets have always, even in spite of themselves, thought and written in terms of human life, and in creating masterpieces their attention has always been directed to some fundamental aspect of human nature or destiny.

In the historical and critical edition of the works we are invited to interpret the title 'Des Meeres und der Liebe Wellen' as indicating the metaphorical relation (if any) between the waves of the sea and those of love, or alternatively, the mythological association of Venus with the ocean waves.[3] But if we consider the annihilating (and, of course, symbolical) part played by the sea waves in Grillparzer's work, as in all other versions of the story of Hero and Leander, we realize that the title has a less superficial meaning than this. It indicates that Grillparzer's philosophic intention, if we may so term it, was to exemplify in his work the strife and the struggle for superiority between two main elemental forces in human life. The waves of the sea are the irresistible forces without; calm and gentle and smooth-flowing at ordinary times, when *duty* is observed; but storm-tossed and angry and powerful to destroy when not reckoned with or ignored. The sea represents in Grillparzer's conception the compelling forces of the world, in all

[1] 'Romantisch' is here used (mainly) in the sense of 'allegorical'.
[2] 'Wke.' I. 16, p. 230. Cf. also T. 3247. [3] Cf. 'Wke.' I. 4, p. 255.

their cruelty, spite, malignance, and vengefulness towards the rash or daring spirits who, yielding to or following *desire*, try to appropriate for themselves a happiness of their own. In so doing they ignore the facts of human life which demand their consideration, and life avenges itself on them for this neglect, as the waves of the sea avenge themselves on the importunate swimmer, or punish adventurers who imprudently set sail in a craft not built to withstand the storms. The title 'Des Meeres und der Liebe Wellen' contains, that is to say, the idea of the contrast between duty and desire.

In the opening acts of the play Hero is at peace with herself and, like a poet not torn away from *his* chosen activity by conflicting desires, she is contented with her lot and willingly takes a binding oath of allegiance to *her* chosen activity, committing herself, inexperienced and untried, to a life-long sacrifice of herself as a priestess. Like a poet who enters into a contract to deliver works at regular intervals to an official body, as we saw that Grillparzer had done to his subsequent regret at the time of planning this work; or like one who for art's sake renounces love and happiness, as Grillparzer was persuaded he did later, when they were to be had for the asking in the person of Marie v. Smolenitz: so does Hero (in whom Marie is incidentally portrayed) confidently undertake to observe demands made upon her before she is capable of realizing what difficulties and sacrifice this may entail. Hero is no more fitted by nature to lead the austere and exalted life of a priestess than Grillparzer came to feel himself to be fitted to carry out his partly self-imposed, partly supra-imposed, duties as a poet during the years of his trials and of the planning and writing of 'Hero'.

When love comes into Hero's life she forgets, true woman as she is, as Grillparzer himself felt tempted to forget, everything else: in the first place duty, then reason, caution, respect, filial affection, and the whole of her environment, in a new world of all-absorbing happiness and desire. Here, too, she is perfectly at peace with herself, and there is no trace of conflict in her. Grillparzer distrusted love for this very reason, that it has such power to blind and betray its victims; he distrusted it as a cruel, irresistible, elemental, and disintegrating force in human nature. It is because Hero, in becoming a victim of this force, so totally forgets her duty, that she is made to suffer in the end; not because of nature's blind or jealous spite as evinced in the storm at sea. Like Hero, Leander too is a victim of love. Like Medea herself in 'Das goldene Vlies', both are betrayed by love and both become involved in guilty conduct. It is surely a too subjective and inadequate pronouncement to say that the love of Hero and Leander was too beautiful to exist in a harsh, cold world, as so many critics, including Volkelt and Reich, have conspired to agree. Nor can we say with Jellinek that the catastrophe is due to the invervention of blind Chance,[1] nor with Mell that it is due to Hero's tired feeling in Act IV.[2] If this were so there would be no excuse whatsoever for the intervention of the priest in the play. This figure is not introduced because Grillparzer was in need of a villain for his piece. Although he naturally had understanding and sympathy for the lovers, he still stood mainly (at this stage) on the side of duty. Hero's conduct (as well as Leander's) was, in his opinion, punishable; and the priest, as we saw, was introduced as the Agent of what was intended to appeal to the audience as Just Retribution. Hero is made to suffer and atone at the hands of the offended and avenging world to which she owed allegiance and which demanded submission to its mandates and duty done. In like manner would a poet suffer the loss of his reputation, and sacrifice his honour and the respect of the world, and his own self-respect, if he deserted his sworn duty and his art. Grillparzer's conception of his duty as a poet, and the difficulty of its fulfilment, is reflected in his representation of Hero and her desertion of her duty as a priestess.

From what has just been said it is easy to appreciate Grillparzer's progress in 1828, after Marie's marriage to Daffinger, from his intimate first MS. to his 'representative' second MS., with a view to eventual stage production: what we have observed is a natural process and the outcome of a fundamental tendency on the part of the author to treat of problems which affected him personally in his struggle to achieve his poetic destiny. He was doubtless convinced that these personal problems had a wider human significance, which it was his mission as a dramatist to convey. The morally didactic or rather hortative tendency of much that he wrote (as exemplified, for instance, in the early plan of this work, as also perhaps in his formulation of its title)[3] forces us to conclude that the dramatist was not merely actuated by a subconscious desire to seek 'Selbstbefreiung von lastenden Seelenzuständen' through his works. We may perhaps be justified in claiming that Grillparzer's conception of his true function as a dramatist, if he ever formulated any such conception, was that he should select and present his material in such a way as to interpret precisely

[1] Jellinek, M. H.: 'Die Sage von Hero und Leander in der Dichtung'; Berlin, 1890, p. 71.

[2] Jb. xviii, p. 18.

[3] The title 'Hero' (or 'Hero und Leander'), like 'Bancban' for 'Ein treuer Diener seines Herrn', is commonly used for the sake of brevity. This should not be taken to imply a criticism of the longer forms, despite their 'difficulty' and consequent misinterpretation. Grillparzer's titles are characteristic and therefore ultimately preferable to any less 'universal' ones.

those general human problems of which he had gained a deep knowledge and experience in his own person.

A third MS., which is fragmentary, followed; but up to February, 1829, 'Hero' has been satisfactorily composed only as far as Act IV, and setting to work upon this Act again Grillparzer found that the Hero he had previously understood was lost to him now (T. 1692). But just at this time he was again becoming interested in Marie. One can observe how his interest grows hand in hand with the progress of this fourth MS., and in less than a week 'Hero' is finished for the first time and Grillparzer is once more under the spell of Marie's great beauty and charm.[1] She is an enigma for him; but the pity still lived on which he had felt for her, because he had distrusted her and forsworn his love, and so caused her great unhappiness and surrendered her to a 'coarse and brutal' husband.[2] It does not seem at all improbable that Marie had complained of Daffinger in similar words at the time of her earlier relations with Grillparzer, as now again in 1829, and had so given him the suggestion for Hero's remarks about her brother in Act I. One might follow up the argument and say that Grillparzer is thinking of himself in portraying Leander as a totally different kind of man from Daffinger[3] or Hero's brother, and as an acceptable lover for Hero or Marie. Apart from this, there are certainly some other undeniable resemblances between Leander and Grillparzer himself, as we shall see. That Daffinger, too, 'der stets Übermütige', as Costenoble called him,[4] served Grillparzer as a model for Naukleros, especially in respect to the latter's relation to Leander, may be regarded as established.[5] But Marie's nature in particular seems to have been admired and studied in an objective way by the poet, to the advantage of his heroine, much as he appears to have studied Charlotte Paumgartten for Medea in 'Das goldene Vlies'. He seems to have observed Marie in a manner which enabled him to make his Hero perhaps the finest of all his women characters and to give her so surpassingly human and intimate appeal.[6]

One of the happy consequences for his work of Grillparzer's renewed interest in and love for Marie in 1829 seems to have been that it influenced and inspired him to re-cast the conclusion (T. 1709) and thus to correct what we have described as his bias on the side of

[1] T. 1695, 98, 1701, 09, 13, 17, 22, 24, 29, 35.

[2] T. 1638: Du bist an die Gemeinheit verkauft, etc. T. 1722: Der Mann malträtirt sie im eigentlichsten Verstande, etc.

[3] Cf. particularly T. 1638 and the poem 'Trennung', G. 84, 9.

[4] Cf. op. cit., I. p. 220, Oct. 8, 1822.

[5] Cf. Backmann, Jb. xxxi, p. 35.

[6] This effect thus results from conditions sharply contrasting with those hitherto supposed to be operative, alluded to in the opening paragraph of this chapter (p. 151).

duty. Hero now dies, convincingly portrayed, of a broken heart. Any bias, since it is beyond the capacity of a poet's human feeling to achieve perfect impartiality, is now in favour of the lovers; and we are disposed, or rather predisposed, to acquiesce in this. It is, indeed, easy to understand that the poet who came to feel such a deep sympathy for Hero as he now conceived her could not remain strictly faithful to the sterner creed of duty. As in the case of 'Sappho', where a lyrical feeling of elation had led to a complete change of attitude on the author's part, Grillparzer seems to have allowed himself to be carried away, fortunately we may say, from the sternness of his preconceived standpoint by the sheer emotional force of what he came to write. One might almost say that the poet in Grillparzer again rises superior to the dramatist in him, as with 'Sappho'—or perhaps rather, in this case, to Grillparzer the moralist.

Thus completed, 'Des Meeres und der Liebe Wellen' was handed over to the copyist on February 26, 1829, and presumably submitted for approval and performance at the Hofburgtheater soon afterwards; but delays occurred, and the work was not produced until April 5, 1831, when it proved a failure. The first three Acts were greeted with 'frenzied applause', the last two were received in stony silence. Laube,[1] who as theatre-manager successfully revived it in 1851, attributed this failure to the inadequate performance of Hero's rôle by Julie Gley (later Frau Rettich), especially in the difficult fourth Act ('a dramatic steppe'). But Laube may have been in part mistaken: the naïve Viennese public, loth to contemplate tragedy, may simply have resented the stern measures of the priest—the explanation of their cold reception of the tragic *dénouement* may be as obvious as that. Grillparzer was at this time inclined to over-estimate the value of the instant popular verdict ('the poet can only be sure that he is properly fulfilling his true mission, if he creates works that are capable of winning popular approval'),[2] and his reaction to this refusal of his masterpiece, which has since become his most popular work, was characteristically drastic (T. 1893):

> 'Sonderbar die Wirkung, die dieses Mißlingen auf mich machte! Anfangs höchst unangenehm, wie natürlich, aber schon den zweiten Tag gewann ein höchst beruhigendes Gefühl die Überhand. Aus der Knechtschaft des Publicums und des Beifalls gekommen zu sein, wieder mein eigner Herr, frei zu schreiben oder nicht, zu gefallen oder zu misfallen,

[1] See his 'Nachwort zu DMudLW' in Cotta [1].

[2] Cf. 'German Life and Letters', Vol. II, Oxford, 1938, 'Grillparzer's Rank as Dramatist' (by the present author), p. 302.

kein obligenter Schriftsteller mehr, wieder ein Mensch, ein innerlicher, *stille Zwecke* verfolgender, nicht mehr an Träumen, an Wirklichkeiten Antheil nehmender Mensch!'

This confession underlines by implication what has been said regarding the universal contrast between the two poles of duty and desire, or more personally 'art' and 'life', as being for Grillparzer the crucial issue and reflected in this, as in all his works. It is as if he were saying here that the sacrifice and self-abnegation reflected in this tragedy had been made in vain. He no longer looks upon his dramatic work, his art, as a duty, at any rate not in the narrow sense of the word; but feels inclined to turn away from it to the pursuit of happiness and contentment, to life. The attitude is similar to that which dominated him when he was beginning to write 'Sappho'. And it was in this mood that he took up a plan dating from that period of his life and completed 'Der Traum ein Leben'.

Yet Grillparzer never completely lost faith in this tragedy as an achievement; for him it seemed to contain that which would justify something of his claim to immortality in the eyes of future judges of his work (T. 1893). With some changes it was printed in 1840; certain emendations of the printed text were made by the poet subsequently: they are incorporated in the standard critical text. The initial failure of this tragedy on the stage, however, was far more harmful to Grillparzer than that of his 'Goldenes Vlies', a failure which he had more than half foreseen at the time of handing over the work to the Hofburgtheater. The failure of 'Hero' brings us virtually to the end of that period in which Grillparzer sought actively after fame and recognition. The refusal of this 'romantic' love-tragedy led ultimately to his divorcement from the stage.

2. LITERARY INFLUENCES AND SOURCES

In formal respects, in structure and diction, as also obviously in setting and choice of subject-matter, Grillparzer's tragedy of 'Hero' conforms to the classical or Hellenistic tradition established in German drama by Goethe and Schiller; it thus reflects and represents the poet's principal aim and ambition in this feld of endeavour:

> 'Ich möcht lieber stehen bleiben
> Da, wo Goethe, Schiller stand' (G. 893).

Whether this cultural (and political) and at the same time aesthetic ideal of Grillparzer's implies too exalted or too conservative an ambition is still debatable; yet in regard to his actual achievement in the field of drama there are many who are prepared to concede even more than Grillparzer himself claimed when again, in his autobiography, speaking of his visit (in 1826) to Goethe, he remarks:

> 'Er ist mir auch in der Folge nicht gerecht geworden, insofern ich mich nämlich denn doch, trotz allem Abstande, für den Besten halte, der nach ihm und Schiller gekommen ist'.

Leaving far behind Grillparzer's own (modest) claim, as also the more local pretensions of his Austrian compatriots on their native poet's behalf, and deprecating his 'comparative neglect' at the hands of critics representative of the German nation, the latest tendency in the objective assessment of Grillparzer's achievement is characterized in the following judgement:

> 'Grillparzer adds to the achievement of Goethe and Schiller whatever Romanticism has to offer of dramatic value, and it would take a very able critic to establish in what respect his poetry,[1] his psychology, or his stagecraft, is inferior to theirs'.[2]

Such an estimate does not rest, of course, on the dramatist's achievement in any one particular work; yet the poet himself was probably right in deeming his 'Hero and Leander' to be the work which (primarily) 'would justify something of his claim to immortality'.

In structure 'Hero' corresponds in the main to classical standards, its subdivision into five Acts permitting conveniently of that gradual and inevitable convergence of the leading protagonists which culminates in the middle Act, leaving two more subdivisions or phases to prepare and compass the catastrophe and our acceptance of it with tears in the *catharsis*. The whole action is compressed within a period of little more than two days, in close observance, not of any derived Rules of the Unities, but of the more fundamental principle of 'continuity' which covers these rules. It is true there are necessary, but strictly limited, changes of scene; these, however, are such as to be well within the range of the characters' movements since they last appeared on the stage. It is instructive to note how at the close of nearly each act or scene of this model tragedy, the characters make their exit (as in 'pre-curtain' classical drama) in anticipation, as it were, of their next dramaturgic assignation. This provision fosters and maintains the illusion of present actuality and continuity of action

[1] By this we are doubtless meant to understand 'dramatic verse for actual stage performance'; see below.

[2] G. Waterhouse: 'Short History of German Literature', Oxford, 1943, p. 116.

despite changes of scene—a continuity which is the flowing life-blood of dramatic presentation.

Features of this kind easily escape notice when a drama, intended to be seen and heard, is merely read. In the same way the diction of a verse-drama may come to be judged as if the criteria normally applicable to literary verse or 'poetic (book-)drama' were valid. In point of fact, this has happened repeatedly in regard to Grillparzer's works, particularly in cases of alleged lapses into Viennese colloquialisms; it should be remembered that the test of their artistic congruency is their effectiveness in actual performance on the stage. There it becomes evident that these 'inequalities' are as purposeful and acceptable as in Lessing's 'Nathan', the work which established blank verse as the appropriate, but not austere nor too exalted, medium of the German poetic stage drama. This form of metrical expression, as used by both these dramatists, while calculated like the verse forms of Greek and Elizabethan drama to lend immortality to memorable speech, is yet so natural and so well adapted to its function as to be not only, as Lessing put it, 'easier to write' than prose; but also realistic and modern enough to merit, in Grillparzer's instance, the discriminating praise accorded it by E. Reich. Referring in particular to the love-scene in Act III, because of its beauty and truth to life, as the best example of a love-scene to cite against Bulthaupt's well-known argument in favour of the poetry and glowing lyricism of the balcony scene in 'Romeo and Juliet', he writes:

> 'Grillparzers Technik schreitet da zwischen gar zu prunkvoller Rhetorik und eigenwilliger Hintansetzung der Bedürfnisse jeder Bühnenkunst mit glücklichem Takt den Pfad gereifter Theaterübung. Er gewährt dem Gefühl passenden Ausdruck, hütet sich aber vor hochklingenden, darum ihm nicht angehörigen Worten, wie sie stets ein äußeres Erborgtes bleiben, und spricht, ohne die "Bescheidenheit der Natur" zu verletzen, doch erhöhten, bewegten Seelenzustand aus. Grillparzer entgeht der Charybdis stolzester Pathetik, ohne der Scylla theoretisch verstockter Naturalistik zu verfallen, auch hierin ein Wegweiser echter, moderner Kunst'.[1]

3. DIE TRAGÖDIE VON 'YORKSCHIRE'[2]

Quite the most fascinating indication of a specific source of literary influence on 'Des Meeres und der Liebe Wellen'—and it is practically

[1] Op. cit. (4th ed.), p. 172.

[2] The main subject-matter of this section was originally printed in the 'Modern Language Review', Vol. XXI (1926), p. 419 ff., under the title, 'Grillparzer's Hero and Shakespeare's Juliet'.

the only one revealed (were it not for a slip[?]) by Grillparzer himself —is to be found among some observations on the characters, supplied as an aid to the actors in preparation for the production of the play.

Though the theme of Grillparzer's tragedy at once suggests a comparison with Shakespeare's 'Romeo and Juliet', the evidence so far assembled would hardly do more than suffice to show that Grillparzer knew the work, and that he was influenced by it in certain of its externals. Of this order of influence are such passages as the one in which Hero, believing her lover to be far away is emboldened to address words to him into the night, whereupon Leander unexpectedly replies (like Romeo: 'I take thee at thy word,' Act II, Sc. 2) from close at hand (l. 1061). There is, too, apart from the general similarity between the balcony-scene in 'Romeo and Juliet' and the tower-scene here, the circumstance of Leander's having climbed the tower without aid, as Romeo had climbed the orchard walls, and the consequent inquiry from Hero parallel to that of Juliet.

E. Groß[1] speaks of the similarity between the functions of Benvolio and Naukleros in the two plays, and of the resemblance between the characters of Romeo and Leander, how they both behave when in love, and how, apart from outwardly hostile circumstances, they both bring about the catastrophe through their blind precipitation. But it is chiefly through a development of the thought contained in the following passage that we shall be able to trace the subtler and more interesting of Shakespeare's influences:

> 'Hero wie Julia wird durch die erwachende Leidenschaft in allen Tiefen ihres Wesens umgewandelt, beide scheinen in ihrem Gesamtdasein auf eine neue Entwicklungsstufe emporgehoben zu sein. Mit der Liebe erwacht ihr eigentliches Weibsein, ein psychologischer Vorgang, den Grillparzer auch an "Esther" und "Libussa" schildert'.

On the same page Groß uses the words:

> 'Nur einen leisen Wiederklang der liebegesättigten Stimmung aus der Abschiedsszene zwischen Romeo und Julia nach gemeinsam verbrachter Nacht (III, 5), wird man in Heros Stimmung am Morgen nach dem genossenen Liebesglück im Turm erkennen, wenn sich in ihr, wie in Julia, die unter tiefstem Erleben erwachte Frau enthüllt' (pp. 31 f.).

It is rather the contrary which seems to be the case. The whole of Act IV is full of this state of feeling in Hero. And she resembles

[1] Groß, E.: 'Grillparzers Verhältnis zu Shakespeare', Shakespeare-Jahrbuch, Vol. LI (1915), p. 1 ff. (Ref. here to p. 31).

Juliet in other respects too. Is she not like her in being 'dämonisch'—in the sense in which Goethe applies the word to Egmont, and in which sense we shall find Grillparzer himself using it below—in her blindness to danger and deafness to warning? Is she not like her in becoming so utterly careless of everything that had previously occupied her mind and affections? Are not both 'possessed'? As a result of real love having taken possession of her whole being, in her complete surrender to passion, Juliet becomes blind to filial duty, to her own and Romeo's danger, careless of all other ties, and capable of deceit. How eloquent of the power of real love to change her whole nature is the way in which Juliet receives the news of her cousin's death at Romeo's hands, and the way in which she behaves while—

> '. . . bloody Tybalt, yet but green in earth,
> Lies festring in his shroud (Act IV, Sc. 3)!

In the same way Hero's nature is changed. She, too, becomes forgetful of her duty and filial affections, becomes deaf to warning, blind to Leander's danger and her own, and capable of wilful deceit. But she is (in the finished work) of a much less passionate nature than Juliet;[1] and Grillparzer's representation of the effect of love upon her, in maturing her to womanhood in the sense in which Juliet is matured, takes forms not essentially different from, though gentler than in Juliet's case.

As far back as in 1820 Grillparzer had planned to represent Hero as being 'matured to womanhood' in Act IV, as is seen in the plan sketched out in his diary during the autumn of that year. This Hero—akin to Charlotte Paumgartten—was of a much more passionate nature than the later one, and the third act was planned to end with a scene in which the chaste, natural and naïve Hero, as we know her now, is nowhere in evidence. She is, in fact, more closely allied to Juliet at this stage. After the second meeting with Leander, she agrees to receive him into her tower at night. They arrange to carry on a clandestine intercourse, and do so. Both of them practise deceit and subterfuge, and, in general, there is very little trace of the finer elements and more attractive qualities of the later work.

Even in January, 1827, as already stated, Grillparzer cannot have had a conception of Hero materially different from that of the early plan. This is clear from two passages referred to by Reich as being

[1] Reich, op. cit. (4th ed.), p. 71, speaks of 'die allzu überhitzte Leindenschaftlichkeit, die Temperamentfülle, wie sie wenig englisch mit südlicher Glut in Romeo und Julïa aufschäumt', in contrast to Hero.

written on one of the numberless pages[1] of Grillparzer's preliminary notes and plans for 'Hero'. This page of Grillparzer's manuscript, which is the only one bearing a date, was written on January 8, 1827. Reich quotes from it (p. 174): 'Hero soll von vornherein einen Zug zur Heftigkeit haben'. This is certainly not applicable to the later Hero; and elsewhere (among those remarks on the characters of the play which are again to be referred to, and which are doubtless of later date) we find Grillparzer writing: 'Hero mit einem durchgehenden Zuge von *Heiterkeit*' (the last word underlined).[2] This passage bears the distinct aspect of being a conscious revision of the above, made by Grillparzer with the earlier notes in front of him.

The second passage referred to by Reich as being written on the same page of Grillparzer's manuscript on January 8, 1827, is the well-known one referring to Charlotte Paumgartten and the lamp-motive.[3] Grillparzer had made a note on this point, in the first place, in his diary for the year 1819, before his work on 'Hero' had begun.[4] Strangely enough, though many Grillparzer commentators have quoted this passage, none of them has remarked that, however well it may suit Grillparzer's earlier conception of a passionate Hero in 1820 and 1827, it does not apply (in the same sense) to the later Hero. Charlotte Paumgartten had set the lamp on the floor in order to have her arms free for an embrace, an act resulting from a state of feeling such as we could understand in the earlier Hero (or in Juliet), but certainly not in the later one; and whereas Grillparzer writes in 1827: 'Nicht gerade die Begebenheit soll dort Platz finden, sondern die Gesinnung, die Gemüthsstimmung,' in the finished work it is the incident itself which is utilized,[5] while the state of feeling prompting Hero's action is entirely different. Maidenly modesty has taken the place of ardent passion.

It seems impossible to doubt that when he first conceived his 'Hero'

[1] Cf. ibid., p. 173. These 'numberless pages' have presumably come to light in the 'Apparatband zur Hero' ('Wke.' I. 19), which was published in 1939, just before the outbreak of the war. I regret that I have been unable to obtain access to it.

[2] First quoted from Grillparzer's manuscript by H. Laube, 'Grillparzers sämmtliche Werke', Stuttgart, 1872, Vol. V, p. 131.

[3] Quoted by Backmann ('Wke.' I, 4, note to Hero, l. 1255) as follows: 'Im 3. Akte zu gebrauchen, wie damals Charlotte, als sie den ganzen Abend wortkarger und kälter gewesen, als sonst, beim Weggehen an der Hausthür das Licht auf den Boden setzte, und sagte: ich muß mir die Arme freimachen, um dich zu küssen. Nicht gerade die Begebenheit soll dort Platz finden, sondern die Gesinnung, die Gemüthsstimmung'.

[4] Cf. 'Wke.' II, 7, p. 239, No. 607: 'Wie sie trotzig war den ganzen Abend und höhnisch fast und unhöflich, beim Fortgehen aber das Licht auf den Boden setzte und sprach: Ich muß dich küssen und mich umfieng und an sich drückte mit all der verzehrenden Gluth der Leidenschaft und des Verlangens. Studiere diesen Charakter genau. Dem Dichter kommt nicht leicht ein interessanterer vor'.

[5] Act III, l. 1255, Hero: (das Licht auf den Boden stellend) 'Die Lampe solls nicht sehen'.

Grillparzer thought of modelling his heroine, not only on Charlotte Paumgartten as he knew her, but also on Shakespeare's heroine. Here we may have the key to a difficulty that appears to have baffled all Grillparzer's commentators and editors. It occurs in a note of Grillparzer's originally published by Laube in his (the first) collected edition of Grillparzer's works, and frequently requoted by later editors—though in some cases[1] without the final sentence, which contains the difficulty in question. The note, written on the same (undated) page of manuscript as the words quoted above: 'Hero mit einem durchgehenden Zuge von *Heiterkeit* (which as has been observed, looks like a revision of an 1827 note), runs as follows:

> 'Im vierten Akte . . . ist sie (Hero) schon wieder ins Gleichgewicht des Gefühls gekommen, aber eines neuen, des Gefühls als *Weib*. Zwar im Gleichgewichte, aber doch höchst gesteigert, sensuell, all das Dämonische, die ganze Welt Vergessende, taub und blind, was die Weiber befällt, wenn eine wahre Liebe eine Beziehung auf die Sinne bekommen hat. Dasselbe, was mir dem Weibe in der Tragödie von Yorkshire eine so furchtbare Wahrheit giebt, nur unendlich gemildert durch Hero's Charakter'.

In the light of what has been said above, the phrase 'unendlich gemildert durch Hero's Charakter' shows this note to have been written after the change in Grillparzer's conception of his heroine. We may therefore regard it, too, as possibly, if not probably, a revision of an earlier note—a possibility which must be borne in mind in attempting to account for the mention here of the 'Tragödie von Yorkshire'.

At first sight it looks as if Grillparzer might have been referring to the so-called *Yorkshire Tragedy*, which he may well have known as a work attributed by some to Shakespeare's pen. But he *could not possibly* have meant to refer to the one woman who figures in this work. In the few glimpses we get of Calverly's wife we can trace no vestige of resemblance in her to either the earlier or the later Hero, whether in her character, in her state of feeling at any time, or in her experiences. She is docility itself, and dutifulness, and wifely devotion, under the most extreme provocation. Nor has any other tragedy with 'Yorkshire' either in the title, or as the name of the author, been discovered which would make the sentence intelligible. And yet there seems to have been a clear, if tacit, admission on Grillparzer's part of a definite literary influence. The use of the word 'mir' must

[1] The sentence is omitted, for example, in Meyer's Klassiker-Ausgabe and even by Backmann in 'Wke.' I. Vol. IV.

surely indicate that he knew at first hand the tragedy referred to and wished to record the vivid impression made *upon him* by the woman character in it, whose portrayal on becoming matured to womanhood, as Hero is matured, he thought 'so terribly true to life'. The problem gains both in interest and significance when we realize that the influence suggested by Grillparzer's words is not only of a fundamental character, but is also of a type which would perhaps only find its way into the writings of a dramatist of his particular perceptions and psychological bent. As a matter of fact, Grillparzer's continuous interest in and employment of this very motive, which he found confirmed in his own experience of love for 'Therese',[1] dates back to the period of about 1810, that of the 'greatest literary experience of his youth, Shakespeare and especially "Romeo and Juliet" '.[2] The influence of this work—so revealing (for Grillparzer) of love's tragic dominion and daimonic power—is reflected in the fragments 'Spartakus', 'Seelengröße', *etc.*, then in 'Die Ahnfrau', 'Sappho', 'Das goldene Vlies', and now, above all, here.

Moreover, since Grillparzer's words, as they now stand, fail to enlighten us as to the actual source of this basic influence on 'Des Meeres und der Liebe Wellen', and in view of the striking parallelism between his Hero (especially the earlier one) and Juliet, the conjecture suggests itself that the word 'Yorkshire' is an error (perhaps even at one remove a deliberate error[3]), and that it should read 'Shakspeare'.[4] An enquiry at the Grillparzer-Archiv in Vienna has elicited the interesting information that the manuscript used by Laube reads 'Yorkschire'.[5] It remains now to offer some possible explanation of the mistaken changing (if such it be) of 'Shakspeare' into 'Yorkschire'. The error might be accounted for in various ways, but perhaps most plausibly by suggesting that if Grillparzer was copying out some notes made by himself at an earlier period of his work upon 'Hero',[6] he might easily have first misread the word 'Shakspeare' as 'Yorkschire' and written it so, in the version we have before us, as a result of over-haste, thoughtlessness,

[1] Cf. Backmann's Intro., 'Wke.' I, 4, p. viii. [2] Cf. ibid.

[3] It need perhaps hardly be recalled that Grillparzer frequently indulged in such prevarications and subterfuges as this might exemplify. This ironical practice is not peculiar to Grillparzer, but belongs to the poet's technique of imparting 'open secrets'; it is not engaged in gratuitously, but as the (ultimately) most memorable form of confession and communication. Of wise teachers, among whom poets rank highest in intuitive mastery of method, Goethe wrote:

> 'Ein jeder weiß zu mehren wie zu mindern,
> Bald ernst, bald heiter klug zu frommen Kindern'.

[4] Grillparzer frequently uses this spelling.

[5] Dr. Backmann kindly provided a tracing.

[6] We saw how probable it was that Grillparzer re-wrote and changed the passage referred to by Reich as being written on Jan. 8, 1827.

or lack of sympathetic contact with his earlier text. In German script, and especially in Grillparzer's handwriting, the words 'Yorkschire' and 'Shakspeare' are strikingly similar in general appearance. There is remarkably little to choose between his writing of 'Y' and 'Sh', or between (and this is how the mis-spelling 'Yorkschire' may arise) 'ch' and 'p'. If Grillparzer's writing of the two words could be reproduced here, it would be seen that they look almost identical, the only noticeable difference between them lying in the vowel before the second 'r'. The error may have resulted from other attendant circumstances as well (e.g. a recent chance reminder of the existence of a supposedly Shakespearian play entitled, 'The Yorkshire Tragedy'), circumstances of which we can have no knowledge. But if we may assume, as in fact assume we must, that Grillparzer had meant to write: 'Dasselbe was mir dem Weibe in der Tragödie von *Shakspeare* eine so furchtbare Wahrheit giebt, nur unendlich gemildert durch Hero's Charakter', we see how reasonable and illuminating, in the light of his preceding remarks on Hero's state of feeling in Act IV, such an observation would be. It would follow that the tragedy in question was '*Romeo and Juliet*', the one love-tragedy by Shakespeare most allied to Grillparzer's in theme, and that the woman referred to was Juliet herself.

An influence of such a kind as has been here deduced, implicitly indicated as it seems to be by Grillparzer himself, is of a highly significant order. Grillparzer's reaction is not merely emulative, unoriginal, or imitative: but congenial with Shakespeare, confirmed by experience, and creative of art. It underlies the root conception of this tragedy.

4. OTHER SOURCES

If we now turn to a consideration of the influence on Grillparzer exercised by previous treatments of the 'Hero and Leander' story itself it will be to bring out those main contributions to the theme's tradition which affected Grillparzer.

Stimulated perhaps, in the first instance, as Backmann suggests,[1] by some impulse imparted by a chance reminder, or by the perusal of a passage on 'Hero and Leander' like Wieland's in 'Schach Lola', Grillparzer seems to have based his 1820 plan—if we except for the moment his underlying personal experience—in large part on hints from Franz Passow's edition[2] of Musaeus' version of the legend (ca. A.D. 500). In virtue of its enthusiastic and perhaps extravagant praise of this poem,

[1] 'Wke.' I. 4, p. ix f.
[2] Leipzig, 1810, containing both Introduction and verse-translation.

Passow's attractive booklet was well constituted to fulfil for Grillparzer this initial rôle. The commentator lauds Musaeus's reconciliation of the classical and romantic ideals, the dramatic qualities and the genuine tragic conception, the figurative plasticity, the impressive setting and human significance of the poem—attributes these which, if not actually present in the measure implied, were at any rate realized to the full in Grillparzer's ultimate response to such encouraging representations.

Georg Knaack unconsciously pays Grillparzer a very high compliment when, in his study on 'Hero and Leander' in classical literature, he remarks, somewhat illogically perhaps, that his own hypothesis that a 'genuine' and highly poetical original epic form of the legend must have existed and served Ovid and Musaeus as a source, receives support from Grillparzer's practical proof that such a genuinely poetical treatment was possible.[1] In other words, he credits Grillparzer with having restored to the world more or less what had been lost, although he makes the reservation that the form ought, strictly speaking, to have been not dramatic but epic, as in the supposed original. What Knaack is chiefly concerned with, is to show how undeserving the grammarian Musaeus's 'epyll' is of the praise which has been meted out to it by such people as Passow, Schwering (and latterly Backmann), and to show that Musaeus's work was nothing but a 'botched version' of an infinitely more poetical original. However that may be, it is significant that Grillparzer too, in his use of Musaeus's epic poem as a source, soon became conscious of its poetic defects. He perceived that in the interests of the work as a whole, and particularly in the interests of his Hero, it would be necessary to proceed from a higher seriousness of moral purpose and a higher conception of love than Musaeus had done, or than was evident in his own plan of 1820 as influenced by Musaeus.

Grillparzer's early plan, in its introduction of the high-priest, may also have been in part influenced by the German folksong, which, in introducing the 'Falsche Nonne' to extinguish the lamp, alone established a potentially 'dramatic' relationship between this event and the catastrophe. In all the other sources the lamp is extinguished without human agency by the 'epic' storm. The reason why the storm itself, as an embodiment of Fate (e.g. in Schiller's unequal ballad treatment) or of Destiny, or Chance, was insufficient, has already been pointed out.

Later, in 1822, as earlier mentioned, Grillparzer noted down that Marlowe had written a 'Hero and Leander'. Though this indication

[1] Knaack, G.: 'Hero und Leander' (in Festgabe für Fr. Susemihl, Leipzig, 1898), p. 82.

has not been followed up by previous investigators, there can hardly be any doubt that this was the most important literary influence subsequent to that of Passow's Musaeus. There is, in fact, more than enough material for a footnote in the following salient features of Marlowe's poem, listed by Kind[1] (p. cxvi, fn.) as differing from Musaeus (and from Grillparzer's early plan), but present in the finished work:

> 'Although there is no documentary evidence available to show that Grillparzer knew the fragment of Marlowe, which was completed by Chapman, there are interesting parallels between the Marlowe-Chapman poem and Grillparzer's drama: The action is confined to three days. There is only one night of love, Hero and Leander love each other at first sight. Leander is depicted as a bashful, reticent youth, inexperienced in affairs of the heart; but his first meeting with Hero completely changes him: he boldly wears her purple hair ribbon about his arm and her consecrated ring on his finger as tokens of his triumph; and he is filled with but one desire—the enjoyment of Hero's love. Despite his father's rebuke and attempt to prevent further meetings of the lovers (in our drama the rôle of Naukleros), Leander surprises Hero by swimming over to her tower. Hero's ideals also undergo a complete change through love. Finally, when she spies Leander's shattered form, she casts herself upon his body, and dies of a broken heart'.

If we add to these significant points the substance of certain relevant observations in the following account of the action of the play, more especially those dealing: with the lovers' first encounter; with love's dominion over its victims; with the precedent in Marlowe for Hero's 'Komm morgen denn!'; with the change in Leander from torpor to vigour; and not least the note relating to the evidence of personal experience as the fundamental source of inspiration in Marlowe's as in Grillparzer's work[2]—little doubt will remain that Grillparzer's tragedy is materially indebted to Marlowe's work, which Swinburne characterized as one of 'rare and even unique poetic accomplishment'.

5. THE COURSE OF THE ACTION

When Hero appears on the stage at the beginning of the play there is from the very first something natural, unassuming, and attractive about her naïvely self-satisfied bearing and words. She embodies the qualities expressed in those words of Grillparzer's in his manuscript in

[1] Kind, J. L.: 'Des Meeres und der Liebe Wellen', Oxford German Series, New York, 1916.
[2] Cf. p. 178 fn. below.

1829: 'Hero mit einem durchgehenden Zuge von Heiterkeit, unbefangen, verständig, gefaßt'. In addition to this there is something quite convincingly Viennese about her. As Sauer puts it: 'Hero ist eine junge Wiener Aristokratin, die Nonne wird'.[1] She betrays her natural 'Schnippigkeit' in her words to Hymen and Amor when adorning their statues with wreaths of flowers: there is something faintly disrespectful but none the less attractive in her manner of addressing them. Scherer pointed out, and Schwering after him, that in this scene, where she appears decorating and putting in order the temple vestibule, we have a reminiscence from the first Act of Euripides' 'Ion', where the hero appears for the first time employed on the same duties. As in Musaeus, Hero wishes to have nothing in common with the frivolity of the rest of the womenfolk about her, but is 'nice of conduct' and 'prudently withdraws from their follies',[2] as befits one of her birth and office. But she is not contemptuous or condescending, and she regrets her anger when she is provoked. She is even careful to shield the mocking and disrespectful Ianthe when the priest appears, deeming the betrayal of Ianthe's name to him an action unworthy of herself. Or perhaps Hero behaves in this manner because of her generous and noble spirit, just as Esther, who resembles Hero in so many other respects too, protects Haman from the king's wrath, praising Haman's ambition, or, as she thinks, his bad judgment, as zeal. Hero has never felt the need for companionship. She is perfectly satisfied with her lot and, far from feeling lonely, imagines that she has enough to do in attending to her duties. She is so self-sufficient and self-possessed, so much at peace with herself and her environment, that she does not wish for friendship; much less does she understand that in suggesting companionship for her the priest had been thinking of companionship and nightly communings with her goddess. When he makes himself clear on this point, she replies:

> 'Verschiednes geben Götter an Verschiedne;
> Mich haben sie zur Seh'rin nicht bestimmt,
> Auch ist die Nacht, zu ruhn; der Tag, zu wirken;
> Ich kann mich freuen nur am Strahl des Lichts'.

There is nothing of self-sacrifice about Hero's devotion to her duty. She has been happy to escape from the disturbed atmosphere of the world without and of her home in particular. She is glad that she has nothing more to do with menfolk, whom she imagines all to be either

[1] 'Wke.' I, 1, 'Zur Einführung', p. xii.
[2] Quotations are taken from Fawkes's Translation of Musaeus.

like her father, petty and tyrannical, or like her brother, boorish and rough. But apart from this she has practically no qualifications to be a priestess, unless it be urged that she is of high birth and of a calm, if not profound, of an understanding, if not prophetic, nature. Before all things Hero is young and without experience of life. But how readily and convincingly she betrays her really loving and womanly nature in her bearing towards her mother, who surely has many traits of Grillparzer's own mother, and in the scene with the turtle-dove! The dove-motive, too, is borrowed from 'Ion'.[1] It conveys a suggestion that she lacks the austerity or seriousness of character befitting a high-priestess. In Musaeus there is of course no trace of it. In Marlowe, Hero is engaged in sacrificing turtle [-dove]s' blood at a silver altar when her gaze falls upon Leander. This suggestion could not have been acceptable to Grillparzer in its entirety, but he seems to have accepted from Marlowe a good many hints as to the circumstances connected with the first meeting of Hero and Leander. What he found in Musaeus was of no use to him, because it was so totally out of keeping with his own conception of the characters of Leander and Hero. But in Marlowe there is a hint of melancholy being 'frighted away' by love which seems to have passed over into the character of Grillparzer's Leander,[2] and Marlowe seems to have visualized the scene at the altar much as Grillparzer did. He describes how Hero and Leander fall in love without a word being spoken and has the famous line, which Shakespeare quotes in 'As you like it',

'Who ever lov'd, that lov'd not at first sight?'

Marlowe's Leander, in the act of kneeling, seems to be kneeling to Hero herself, as in Grillparzer's work. But Grillparzer's setting is marked to an even greater extent with symbolical traits. Leander kneels at the altar of Hymen as Hero approaches, and her confusion, when she sees him, leads her to perform her duties as priestess imperfectly. We see here, from the very first, of what far-reaching and fateful effect this disturbing new emotion is to be for Hero; and when she pours incense into the fire, she does it absently and with a shaking hand, so that a vivid flame shoots up, symbolical of the sudden flaming up of love within her. Before she goes away she takes another opportunity of gazing at Leander, looking round as if there were something wrong with her shoe. The suggestion for this motive may quite as

[1] Cf. Scherer, W.: Vorträge und Aufsätze, Berlin, 1874, p. 255. Ion drives away a bird that has come to make its nest; but he is afraid to kill it. Later his parents arrive, like Hero's. Also Schwering, J.: Franz Grillparzer's 'Hellenische Trauerspiele', etc., Paderborn, 1891, p. 94.

[2] Marlowe, 'Hero and Leander', I, l. 99. But Leander's 'Trübsinn' is also a condition of torpor and depression like Romeo's, prior to the vitalizing experience of love.

well be assumed to come from Marlowe in the opening lines of the second Sestyad, as from the scene in Mme. de Stael's 'Corinne' referred to by Sauer.[1]

Such scenes as this, and there are many others in the remaining acts of the piece, were not written by Grillparzer in the hasty manner in which he wrote his 'Sappho'. They are written with the greatest care even for their tiniest details. Grillparzer laid great stress on the 'figurative plasticity' of the various scenes, that quality of the dramatic art of Lope de Vega which was so much admired by him. He felt the need to make his settings and the attitudes and actions of his chief figures eloquent of what was going on within them. In 1829, when he was at work on his 'Hero', correcting and improving, he writes: 'Ich rechne auf die große Bildlichkeit des Stückes' (T. 1709). Later on, in 1834, long after the work had been finished (T. 2132):

> 'Ich erinnere mich noch, daß ich nichts mit größerer Anschaulichkeit gearbeitet, als dieses Stück, aber das Äußere, die aufeinander folgenden Tableaux, ward mir dadurch gewissermaßen die Hauptsache, wo noch besonders dazu kam, daß ich in der ersten Figur immerfort Marien vor mir sah in aller ihrer damals wirklich himmlischen Schönheit'.

Hero does not appeal to us so much by what she says, as by what she does, and it is her actions that we find so charmingly naïve and attractive. She does, indeed, seem to be modelled from life. In his 'Briefe an Marie' Grillparzer speaks of 'jenen langen tiefen Blick, den du mir beim Scheiden in die Brust senktest' (T. 1639), the same look which Hero gives Leander at the close of this Act and which Erny had given Otto when first they met in the 'Treuer Diener'. The fact that there is a resemblance between this action on the part of Grillparzer's Hero and Marlowe's Hero or Mme. de Stael's Corinne may help to explain its presence in Grillparzer's piece. But on the other hand its presence here and in the 'Treuer Diener' might be accepted as further evidence of the fact that Grillparzer almost invariably went to work with an eye to his own experience. As a dramatist he nearly always called visualization and actualities to his aid. Further instances of such living, expressive, and unforgettable pictures occurring in the piece will be mentioned; they never fail to cast an illuminating light on the character of the heroine and contribute in a large degree to her intimate charm and appeal.

The scene in Act II where Hero and Leander meet for the second time, this time in the temple grove, formed part of Grillparzer's plan

[1] Sauer's review of Schwering in 'Anz. f. d. Alt.', Vol. XIX, p. 236.

from the very first; but Leander's character is remodelled. According to the 1820 plan he was to draw water for Hero, whereas in the finished work, he is, at this stage, far too shy and inexperienced to be capable of such gallantry, suggestive rather of Musaeus's lover. Marlowe's Leander, on the other hand, had not possessed the initiative or the experience to pick up Hero's 'painted fan of curled plumes' for her. Grillparzer's Hero passes by with her water jugs singing to herself, significantly enough, like Psyche in the 1811 dramatic fragment, the song of Leda and the Swan. Like Psyche's father, Hero's uncle and guardian has told her not to sing this song, for some unspoken reason which she, like Psyche, cannot guess. She pays no more attention to the words than Kreusa did in singing Jason's song to Medea. In the conversation which Hero holds with Naukleros and Leander, when she is so struck with pity for him, she betrays not unguardedly, but naturally and naïvely, her love for him. If Leander had come a day earlier it might not have been too late. But now she has promised and will keep her word. But she asks Leander to appear again at the next year's feast, and every following year, and asks him not quite to forget her. And she promises to do the same. Then follows, on the approach of her uncle, the 'wicked' uncle as Naukleros thinks, the charming little deceit, the expressive and unforgettable picture of Hero ministering to the supposedly sick Leander, giving him to drink:

> Leander (Naukleros wegstoßend)—
> 'Nicht du! Ich, ich!'
> Hero (ihm den Krug hinhaltend aus dem er knieend trinkt)—
> 'So trink! und jeder Tropfen
> Sei Trost, und all dies Naß bedeute Glück',

—as indeed it does for Leander.[1]

It is evening when, at the beginning of Act III, Hero reappears. For the first time she sees her newly-appointed dwelling place in the tower, where she is to live the lonely life of a priestess for the rest of her days. This circumstance gives scope for the excellent dramatic device of the priest's description. He indicates among other things the situation of Hero's bedroom through the door to the right and describes the nature of her future life in these rooms. But Hero is not listening; she is distrait, and is disquieted at the thought of her loneliness. How different is her state of mind now! And we see and feel how changed it is since the morning of the same day, without her needing to express

[1] In view of the symbolism of this action, it is not inappropriate to recall the poems 'Wunderbrunnen' and 'Todeswund' referred to on p. 88.

the change in words. But she believes that she will be herself again on the following day, though here, too, this promises nothing more than was indicated in Act I. Really, in fact, it promises rather less, and such a Hero would even less nearly approach what the priest requires of her; for she means now that she will soon have the strength to become reconciled to her lot, a lot which she had previously welcomed with confidence and contentment. The priest speaks the philosophy of Grillparzer when he preaches tranquillity and concentration of mind, and the studied avoidance of everything that distracts. Ordinary human beings, engaged in the restless activities of life, may carelessly expose themselves to dangers from without:

> 'Doch wessen Streben auf das Innere führt,
> Wo Ganzheit nur, des Wirkens Fülle fördert,
> Der halte fern vom Streite seinen Sinn,
> Denn ohne Wunde kehrt man nicht zurück,
> Die noch als Narbe mahnt in trüben Tagen'.

It is Grillparzer speaking from his own experience and with conviction. But such teaching is not for Hero. In her there is no awareness of conflict between duty and desire, and she is without personal ambition. She is a woman and a child of nature, and like Marie Daffinger she is a child; not impulsive but irresponsible, controlled from the heart, not from the head. It is the priest who represents duty and is destined to avenge its neglect and infringement. Hero feels that she has done wrong when she notices her uncle's suspicions; but she cannot help regretting that she has now pledged herself and is answerable to her goddess and to him. She looks round her apartment. How wide and bare it is! 'Horch!—es war nichts—allein, allein, allein!' She places the lamp near the window and stands by it looking out into the peaceful night and listening to the whispering of the waves. But she takes away the lamp again when she thinks that Leander might see it from the distant shore. Such gentleness and modesty belong only to Grillparzer's Hero, who differs entirely in this respect from the earlier ones. And then, with charming naïveté, in recollection of her childhood, she addresses to herself the words:[1]

> 'So spät noch wach?—Ei, Mutter, bitte, bitte!—
> Nein, Kinder schlafen früh!—Nun denn, es sei!'

and commences to take down her hair. And again she finds herself humming the words of the song of Leda, and her thoughts turn again

[1] Sauer wrote in his review of Schwering, p. 337, that Hero is addressing the lamp, but this does not seem to be an altogether justifiable assumption.

of their own accord to Leander. She thinks of him with a wonderfully expressed tenderness and sends her greeting out to him across the night.

Everything seems to have been waiting for this moment.

Suddenly Leander, whom she thought so far, appears with his head at the window, as if in answer to her call; the motive is from Shakespeare, yet more boldly handled. In Musaeus and in Grillparzer's early plan the meeting was pre-arranged. Musaeus's Hero runs out to meet Leander, not so far as to wet her feet in the waves, a trait occurring in Ovid, but she runs out eagerly and leads him to her tower. Marlowe's Leander finds the door of the tower open and 'needs not to climb'. The suggestion for Leander's feat in climbing the tower in Grillparzer's piece is perhaps to be found here. This trait was not present in the early plan, where Hero throws him down a cloak, in which to conceal himself. The Hero of the finished play, in which there is no question of a tryst, has, indeed, little enough in common with the Hero of the early plan. When she gets over her first fright at seeing Leander, she is filled with pity for him in his shivering and breathless state; and questioning him as to how he had climbed into her room, learns of the dangers he has faced on her account. Grillparzer's Hero betrays a deeper and more natural love than her predecessors in showing her anxiety for Leander if he should return by the way he had come. She fears for his safety, and Leander has no need to plead for her pity, although (like Marlowe's lover)[1] he soon learns in his wooing that this is the readiest way to her susceptible heart. It is for him that she trembles, shuddering at her own weakness, when the watchman approaches; and she sends him, in spite of what it costs her, to hide in her bedroom, bidding him take the lamp with him until the danger is passed. Hero's attitude meanwhile:

> ('Sie senkt sich in den Stuhl, mit halbem Leibe sitzend, so daß das linke herabgesenkte Knie beinahe den Boden berührt, die Augen mit der Hand verhüllt, die Stirne gegen den Tisch gelehnt')

is another of Grillparzer's studied postures, expressive of remorse and

[1] Backmann sees in Leander's previous inexperience of love Grillparzer's most noteworthy departure from Musaeus. But Grillparzer had in Marlowe a predecessor in this respect: Marlowe's Leander is a 'novice' (Sest. II, 13, 63 f.). In respect to this motive and all that pertains to it in Marlowe's poem we feel perhaps most surely the justice of an observation by its latest editor to the effect that (as with Shakespeare) basic personal experience and near connection with real life and thought infuse a new vitality into the work, as with the greater achievements of the Elizabethan dramatists (cf. *Marlowe's Poems*, ed. L. C. Martin, London, 1931, p. 4). This applies in full measure also to Grillparzer's treatment of Hero and Leander's 'slender classic theme'; in this direction Marlowe may be said to have set him a noteworthy example.

shame and emotional exhaustion; it is hardly a listening attitude, as Backmann contends; but there is an element of resigned expectancy, coupled with an impulse to seek composure and power to dissemble, before the dreaded ordeal of discovery and exposure. Realizing now that she loves Leander, because it is for him that she fears, she bursts out with reproaches against him for so coming and disturbing her peace of mind. But she realizes that he is as helpless to resist the force of this new emotion as she is, and at the very pity and horror of the thought she takes back her wish that he had perished in the waves or fallen from the tower in his hazardous climb. It is then that she speaks out his name for the first time. She has known it since the moment when their eyes first met and she heard Nauhleros call him by name. And now she betrays her knowledge and with it her love all unawares. It is impossible to assume that Grillparzer was not writing this beautiful scene from his most intimate experience and with the whole wealth of his poetic genius and psychological insight. Nowhere does there seem to be a false note or a word out of place, and every action and gesture is expressive and symbolical of what is going on in the hearts of the lovers. There is nothing of oratory or unnaturalness about the dialogue, the words do not flow with logic or eloquence; but all belongs of inner necessity to the ebbing and flowing of the emotions within, and everything is spoken from the heart. There is no doubt that Grillparzer was thinking of this scene when he selected from Diderot's 'Discours sur la poésie dramatique', the following 'Motto zur Hero':

> 'Je ne connais rien de si difficile qu'un dialogue où les choses dites et répondues ne sont liées que par des sensations si délicates, des idées si fugitives, des mouvements d'âme si rapides, des vues si légères, qu'elles en paroissent décousues, surtout à ceux qui ne sont pas nés pour éprouver les mêmes choses dans les mêmes circonstances'.[1]

It is this that makes Grillparzer's love-scene so worthy of the praise accorded to it by Emil Reich, namely that it is beautiful and truthful in a way which gives it a place of its own in the world's literature, by the side of the balcony scene in 'Romeo and Juliet', but different from it in being more realistic; just as it is more modest and even more truthful to life than any naturalistic rendering of such a scene could be.

Love is depicted by Grillparzer as the most magical and romantic, but on the other hand the most irresistible and dangerous of human passions. With Hero to a greater extent than with other characters in his dramas Grillparzer observes the effect of love upon her whole

[1] 'Wke.' II, 8, T. 1763 (Summer, 1830).

nature and being, just as he does with Leander. The latter (like Phaon) is awakened to manhood and even heroism, and seems to live his complete life for the first time, a new world opening up before him when he loves and is loved in return. Hero in Act III, like Medea, feels herself powerless against the irresistible force of love within her, but she is truly womanly in quickly turning her thoughts to pity for Leander and anxiety for his safety, not her own. She only thinks of the dangers to which Leander is exposing himself now, and is anxious to lead him back safely out of the tower. But when Leander pleads with her to give him permission to come again, he little realizes how disposed she is to risk everything to see him again and to grant perhaps more than ever he has dreamed of asking. She can no longer bear the thought of life without Leander, and, as with Medea, her resistance breaks down suddenly and just as unexpectedly. She outbids Leander in a manner which is wonderfully true to woman's nature with her unexpected reply:

'Komm morgen denn!'[1]

After that her granting of the parting kiss is motivated almost independently of further pleading. But the charming modesty with which she grants Leander's naïve request in the wonderful picture where he kneels with his hands behind him and she puts the lamp aside so that it shall not see is another of the treasures which this fascinating third act has in store. The picture itself is unforgettable and remains imprinted on the mind as entirely expressive of Hero and Leander's modest and unsophisticated love, and descriptive of its intimate and romantic appeal. Charlotte Paumgartten had put down the lamp in order to have her arms free for a passionate embrace. Marie Daffinger had steadfastly denied a first kiss, because it meant for her a 'breach of faith'. In Hero's case it means no less, but Hero is not thinking of her duty and acts as she does because it is her nature to be modest and because it is really a first kiss. Immediately afterwards Hero vanishes frightened through the door, yet scarcely thinking that Leander will

[1] Grillparzer's probable source, alongside actual experience, for this motive is to be found in Marlowe (I. 341 ff., italics mine):

'With that, Leander stoop'd to have embrac'd her,
But from his spreading arms away she cast her,
And thus bespake him: "Gentle youth, forbear
To touch the sacred garments which I wear.
Upon a rock, and underneath a hill,
My turret stands and there God knows I play
With Venus' swans and sparrows all the day, . . .
Come thither'; *As she spake this her tongue tripp'd,*
For unawares "Come thither" *from her slipp'd*;
And suddenly her former colour chang'd, . . .

follow her, expecting to find beyond that door the way out of the tower. In an earlier conception of the play she was to remain standing in the doorway with bowed head while the curtain fell; but now she disappears and after a pause is heard by Leander to be returning on tip-toe. At this point the act closes. The latter version seems preferable, because Hero is modest and perhaps ashamed, but is not intended to convey the impression that she is burdened with any sense of guilt. The lighter and more playful touch is more in place at the end of such a graceful and charming act.

Quite in accordance with Viennese tact and instinct is the largely sensuous yet modest nature of this piece. In this respect Act IV, which has so little of external action in it, but which embodies so much psychological insight into Hero's nature and state of mind, is particularly worthy of note. 'Sonderbar!' writes Grillparzer, because of the lack of understanding with which this very act had met, 'Diesen 4-ten Akt schrieb ich gerade mit der meisten Innigkeit, dem nächsten Einleben....' The words that follow would seem to indicate beyond all doubt that the task which Grillparzer had set himself was not so much to portray the tragic fate of Hero and Leander as to characterize the effect of love upon those who come under its powerful dominion and to emphasize the dangers to which its hapless and deluded victims may become exposed.

> 'Das Ganze ist offenbar . . . mehr mit einer allgemeinen, als mit einer besonderen, mit einer Stoff-Begeisterung geschrieben. Mehr Skizze als Bild. Die Aufgabe war ungeheuer. Wenn die Lösung gelang, war der Gewinn groß für die Poesie. Sie gelang nicht und doch und doch! . . . Es möchte leicht eine Zeit kommen, wo man den Werth des, wenn auch nur Halb-Erreichten in diesem 4-ten Akte einsehen dürfte' (T. 1893).

What he strove to achieve in the fourth act is indicated in the words which he wrote in his 'Hero' manuscript:

> 'Im vierten Akte . . . sind Heros Gedanken nur auf das neu erwachte Gefühl und dessen Gegenstand gerichtet. Keine Furcht mehr vor Entdeckung, für Namen, Ruf. Der Priester läßt ihr seinen Verdacht nur allzu deutlich merken; sie bemerkt ihn nicht. Man spricht von einem Sturme, sie zündet doch die Lampe an. Träumerisch, sensuell'.

Here there can be no doubt that the task which Grillparzer had set himself was as described above; to emphasize the dangers of love for those who are in its power. But it would be scarcely reasonable to assume that the 'half-achieved in Act IV' is a criticism of Grillparzer's as to the adequacy of his portrayal of love's dominion over Hero; it refers more probably to the inadequate representation of love's inevitable danger for her. In other words, as Grillparzer himself said: 'Die Figur des Priesters ist zu kurz gekommen'. The priest does not seem to act in a manner so entirely free from personal motives and bias as Grillparzer must have desired of him in his capacity as an agent of Retribution or avenging Fate. In other words, he unfortunately has a suggestion of the villain about him and does not quite succeed in covering himself and justifying his action in the eyes of the spectator.

Act IV opens with broad daylight at the point where Hero has at last succeeded in getting Leander away, as she imagines, unseen. When the temple-guard convinces Hero by his questionings that he already suspects a great deal, she is not, however, in the least concerned, but replies in a light, mocking tone, without attempting to ward off his suspicions. She is simply courting disaster. With the arrival of the priest she declares tht she is going into the tower, to sleep. The temple-guard can account for her tiredness and relates everything that he has seen and heard during the night. To the priest's credit be it said that he is not quick to believe everything he is told, and it is only when he hears that the swimmer whom the temple-guard has seen has made off in the direction of Abydos, that he begins to have his suspicions too.

When Ianthe is called she betrays by her whole strange manner that she, too, has some knowledge of what has happened; but Hero returns, for the priest sends for her as well, and very quickly attracts attention to herself by her still more striking and unusual behaviour. The tone in which she speaks to her uncle, when he says it is certain that a stranger has been seen at the tower, is no longer the respectful tone of the Hero of the earlier acts:

> 'Nun Herr, vielleicht der Überird'schen Einer!
> Du sprachst ja selbst: in altergrauer Zeit
> Stieg oft ein Gott zu sel'gen Menschen nieder.
> Zu Leda kam, zum fürstlichen Admet,
> Zur strengverwahrten Danae ein Gott;
> Warum nicht heut? Zu ihr; zu uns, zu wem du willst'.

The priest can scarcely believe his ears. Hero speaking of sacred things in such a mocking tone! But Hero moves away and sits on a stone bench near at hand, lost in day-dreaming. Again the song of Leda is on her lips. Its significance is known to her now. She is quite lost to her immediate surroundings. Startled by her uncle's stern insistence on her attention, she rouses herself to protect Ianthe from her accusers and shows for her a new-found tenderness, kissing her repeatedly.

Medea had believed, as Hero is pleased to believe, in the divinity of her lover and had shown a new affection, in her case for Peritta, whom she has previously thought foolish and weak. The priest notes this change in Hero's nature and seeks to explain it; but his questionings of Hero only provoke such replies as that the breezes know her secret and that they will keep it to themselves. She wonders what time it is and how long it will be till evening; the next moment she is lost entirely to her surroundings again. Roused once more she perceives that everything is not as usual about her, but cannot comprehend it all. The priest, however, will not give her leisure to go and think things out, as she would like, but reminds her that she has duties to perform. Hero, whose days had previously been so full of many things to do, is quite astonished at the idea. But the priest has made up his mind to give Hero no chance to rest, and realizing that the mere reading of a letter from her parents will not engage her attention very long, sends her off on a wild-goose chase to seek a messenger from her parents and to attend to similar urgent duties. Hero is not sufficiently alive to what is going on about her to question the probability of his story and goes off with Ianthe, her new-found friend. Her unwelcome errand is destined to keep her occupied all day and render her incapable of the watchfulness at night on which so much now depends.

Meanwhile Leander and Naukleros in Abydos, it may be observed, have changed their rôles. Now it is Leander who is bold and Naukleros fearful. There is a resemblance between Leander and Phaon (and Romeo) in this respect, as has already been indicated. Phaon, too, displayed unwonted heroism as a lover, though not heroism of a very high order, it is true. Leander behaves towards Naukleros in a manner very suggestive of Marlowe's Leander:

> 'But love resisted once grows passionate,
> And nothing more than counsel lovers hate;
> For as a hot proud horse highly disdains
> To have his head controlled, but breaks his reins,
> Spits forth his ringled bit and with his hoofs
> Checks the submissive ground; so he that loves,
> The more he is restrained, the worse he fares;
> What is it now but mad Leander dares?'

Like Marlowe's Leander, too, he possesses a love-trophy from Hero, his lady's colours,[1] and there are numerous other reminiscences of Marlowe, which do not occur in Marlowe's principal source, Musaeus, or elsewhere.

[1] Jellinek, loc. cit., p. 68, noted this.

When Hero returns it is almost evening. In spite of her great weariness she realizes by now that she has been plotted against, but cannot think to what end. But her spirit is defiant, and she is determined to take no more orders from any one, but to act as she thinks fit. She asks Ianthe to go and prepare the lamp for her, and she thinks again of Leander's coming, the one bright spot in all her future. It is true that she cannot look very far ahead. For the future beyond to-night she has no plans and no cares. Leander is only to come this once, she promises herself. There will be time to think of other things afterwards. But for the time being she feels only her own unstilled passionate longing and is aware only of the need for watchfulness until Leander's late approach. Resting her head in her hand she immediately falls asleep, and when she is awakened the next moment by the priest she thinks he is Leander come to her. The priest is as unrelenting as before and embarrasses Hero with questions and demands. Will she not go and fetch her parents' letter? Hero would like to postpone this until to-morrow. She is not anxious about her parents. She feels that they are well. The priest asks her in an ironical tone whether her feeling convinces her of Ianthe's innocence too. Yes, she replies, and gently but confidently points out to him further that it rests with her whether Ianthe is dismissed or not. She knows what are her rights and what her——, here she hesitates; she was going to say that she knew what her duties were, too. But she quickly recollects herself:

> '. . . : auch meine Pflichten kenn' ich;
> Wenn Pflicht das alles, was ein ruhig Herz,
> Im Einklang mit sich selbst und mit der Welt
> Dem Recht genüber stellt der andern Menschen'.

It would be difficult to conceive a less adequate definition of duty—and Hero knows it; she renounces all endeavour to serve her goddess, and as for being even 'at harmony with herself and with the world', she is 'dämonisch, weltvergessend, taub und blind', in spite of what she may think. It is because she is entirely oblivious to the duty that the world (and the gods, as the priest would like to add) can justly demand of her that she is made to suffer. Grillparzer is teaching, by Hero's example, that to neglect duty in this sense is a fault, a crime which selfish desire or love's tyranny may mislead us to commit, but which our world will surely avenge.

It is Hero's self-confidence, her independent, self-reliant spirit which prevents her from heeding the priest's warning: 'Hero, Hero, Hero' !—Hab Mitleid mit dir selbst!' But he is bent on punishing Leander and is scarcely conscious of what the results of his action will be for Hero. Just as he feels that she would be capable of saving Leander if she learned in time what threatened him, so does he expect her to have the will to submit to the inevitable later on. It is because of his insufficient knowledge of human nature, or his lack of a completer understanding and sympathy for Hero, that he is ultimately unfitted to be her judge.

When Hero lights the lamp in her tower and places it at the window the priest becomes convinced that it is she who is really responsible for what has taken place and he is determined that she shall be punished for her guilt. He leaves the scene and Hero returns. The letter which she had gone to fetch is forgotten now. In itself it has been too insignificant an object to support practically the whole action of Act IV, the whole external action, that is; and one feels that a more convincing motivation ought to have been found for Hero's almost purposeless comings and goings the whole day long. But we may modify this judgement if we assume that the *warning* referred to in l. 1744 as being contained in this missive, having clearly something to do with Hero's recent conduct (in Acts I and II), was probably the reason why the letter was sent; it seems that Hero's father, too, has written a letter (cf. l. 1708): what, then, is more likely than that both letters were written at the priest's request, as an urgent and timely warning.[1]

Finding herself alone Hero decides to stay outside in the cool night air. Already there are signs of a fresher wind blowing up from the sea; but the thought only serves to remind Hero of her Leander, because the wind blows from him and will bring him all the more quickly to her side. She is troubled with momentary doubts as to her wisdom in letting him come, now that suspicions are aroused; but above all things she longs to be near him, and in thoughts of Leander she sinks slowly off into the sleep which has been besieging her senses since the dawn.

The act closes with forebodings of what the night has in store. The priest, finding Hero asleep, creeps up to the tower and either extinguishes her lamp or moves it so that the wind, 'der Götter Sturm', will extinguish it. His action is not so entirely free from blame as Grillparzer would have had it appear. The priest must be assumed to act in deep religious faith; but to a modern audience it looks almost as if he were at best afraid of his own conscience and were at bottom a moral coward after all. Yet it has been seen that in the interests of Grillparzer's dramatic theme the priest must have been intended to appear, not as acting of his own free will, but as the agent of a higher

[1] This explanation may help to dispel the doubts expressed by some commentators as to the plausibility of the letters ever having been written at all.

Causation, so far as this idea was reconcilable with modern dramatic demands.[1]

With the opening of Act V it is morning, and the storm of the night has abated. Hero is found standing in the middle of the stage with her head in her hands, staring blankly in front of her. This attitude is intended to convey the impression that Hero reproaches herself for her lack of vigilance and that in her conscience-stricken state and desperate anxiety she fears the worst. It is important that she should never come to see clearly that her happiness has been conspired against or that she is being punished for breaking her vows. As Grillparzer puts it: 'Nie soll Hero daran ein besonderes Gewicht legen, daß jenes Verhältnis verboten, oder vielmehr *strafbar* sei'. Only the other persons on the stage and the spectators are to realize this to the full. It follows from this circumstance that though the whole truth is not contained in Mell's statement that the real cause of the tragedy lies in Hero's tiredness in Act IV, it is essential in the interests of what Grillparzer unjustly terms the 'too theatrical conclusion' to the play[2] that this should be Hero's view. Her character is such that, had she felt herself to be without real responsibility for Leander's death, she would not have died of a broken heart, but would have lived on, her outraged sense of justice and her desire for revenge supplying her with a new lease of life. There is a certain danger for the successful motivation of the catastrophe in the final version of the play even in such passages as:

> 'Verschweigen ich, mein Glück und mein Verderben,
> Und frevelnd unter Frevlern mich ergehn?
>
> . . . . . .
>
> Du warsts, du legtest tückisch ihm das Netz,
> Ich zog es zu, und da war er verloren',

words addressed to the priest, her uncle, in which Hero shows that she

[1] It is interesting to speculate what might have been the effect of allowing the lamp to be blown out by the storm before the priest could fulfil his expressed intention to extinguish it. He would not have been expected to re-light it! In this way the poet might have spared his priest the condemnation implied in his final judgement of this Act: Vor allem ist die Figur des Priesters zu kurz gekommen.

[2] Cf. 'Wke.' II. 8, T. 1709. But it should be remembered that on the face of it Grillparzer had little reason to doubt the possibility of death resulting from a broken heart after his experiences with Marie Piquot and Charlotte Paumgartten. Incidentally, in Marlowe-Chapman, too, Hero does not commit suicide, but dies of grief.

The version of the German folksong in Des Knaben Wunderhorn (cf. p. 152, fn. 1) which Grillparzer may well have consulted, suggests a like ending:

> Sie nahm ihn in ihre Arme
> Und küßt ihm seinen Mund:
> Adie, mein Vater und Mutter,
> Wir sehen uns nimmermehr.

is conscious of having been wronged in addition to being herself in part responsible. To Naukleros she says:

> 'Und fragst du wers getan? Sieh! dieser hier,
> Und ich, die Priesterin, die Jungfrau—So?—
> Menanders Hero, ich, wir Beide tatens'.

These passages betray perhaps traces of a different and differently motivated conclusion in accordance with Grillparzer's earlier plan; he has indicated himself that the present conclusion is not the originally intended one. Hero is made to say further on:

> 'Laß mich! Der Mord ist stark. Und ich hab' ihn getötet',

and it is in this belief, broken in spirit and overcome with sorrow and desolation, that she dies.

When Hero had first caught sight of Leander's corpse her cry of terror had attracted the attention of the priest. She had believed that she still had need to guard her own and Leander's secret, and in her fear of betraying it she had attempted to suppress her surging emotions and to put on an easy manner. For Hero to attempt deceit and concealment at such a moment is a task beyond her powers, and she collapses in a swoon. Nothing can equal the skill with which Grillparzer accomplishes the task of making Hero's death upon the stage seem probable. He proceeds realistically and with unfaltering understanding of the most hidden secrets of woman's nature. There is no call for Coleridge's 'willing suspension of disbelief for the moment which constitutes poetic faith', when Hero is made to die of a broken heart. If the expression 'to die of a broken heart' has any meaning, that meaning is here conveyed. Not even in Shakespeare's tragedies is there to be found an intenser moment and more pregnant climax. Hero's piteous attempt to keep her secret, her instinctive effort, in this terribly true situation, to dissemble her agony of grief, is more than her life can withstand. It seems as if her heart would burst, and it is, indeed, at this moment that it suffers its most vicious stab. From this cruel moment onwards we actually witness the inevitable approach of that ending, when like the Hero of [Marlowe-]Chapman:

> 'She fell on her love's bosom, hugg'd it fast,
> And with Leander's name she breath'd her last'.

Later on Hero's despairing efforts to call Leander back to life, and then the sudden silencing of her lamentations, are the outward signs of her terrible sufferings in her grief. She has not comprehended the magnitude of her loss because of its stunning effect upon her senses, and she is found half-lying on the steps, looking at Leander as if in curiosity. When Leander is to be taken away she realizes what she has lost in him, and looking into the future she laments:

'Nie wieder dich zu sehn, im Leben nie!
Der du einhergingst im Gewand der Nacht
Und Licht mir strahltest in die dunkle Seele,
Aufblühen machtest all was hold und gut;
Du fort von hier an einsam dunkeln Ort,
Und nimmer sieht mein lechzend Aug dich wieder.
Der Tag wird kommen und die stille Nacht,
Der Lenz, der Herbst, des langen Sommers Freuden,
Du aber nie, Leander, hörst du? nie!
Nie, nimmer, nimmer, nie!'

Now there is nothing left of Hero's former independence, and all her inner harmony is shattered. Now she can speak of turning to her goddess for advice. The hand which she gives to Naukleros is cold, and she begs Ianthe to remove the veil from before her eyes. While Hero's back is turned the priest relentlessly insists on the carrying away of Leander's bier. Hero feels this cruelty like a last wrench at her heart-strings and, throwing up her arms in one last unheeded appeal, she begins to sink, and her life ebbs out as Leander is carried further and further away.

Poetic justice is done to the priest; he is not allowed to escape without the accusation of personal guilt after all. But to offset the effect of the priest's exit ('er geht, sich verhüllend, ab'), the last line was necessary. Divesting the statue of Amor of the wreath with which Hero had adorned it at the beginning of the work, Ianthe utters the words:

'Versprichst du viel, und hältst du also Wort?'

Interpreting Aristotle, we may hold that it is ultimately the function of tragedy to reconcile us to the middle course our lives must keep between duty or Necessity and desire or Freedom. This tragedy would have defeated its own purpose, had we been left with the humiliation of duty's representative as a final impression, with no corresponding derogation from the conflicting principle, as in this concluding line. Earlier editions of Reich's account of this work stated: 'Die Rechte des Herzens rangen mit den Rechten der Götter und erwiesen sich stärker'. Were it indeed true that we are left at the end of 'Des Meeres und der Liebe Wellen' thus biased in favour of the lovers, that would be natural, yet contrary to the poet's intention. Reich's final revision of the passage in question, as if in tacit denial of his earlier assumption, reads as follows (p. 192): 'Die Rechte des Herzens rangen mit den Rechten der Götter'.